LA CUCINA DI TERRONI

THE COOKBOOK

Cosimo Mammoliti
with **Meredith Erickson**

Published by Simon & Schuster

New York Amsterdam/Antwerp London
Toronto Sydney/Melbourne New Delhi

SIMON &
SCHUSTER
CANADA

A Division of Simon & Schuster, LLC
166 King Street East, Suite 300
Toronto, Ontario M5A 1J3

For more than 100 years, Simon & Schuster has championed authors and the stories they create. By respecting the copyright of an author's intellectual property, you enable Simon & Schuster and the author to continue publishing exceptional books for years to come. We thank you for supporting the author's copyright by purchasing an authorized edition of this book.

No amount of this book may be reproduced or stored in any format, nor may it be uploaded to any website, database, language-learning model, or other repository, retrieval, or artificial intelligence system without express permission. All rights reserved. Inquiries may be directed to Simon & Schuster, 1230 Avenue of the Americas, New York, NY 10020 or permissions@simonandschuster.com.

Copyright © 2025 by Terroni I.P. Holdings Inc.

Photography copyright © 2025 by Jim Norton Photography,

except where noted below.
p. ii: Photo by Ivaan Kotulsky
p. 7, top: Photo by Mauro Abballe
p. 22, bottom right: Photo by Bryan Portfield
p. 24, top: Photo by Stephanie Palmer D'Andrea
p. 25: Photo by Stephanie Palmer D'Andrea
p. 83: Photo by Stephanie Palmer D'Andrea

All rights reserved, including the right to reproduce this book or portions thereof in any form whatsoever. For information, address Simon & Schuster Canada Subsidiary Rights Department, 166 King Street East, Suite 300, Toronto, Ontario M5A 1J3, Canada.

This Simon & Schuster Canada edition September 2025

SIMON & SCHUSTER CANADA and colophon are
registered trademarks of Simon & Schuster, LLC

Simon & Schuster strongly believes in freedom of expression and stands against censorship in all its forms. For more information, visit BooksBelong.com.

For information about special discounts for bulk purchases, please contact Simon & Schuster Special Sales at 1-800-268-3216 or CustomerService@simonandschuster.ca.

Interior design by SMALL PROJECT STUDIO /
Andrew Di Rosa & Bartosz Gawdzik

Manufactured in China

10 9 8 7 6 5 4 3 2 1

Library and Archives Canada Cataloguing in Publication data is available.
OCLC: 1438665009

ISBN 978-1-6680-2426-3

Per la mia
mamma, Rita

e Papà Vincenzo

Elena, ti amo

Simona, Sofia,
Matteo, Olivia

la mia forza

Paolo

mi manchi

SOMMARIO
CONTENTS

LA NOSTRA STORIA
OUR STORY 1

COLAZIONE 27
BREAKFAST

Uovo sbattuto con caffè 28
Whipped Egg with Espresso

Biscotti da inzuppo 31
Dunking Cookies

Maritozzi 32
Sweet Buns

Bomboloni 36
Italian Donuts Filled with Pastry Cream or Nutella

Cornetti 40
Italian Croissants

Crostata alla marmellata di albicocche 45
Apricot Jam Tart

Panettone French Toast 48

Tartine con scarola e uova 51
Escarole Tarts with Poached Eggs

Panino all'uovo 55
Scrambled Egg Sandwich

Uova al purgatorio 56
Eggs in Purgatory

Frittata alla 'nduja, cipolle e fontina 59
Frittata with 'Nduja, Onion, and Fontina

PIZZA E PANE 61
PIZZA, FOCACCIA, PANINI

Pizza San Giorgio 62
Pizza with Button Mushrooms and Soppressata

Pizza Bufalina 65
Pizza with Mozzarella di Bufala

Pizza Santo Spirito 66
Pizza with Anchovies, Capers, and Fior di Latte

Ciccio farcito con verdure 71
White Pizza with Greens

Panzerotti 73
Fried Pizza Pockets

Focaccia barese 76
Bari-Style Focaccia

Pane pugliese 80
Apulian Bread

Ciabatta di Terroni 85
Ciabatta Buns

Panini con salsiccia e cime di rapa 89
Sausage and Rapini Sandwiches

Panini con branzino e peperonata 90
Sea Bass and Red Pepper Sandwiches

APERITIVO 93

Grissini 95
Long Thin Breadsticks

Taralli 99
Round Breadsticks

Crostini di mais 103
Rita's Corn Crisps

Pane e acciughe 104
Bread and Anchovies

Gnocco fritto 107
Fried Dough Pockets

Bombolini salati 108
Fried Mini Panini

Salatini di pasta sfoglia 111
Savoury Puff Pastry Snacks

Panettone gastronomico 115
Stuffed Savoury Brioche

COCKTAILS 118

CAVINONA: INTRODUCING ITALY BY THE GLASS 122

ANTIPASTI, APRISTOMACO E INSALATE 127
STARTERS, OPENERS, AND SALADS

Funghi assoluti 128
Baked Oyster Mushroom Salad

Calamari alla griglia 131
Grilled Calamari

Farinata con insalata di barbabietole 132
Chickpea Pancake with Beet Salad

Nizzarda 136
Italian Niçoise

Mozzarella in carrozza 139
Fried Mozzarella Sandwiches

Fave e cicoria 140
Fava Bean Purée and Dandelion

ZUPPE 143
SOUPS

Minestrone 144
Vegetable Soup

Pasta e fagioli 147
Pasta and Beans

Zuppa di lenticchie e 'nduja 148
Lentil Soup with 'Nduja

Verdura di Mamma Rita 151
Cosimo's Mom's White Bean and Chard Stew

Zuppa di castagne 152
Chestnut Soup

Vellutata di finocchio 155
Cream of Fennel Soup

PRIMI 157
FIRST COURSES

Ciceri e tria 159
Tria with Chickpeas

Pappardelle alla iosa 163
"Pasta Mayhem": Sausage, Peas, and Mushrooms

Rigatoni arcobaleno 164
"Rigatoni Rainbow": Zucchini, Cherry Tomatoes, and Buffalo Mozzarella

Spaghetti al limone 167
Spaghetti with Lemon Sauce

Ravioli di Zio Paperone 168
Duck Confit Ravioli

Sugo della domenica 174
Cosimo's Sunday Sauce with Rigatoni

Calamarata al sugo di polpo 179
Calamarata with Octopus Sauce

Orecchiette con cime di rapa 180
Orecchiette with Rapini

Garganelli Geppetto 183

Geppetto's Sausage and
Dandelion Garganelli

Gnocchi alla Simi 184

Gnocchi with Tomato Sauce
and Fresh Ricotta

SECONDI 187
SECOND
COURSES

**Frittura di pesce
e frutti di mare** 188

Fried Seafood

Polpo scottato 191

Seared Octopus

Pesce al cartoccio 192

Seafood in Parchment Packets

Baccalà 195

Mamma Rita's Salted Cod

Parmigiana di Titina 196

Titina's Eggplant Parmigiana

Porchetta di Terroni 199

Pork Roast

Salsiccia e patate 202

Terroni Sausage with Potatoes

Semicalda di Terroni 205

Sausage, Bean, and Radicchio Stew

Polpette 206

Meatballs

Brasciole di manzo 211

Braised Beef Roulade

Stinco d'agnello 217

Lamb Shanks

**Fiorentina stile
Terroni** 218

Florentine Steak, Terroni-Style

CONTORNI 221
SIDES

Pipi e patate alla Rita 222

Mamma Rita's Potatoes and Peppers

**Verdure saltate
in padella** 225

Braised Greens

Fagiolini alla Elena 226

Elena's Green Beans

**Cime di rapa saltate
in padella** 229

Sautéed Rapini

Peperonata alla Piera 230

Piera's Stewed Peppers

**Pasticcio di zucchine
con le uova** 233

Zucchini and Egg Hash

Scarola alla Titina 234

Titina's Endive with Olives,
Pine Nuts, and Raisins

Sformato di Fontina 237

Fontina Cheese Soufflé

Finocchio gratinato 238

Fennel Gratin

GLI AVANZI 241
LEFTOVERS

Insalata di pollo 242

Chicken Salad

**Verdure come
le faceva Terri** 245

Terri's Swiss Chard, Meat,
and Cheese Casserole

Gattò di patate 246

Neapolitan Potato Cake

Frittata di spaghetti 249

Spaghetti Frittata

DOLCI 251
SWEETS

Panettone classico 252
Terroni's Panettone

Torta di ricotta 261
Ricotta Cheesecake

Cannoli 262
Traditional Sicilian Cannoli

Crostata di Nutella e crema 266
Nutella and Custard Tart

Sporcamuss 269
Pastry Cream Puffs

Pasticciotti leccesi 270
Flavoured Custard Tarts

Biscotti di Mamma Rita 274
Mamma Rita's Cookies

I ricciarelli di Sud Forno 277
Chewy Almond Cookies

Zeppole di San Giuseppe 278
Fried Choux

Torta della Nonna Lucia 282
Nonna Lucia's Cake

Il tiramisù di Terroni 285
Terroni's Tiramisù

LA DISPENSA 286
THE TERRONI PANTRY

Lievito madre 287
Sourdough Starter

Impasto per pizza di Terroni 288
Terroni Pizza Dough

Bruschetta all'olio 290
Bread Crisps

Base Brioche 291

Pasta all'uovo 292
Fresh Egg Pasta

Pasta agli spinaci 292
Spinach Pasta

Pasta di semola 293
Fresh Semola Remacinata Pasta

Base di pomodoro 294
Terroni Tomato Base

Salsa di pomodoro 294
Classic Tomato Sauce

Besciamella 294
Béchamel Sauce

Brodo di pollo 295
Chicken Broth

Salsiccia di Vincenzo 296
Terroni Sausage

Pasta sfoglia 298
Puff Pastry

Crema pasticcera 301
Pastry Cream

TERRONI SPECIALTY PRODUCTS 302

ACKNOWL-EDGEMENTS 305

INDEX 307

WHAT IS A "TERRONE"? IS IT A PLACE? IS IT A PERSON?

A *TERRONE* IS HOW A NORTHERN ITALIAN MIGHT REFER TO A PERSON FROM SOUTHERN ITALY A COUPLE GENERATIONS AGO. ROUGHLY TRANSLATED IT COULD MEAN "FROM THE EARTH" BUT COULD ALSO BE CONSTRUED AS "FROM THE DIRT." ANOTHER WORD? PEASANT. AS YOU'VE GATHERED, IT WAS HURTFUL AND DEROGATORY AND FOR, SAY, MY PARENTS' GENERATION, SERIOUSLY OFFENSIVE.

And yet, at the age of twenty-six when I was starting this business with my partner, Paolo, I was proud to wear this slur as a badge. I was proud that my family comes from southern Italy. I'm still proud. The original idea was to call our deli-shop *I due terroni*, "the two peasants," but Bernie, the antiques dealer just across from us on Queen Street in the original location, thought that just Terroni was a better name for a restaurant. "Catchier," he said.

1992 · TERRONI QUEEN

But calling it a restaurant is generous. My dream was always to open a restaurant, but we couldn't afford it in the beginning. That came later. It was simply a *piccolo negozio*, a small shop where we sold Italian food goods, along with panini and espresso.

The kids I grew up with in Toronto were all first-generation Italian Canadians. One was from Genova, one was from Napoli, one was from Rome, and one—whose name was Paolo—was from Puglia.

They were immigrants whose parents had fled the Red Brigades and came to Toronto for a calmer life. But of course, they still lived the Italian life, they just did it in Canada. They spoke Italian. They drank Italian coffee. They watched Italian films. They listened to Italian music. And like all impressionable teenage boys, I did the same. But for me, school ended in Grade 12 when I dropped out. I was terrified to tell my father. Although he only had a fifth-grade education, he expected me to go all the way. In the end, his response was fair. He told me in the coming months I would be paying rent and so I had better find work, and quickly. That didn't bother me at all; I was just happy I wasn't in dire straits with my parents. And so I started hustling.

Immediately I got a job working as a dishwasher at The Keg. And then also part-time I would work at this depressing shoe store at Yonge and Eglington, which I hated. As agreed, I would pay my dad rent and then (not as agreed) my mom would sneakily put the money aside, which she handed me much later in life.

TERRONI STORY

Around this time the Rota family moved across the street from us, a nice Italian family who came to Canada from the UK. They had a son named Carlo, and to this day we are still great friends. The family took over a restaurant called Noodles, on the corner of Bay and Bloor, and asked me to come in as a barback/food runner, which was all I needed to say *arrivederci* **to the shoe shop.**

This was my first real introduction to the restaurant business. I worked at Noodles for a few years, eventually climbing my way to bartender where I began to make serious money as a teenager in the mid-eighties. From 1984 until 1988 I would work behind the bar at Noodles for nine months of the year, making (and saving) $600 to $700 cash per week, and then spending three months in Italy. This time spent in Italy was eye-opening. The food! The wine! It opened me up to so much culture from across the country. I was a total sponge. One year I had a Roman accent, the next year I was Milanese, and the following year anyone could mistake me for a gentleman from Rovereto! My real Italian background though? I'm a terroni! My hometown is in San Giorgio Morgeto, Calabria.

1994 · TERRONI VICTORIA

TERRONI STORY

And let's just say this about my Italian hometown, at nighttime there was one thing to do: walk down the street to the end of the piazza, turn around, and walk back. And this is what men—never women—did every night, all night. So, I would alternate my time in San Giorgio walking to the end of the street and walking back OR eating at the *pizzeria locale,* a completely family-run business, kids and all. After about three nights of this, I would have to tap out and find some action. Enter my love of Puglia, where my best friend from Toronto, Paolo Scoppio, had a summer home, in Santo Spirito.

TERRONI STORY

2006 · CAVINONA WINE AGENCY

Paolo's family had a beach house, near Bari. It was a villa in a gated community by the sea and it was mostly people from Bari who had a second home there.

I remember a very rocky beach where part of the appeal was finding your way to the water without falling between the rocks. We would hang out at the beach, play tennis, and look for girls. This was my first real experience with taralli (traditional circular breadsticks), fresh Parmigiana, and catching crabs on the beach.

Paolo's dad (Mimì Scoppio) started a small business in Toronto importing pugliese things like taralli, dried tomatoes, olives, and olive oil. At this time Paolo wasn't having fun working for his father and I wasn't having fun working for other people. For better or for worse, "fun" was the only driver in what motivated us in our teens and early twenties. I wanted to open a restaurant, that was the dream for me . . . but we didn't have the money. So, we opened what we could afford, a small storefront to sell Italian products.

Before I tell you about the original Terroni, let me paint you a picture of what Queen Street West was like in the early '90s: In the light of day there were prostitutes and junkies outside and, in the evening, there were *more* prostitutes and junkies outside! Sure, there were some gems. There was one interesting place directly across the street from us called The Squeeze Club, which was like a pool hall/bar and apparently had been a really fun spot in the mid-eighties, but by the time we arrived it was on its last legs. A few blocks away there was an exciting restaurant called Lotus, which had been opened in 1987 by a young chef named Susur Lee. There was also a wonderful restaurant owned by a chef named Greg Couillard called Stella. Other than that, the street was littered with junk shops, a few nicer antiques shops like Bernie's, and that's about it. Overall, it was rough.

But we found our space at 720 Queen West. My dad built the shelves for us to hold all the olive oil, olives, dried pasta, biscotti, etc. The main attraction was the little deli counter where we sold salumi by the pound, using our very old and very used automatic meat slicer.

TERRONI STORY

2000 · TERRONI BALMORAL

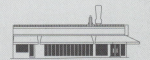
2007 · TERRONI W. HOLLYWOOD, LA

TERRONI STORY

We made $4 sandwiches where the customer could choose one meat—no portioning, just slice away!—one cheese, and two vegetables.

We would wrap the sandwich in butcher paper and *basta*, that was it.

In the beginning, the neighbourhood Italian signore would come in and would be bargaining: "I'll take the whole salami . . . but I want a deal!" Whereas the polite Canadians would order "two slices of provolone and a slice of prosciutto, please." Word on the street grew, as did the lines for sandwiches. A lot of our customers were older Italians in their seventies, and my brother, Vince, started doing deliveries to bring them "good" (i.e., ripe and flavourful) tomatoes to their porch because they could no longer walk to the shop.

Everyone who was working there was family or friends. Vince joined pretty much from the start, slicing meats, working that very used automatic slicer. He began with us part-time as he was finishing school, then he fell into the restaurant vortex, and later he took over the deli and became the head deli boy while Paolo and I were on pizza duty. Vito Scoppio, Paolo's brother, made coffees and helped wherever he was needed. We had a classic old Gaggia, and our espressos were in line with Italian coffee prices: one dollar per shot. In typical Italian style, we were happy to serve cappuccino—up until 11:30 a.m.

TERRONI STORY

2007 · TERRONI ADELAIDE

I also had my blue books that I would buy from Grand and Toy where I would write down the sales every day.

$170 on Monday.

$235 on Tuesday.

$300 (big!) on Saturday.

We had a rhythm—we worked doing whatever was our thing (cleaned/washed floors), then partied together and did it again the next day. We closed at 6 p.m. and were in there for a couple of hours afterward, with loud music on, and we went full speed so we could get out of there to go to the local bar The Messiah for beers and Jack Daniels.

I met my wife, Elena, in the summer of 1992, before we opened. She was an acquaintance of Paolo's and was going to travel to England, but Paolo (thankfully!) convinced her to come to Canada instead. She visited under the guise of practicing her English, but instead we fell madly in love. She went back to Italy to go to school in the fall but came back to Canada for the opening of Terroni in December 1992. But of course, she was still in school so she had to go back—it was her last year. There was a food show in Rimini in February and the Italian trade commission offered one of us (Paolo or me) the opportunity to go. We had to decide which one of us was going. Paolo and I decided on a game of foosball to sort it. The winner would go. One game. Dude, I played my ass off and got to visit her. She got out of school because I used her as an Italian interpreter. We've been together ever since.

It is funny to say, but the truth is we started making real money when this Russian gentleman named Ivan offered us a *calciobalilla* table (foosball table) to have in the shop. Over espresso, perhaps even a "special shot" (i.e., with grappa), we decided to move the boxes of product (we used half the shop as storage, boxes stacked on ugly grey Canadian Tire shelves) somewhere else and put the table behind the shelves. This machine brought everyone in. We were open at 9 a.m. and we closed at 6 p.m. Everyone smoked cigarettes constantly, the ashtray at the end of the bar having to be cleaned hourly. We were making a lot of panini, espresso, and cappuccino, selling deli meats, that's about it—which was fine, as our rent at this time was $800 per month. The foosball machine alone brought in $600 per month. We thought we had won the Powerball. In 1993 we saved enough to do our first renovation—the first of literally hundreds in my life. It was quite a simple job; we added twenty-two seats and installed our Bari pizza oven.

Almost immediately we began importing our own flour for pizza dough. There weren't many people bringing in their own flour, but we wanted every step to be authentic. We only sold "house wine," which was Montepulciano d'Abruzzo and Trebbiano in 1.5-litre formats. We wanted cheap and cheerful, because our customers wanted that and, frankly, I didn't have the bandwidth to take on wine. Not yet anyway.

The Toronto dining scene at that time was coming to the end of the "fine-dining" era. There were places like Pronto, Centro, Winston's, Fenton's, and, of course, Lotus. I think an ingredient that really sums up that era is sun-dried tomatoes. Anyone of a certain age will know exactly what I'm saying. That was the flavour of that era; it was evocative of, or synonymous with, the era. I had a lot of respect for what was going on in Toronto during that time, and part of me misses it! But we were not a part of that scene.

In our genesis, we were more of a store than a restaurant. But that Italian product importation set us up for what we became.

TERRONI STORY

Obviously, we weren't making much in sales, but we could tell we were onto something. People loved the sandwiches, so we added salad. People loved the salads, so we added pizza. It was unique and cool, very spur of the moment. We were going with the flow and the next steps felt very natural. Success was only defined by the fact that it was *ours*. As our needs grew, we started importing what we needed though Paolo's dad's importing business. But of course, as things grew to critical mass, we opened our own importation business, now called Scorte Alimentari.

Eventually the apartment above the shop became available. We rented it immediately and it became our prep/pasta kitchen. Suddenly we could expand our menu! Everything we made was "al forno," because that was the only way we could prepare it to order. We would serve in these beautiful terracotta vessels. Miriam, Paolo's mom, would use the space to prepare fresh pasta, soups, parmigiana, peperonate, gatto' di patate, verdure—all sorts of stuff for us. And now we were a real live restaurant, and you know, it felt good. But we didn't even have time to *feel* so much, because we got extremely busy. There were waiting lines. Like, all the time. I cringe to think of it, but there were times when we had to ask people to leave after they ate.

We opened Terroni Victoria (106 Victoria Street) in 1994.

2008 · OSTERIA CICERI E TRIA
2010 · LA BETTOLA

11

Once we had two restaurants, Paolo and I could split the time between us and give one another more space in each location. Selven, our chef who to this day runs Terroni Adelaide, started on our first day at Terroni Victoria. The experience of opening Victoria Street was the opposite of opening our first location on a sleepier Queen Street, mostly because it is central in the financial core. We got completely slammed. So, after our first lunch, we closed the door after the last customer, and did not reopen for dinner that night. Nor for another four or five days. No excuses, we were simply not prepared for a lunch of two hundred bankers all arriving at the same time to a sixty-seat restaurant, and who wanted to be out in forty-five minutes. So, in the days that followed, we shotgun-hired a bigger staff and reworked menu items. It was better when we reopened, but the problem with this location was that it was out-of-control busy during the day and then completely dead at dinner. And that was just kind of the flow there, for the first three or four years. This was all made much easier with the help of Larry D'Andrea, my right-hand man. He built our first restaurant on Queen as a contractor and then when Victoria Street opened, he also started *managing* the actual restaurant. Since then, he has become our in-house contractor, building every restaurant for us to this day. It was around this time, about 1995, that Karilynn Watson (who prefers her Italian name of *Karina Watsone*) joined us and started doing all our books, making sure that all our *T*s were crossed, and everything was in check. She has done that ever since and today she is our CFO and still overlooks every penny that comes in and out of all the businesses.

TERRONI STORY

2010 · BAR CENTRALE
2011 · TERRONI PRICE

The year 1996 was a defining year for me. It was the year my first child, Simona, was born, and it was the year that my best friend and business partner, Paolo, tragically died.

Between 1996 and 2001 was a complete blur.

Elena and I were building a family, and the years flew by. Most days I would get up at 5:30 a.m. to be at the Etobicoke Food Terminal by 6 a.m. so I could buy all the vegetables and drop them off at the three restaurant locations. Yes, that's right, we are now three. I opened Balmoral (Yonge and St. Clair) in the year 2000, and it was the first place that I truly opened on my own after Paolo passed away. It was a big deal for me. Even though my sister, Anna, joined Terroni during this time to support me, it still felt risky.

Now, I should tell you: Every restaurant that I opened was because an opportunity arose that I couldn't refuse. Sometimes it was a staff person I needed to open for. Often, it was (and is) because of a location I fell in love with, as is the story of the Balmoral location. This space was beautiful—someone had just spent an outrageous amount of money on it, and it hadn't worked out—it was the old Ace bakery and so it was clean and nicely designed. It needed money for a kitchen, but it had beautiful concrete floors, lots of windows, corner space, outdoor patio. Great bones, as they say.

The most attractive thing was that the area was thriving: It was a great residential area. The buildings around it brought lunch and dinner business. At one hundred seats, it was the perfect size, and the building was owned by local restaurateur legend Franco Prevedello (of Centro fame, etc.). My dad built the banquettes, we had incredible customers, and it was a busy lunch with an even busier dinner service.

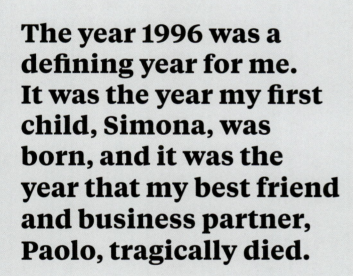

SCORTE
ALIMENTARI
IMPORTING

2011 · SCORTE ALIMENTARI

13

TERRONI STORY

2013 · SUD FORNO QUEEN

I had the legitimacy for the first time ever, that I could make something on my own, and for once (!) an opening came easily to me.

But man, were the days long. It's like what they say about having young children . . . the days are long, but the years fly by. After I would go to Etobicoke Food Terminal, I would make the pizza dough for the day for all locations, and then work lunch service at Balmoral, and then clean up right in time to prep for dinner service. I would come home, and Elena would pass me Simona or Sofia or Matteo, with whom she had spent the last twelve hours. In 2003 we rounded it out to an even four, with the birth of our fourth child, Olivia. It felt like complete madness, but something very sobering was right around the corner.

T

In 2004 we had just renovated Queen Street for the third time and opened a second addition to the first space. We decided to have an opening night for the new space, but unfortunately the only memory I have of that night is being in so much pain I could barely stand. After this pain continued for two weeks, I went to the doctor where, after the exam, he put me in the "bad news room" and told Elena and me that I had stage three colon cancer. I remember the day; it was August 25, 2004.

I went straight from the doctor's office to my parents' house. I don't know why, but my first instinct was to tell them. And the very next day Elena completely took over. It was awesome to witness; she was so amazing and composed and so strong. She made sure I ate and drank well. She made sure I went to every medical appointment, which when you have cancer becomes your total existence. She took care of absolutely everything. She was essentially a single parent of four small children. I was completely down for the count as they gave me a PICC line of twenty-four-hour chemo for one month. And even with my IV drip, we didn't want to tell the kids what was going on because they were so young. I was diagnosed in August and in December I had a very invasive surgery. After that, another five months of chemotherapy. During this time Elena only encouraged me and made plans for when I was better. I cannot convey in words how meaningful this was for me in that time, and still is now.

TERRONI STORY

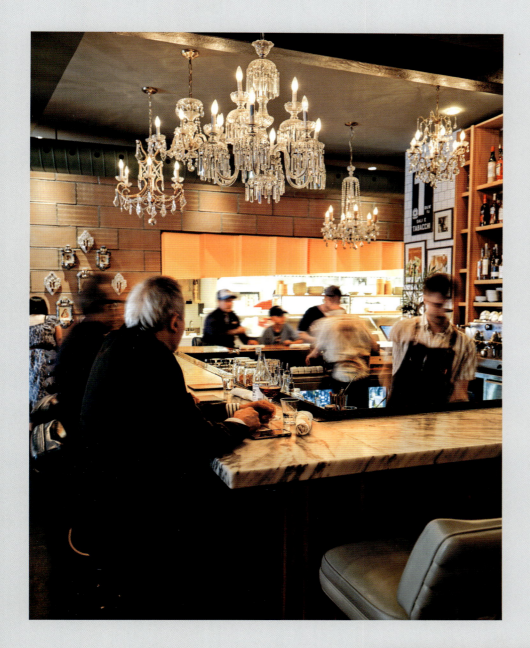

2013 · TERRONI DOWNTOWN, LA

TERRONI STORY

LA BOTTEGA
DI TERRONI
2016 · LA BOTTEGA, ONLINE

2016 · DOPOLAVORO, LA

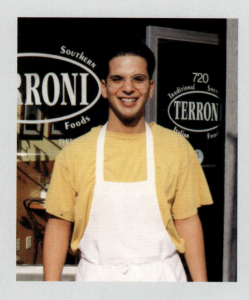 

My siblings, Anna and Vince, along with my close friends and colleagues like Kari and Gio (more on her soon), took over the business along with help from Larry D'Andrea.

I was very young when this all happened, and it was a wildly rare and aggressive form of colon cancer. All in all, I was out of the game for two years. I went from thinking of work twenty-four hours a day to not thinking about work at all. All I thought about was getting healthy. I was incredibly lucky to be so taken care of and to be given this time to try to heal my body.

A good friend of mine, Geddy Lee (yes, national treasure Geddy Lee), recommended this energy worker whose name is Cris Zavarce. Cris really helped me a lot. He taught me to visualize, self-heal, eat well, and stay positive. He did reiki on me and instilled a passion for removing negative thoughts and energy. I like to think that time instilled in me some good habits and they have continued. I've been healthy ever since. I wouldn't wish this on anyone and I'm one of the lucky ones.

A much more positive punctuation in the timeline of Terroni, and my own life, was the arrival of Giovanna Alonzi. We had posted a job opening for Terroni in the Italian Canadian newspaper *Corriere Canadese* and Giovanna saw it. She had just "blown her tuition in Nova Scotia for the summer" and was staying at her mother's house when she saw the posting. When she called the number in the paper, Vince picked up and told her he was just looking for someone "who speaks Italian and can grill some peppers." She arrived for the interview at 9 a.m. on a Saturday morning and remembers telling Vince she could "make things with Nutella." The selling point won him over. He didn't even ask to see her CV. Giovanna's training was hanging out with the older Italian ladies in her neighbourhood. They would call her when they were making cookies because she loved learning how to bake. "I was about eleven years old, and I had just come from Lazio and found a lot of comfort in these kitchens."

From day one, if you asked Giovanna to do something—and even still today—her answer is yes, no problem. Even if it's something she has never done—or especially if it's something she hasn't done! She will always say yes. It's never a "no." She is up to try any recipe and take on anything new in the kitchen. Giovanna is a key component to the growth of the Terroni family. We've been together for a long time, and she is a wonderful human being. And wow, did I ever need Giovanna, because when I got the green light after my sickness, I never looked back. I went faster. I love restaurants. (I still do!) I love Italian products and I was, and am, so much more motivated.

2017 · SUD FORNO TEMPERANCE

TERRONI STORY

In 2006 I started Cavinona Wine Agency, because—like everything we do—if we couldn't find a product we liked, we just skipped the hassle of trying to buy it from someone else, and we began importing it ourselves. And this was especially true when it comes to Italian wine (see "Cavinona: Introducing Italy by the Glass," page 122, for more).

It was also around this time that Elena and I went to visit our friend Shereen Arazm who had left the Terroni Group (yes, we are a "Group" at this point) to pursue an acting career in New York. But while there she decided to work in cool bars and nightclubs instead and then moved to the West Coast, to Los Angeles, to do the same. We had the most wonderful few days together and a very glamourous Hollywood visit. During the trip we spoke about how *maybe* we could do something together, in a while, in the future. I flew back to Toronto and *when I land* Shereen calls me and says, "I found a space, you have to fly back." This is just how Shereen works.

2019 · SPACCIO EAST

I flew back to see a location on Beverly and Curson in West Hollywood. And she was right, it was just perfect.

TERRONI STORY

2020 · STOCK T.C

We opened in 2007, which was wild, because only two weeks later we opened Terroni on Adelaide Street, still the behemoth of all our restaurants (over five hundred seats with patios and private spaces and we often seat over one thousand per day). Terroni on Beverly has continued to be bananas since we opened the doors. I love that restaurant. My point here is two of our biggest restaurants to this day opened within weeks of one another and ergo, it should have been a disaster, but it totally worked. Soon after, another one of our important Terroni family members joined us, Patti Shaw, who worked on all events and PR for Terroni. I love Patti like family. She drives me nuts and keeps me sane, simultaneously.

Downtown LA is the only time we had to close a restaurant. It still stings. But for all the success we have had, often it simply comes down to "right place, right time." Downtown LA can be summed up for Terroni as wrong place, wrong time. We opened in 2013, and the end point for us was COVID—and the riots in front of our downtown location and resulting damage didn't help. The downtown area just never really embraced us and ultimately, we closed. It was no longer safe for our staff. The juice wasn't worth the squeeze. To be honest, I don't really see it as "closing," I see it more as relocating, which we did, to Brentwood in 2024. So, in some ways the win in Brentwood has been extra sweet, as we didn't get there the way I thought we would. But we still got there.

Every Italian has an intense bond with their local *pasticceria* (pastry shop), and we always wanted to create our own.

Enter Sud Forno, which in 2013 opened two doors down from the original Terroni on Queen Street. I'm still very much in love with Sud. I feel we were successful with creating a relaxing atmosphere for the customer as soon as they walk in—the fresh bread smells, the abundance of options, the warm feeling. It felt like when we first opened Terroni. And you know, as Terroni grew, our panini selection disappeared, so with Sud we wanted to get back to making those again. Things like Italian sourdough with Italian wheat, Roman pizza (which didn't exist in Toronto at the time), Cornetti (page 40), Bomboloni (page 36), and Maritozzi (page 32). And it had retail shelves!

As Sud grew—and with our other now eleven locations—we were making our food all over town.

It felt chaotic. We had two separate bakeries, and the scheduling for breadmaking alone took hours and was just overly complicated. Over the years I looked for an industrial space so we could centralize some of the production, but often I was driving out to Etobicoke or Markham or Scarborough to see these huge facilities, and sure, they had the space but . . . with absolutely no charm. And as staff—a lot of staff—would be working here, it had to be beautiful, and it had to feel good to be there. Whenever I'm looking at a space, I always think, *Would I actually want to hang out here? Would spending time here make me happy?* And so, in 2018, when this space came up on the east side of downtown on a one-way residential street (Sackville), and I visited it, I was ready. A onetime sound studio that kind of degenerated into a warehouse, it had all the right bones and a lot of natural light. At 16,000 square feet it was perfect. We originally conceptualized it as a commissary to feed all our restaurants. Just before we opened Spaccio, in February 2019, we were so lucky to have Daniel Mezzolo, an incredible Friulian chef, join the family as Terroni's executive chef. What a relief it was to have him spearhead the Spaccio project.

TERRONI STORY

2022 · SPACCIO WEST
2023 · TERRONI STERLING

TERRONI STORY

2023 · LA BETTOLA, LA

Today, everything gets made there: all our pastries, all our biscotti, all our restaurant desserts, all our bread, all our pizza dough, butchery, gelato, all our five-hour sauces, all our pastas, and five thousand panettone at Christmastime . . . do you want me to keep going? Because I can!

We were going to keep it just as production and retail, but then we realized it was beautiful to watch all the happenings in the kitchen, and so we created a tiny restaurant within Spaccio on the mezzanine floor. And I have to say, a lot of my guests who've been eating with us for over thirty years say this is their favourite location. I love that.

One minor note: As soon as we opened Spaccio, COVID hit. Instead of tables and chairs for the restaurant, we were buying refrigerated shelving units to showcase fresh salami, wines, and cheeses. As soon as products would hit the shelf, the goods would fly off. Instead of a central bakery and restaurant, Spaccio morphed into a commissary and Italian grocer. It wasn't what we had envisioned, but it's what the times called for. And that's the adjustment all restaurants, big and small, had to make. During COVID we brought many of our restaurant chefs to work at Spaccio. It was like having the triple-A team under one roof. All our head chefs (and I want to mention them by name here: Marco Bruno, Fabio Moro, Luca Rotatori, Selvendran Thiruchelvam, Ravikumar Arumugam, Sanjeevan Sriganesan, and Maggie Lee) worked under incredibly difficult circumstances to manage a very challenging time. I'm proud of this, and though it wasn't fun or easy, we learned a lot and grew tighter as a team.

The final Toronto opening (at least as of the publication of this book) and an interesting moment in Terroni history is STOCK T.C. This beautiful restaurant and grocery space is a culmination of my friendship with Stephen Alexander. For those who don't know, Stephen Alexander is a third-generation gentleman butcher, Australian born, Canadian adopted. I was running Terroni, opening new spots. He was running Cumbrae's. We would travel together to eat around the world. And then right beside Sud Forno, a place opened for him to open a new shop on Queen Street. We didn't want to mess up our friendship by bringing business into it really, but finally it was obvious, we should do something together. It felt like NOT doing something was stranger in a way.

TERRONI STORY

The concept of STOCK T.C (the initials stand for Terroni Cumbrae's) is everything we love under one roof: a Sud Forno, a Cumbrae's, and a restaurant. STOCK has the best of both of our worlds.

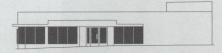

2024 · TERRONI BRENTWOOD, LA
2024 · FORNO TERRONI BRENTWOOD, LA

At STOCK you'll find all the Italian things I love but also all the not-Italian things I love, such as rotisserie chicken, a decadent mac and cheese, foie gras, beef Wellington, duck confit, dry-aged rib eyes, burgers, and lots of French desserts. You get the picture. Also, something you'll never find at Spaccio . . . a very good bottle of Burgundy on the wine list.

It felt very right when this beautiful building came up for lease at Yonge and Eglinton. The broker—you can imagine at this point I've met many brokers—on the building wanted us to take the ground space and then eventually we took the whole thing, all 20,000 feet. The ground floor is the beautiful shop while the second and third floor is our restaurant. Ralph Giannone, who has conceptualized the architecture of all my restaurants, is also Stephen's architect. And so, Ralph created this unbelievable space combining both of our sensibilities. Not an easy feat! The food is Italian American Bistro.

T

Through all of this—from 1992 until present day—selling Italian products and telling the story of Italy through every meal is what drives me. I have the same feeling walking into Terroni now as I had in 1992. It still excites me to see people sitting in my restaurants, laughing, eating, drinking, and having fun. That's everything for me. Still to this day, I walk in, I automatically check the music, dim the lights, and check the plates arriving at tables.

**These fundamentals for me—
through good times and bad—
have always stayed the same.**

UOVO CAFFÈ CIOCCOLATO MARMELLATA ZUCCHERO BURRO LIMONE SALE MANDORLE NOCCIOLA UVA SULTANINA FARINA CREMA LATTE NUTELLA PROSCIUTTO POMODORO OLIO D'OLIVA

COLAZIONE
BREAKFAST

1

COLAZIONE

Uovo sbattuto con caffè

WHIPPED EGG WITH ESPRESSO

SERVES 4

YOU WILL NEED

- Whisk or handheld mixer
- 4 small water glasses or
  4 espresso cups for serving

- 4 very fresh egg yolks
- 5 tablespoons
  granulated sugar
- 1/4 cup (60ml) freshly
  brewed espresso

One of my all-time favourites! We had it every Saturday growing up in North Toronto where I was raised.

My grandmother used to make this economical breakfast treat with the whole egg, instead of just the yolks, because like a typical nonna, she did not want to waste a thing. My mother made the best uovo sbattuto, however. As kids we immediately tasted the difference because she used only the yolks. You need to beat the yolks until very pale, which of course means a lot of sugar. And as we grew older, we added a scandalous drop of espresso.

In a small bowl, combine the egg yolks and sugar and whisk until light and creamy, 4 to 5 minutes. Divide the creamy egg mixture into 4 small water glasses or espresso cups, top each with as much of the hot espresso as desired, and serve immediately.

NOTA BENE This drink contains raw eggs.

COLAZIONE

Biscotti da inzuppo

DUNKING COOKIES

MAKES 30 BISCOTTI

YOU WILL NEED

- Baking sheets
- Parchment paper
- Stand mixer fitted
  with the paddle
- Rubber spatula

BASIC DOUGH

- 2 sticks + 5 tablespoons
  (10½ ounces/300g) unsalted
  butter, at room temperature
- 1½ cups (300g)
  granulated sugar
- Grated zest of 1 lemon
- 1 vanilla bean, split
  lengthwise
- 3 eggs
- 2½ cups (315g) pastry flour
- 2½ cups (315g) all-
  purpose flour
- 1 teaspoon baking powder
- Fine sea salt

VARIATIONS

- 1 cup (150g) hazelnuts,
  lightly crushed
- 1 cup (150g) almonds,
  lightly crushed
- 1½ cups (170g) chocolate
  chips (milk, dark chocolate,
  or a mix works well)

NOTA BENE You can use the Basic Dough in recipes such as the Apricot Jam Tart (page 45). This dough can be made a day ahead and refrigerated or even frozen for several weeks.

This is the most versatile cookie dough there is and comes from our Sud Forno kitchen where the recipe was relentlessly perfected. You can use it for a tart crust, or you can use it for a cookie dough. In Italian we call it *impasto da battaglia*, which translates to "battle ready dough." In this version, the base is simple vanilla, which we can build out to four different flavours: vanilla, hazelnut, almond, and chocolate chip. This cookie may feel like plain vanilla wafer, but it has a lot more flavour and it's tastier because you've made it yourself.

Preheat the oven to 350°F (180°C). Line a baking sheet with parchment paper.

Make the dough: In a stand mixer fitted with the paddle, combine the butter, sugar, and lemon zest. Scrape in the vanilla seeds. Mix until light and fluffy, stopping and scraping the bowl with a rubber spatula as needed, for about 5 minutes. In a separate bowl, lightly whisk the eggs. Set the mixer on medium speed and slowly add the eggs to the butter mixture until well combined. In another bowl, whisk together the pastry flour, all-purpose flour, baking powder, and a pinch of salt. Carefully add the flour mixture in several additions to the mixer and beat until combined. Finish mixing by kneading the dough on a work surface for 5 to 8 minutes until smooth. Set aside briefly while you toast the nuts.

Spread the hazelnuts and almonds on the lined baking sheet and toast until fragrant, 8 to 10 minutes. Set the nuts aside to cool.

To finish: Divide the dough into 4 equal portions. Knead the hazelnuts into one portion, the almonds into another, the chocolate chips into another, leaving one of the portions plain. Shape each portion into a log about 12 inches (30cm) long and 2 to 3 inches (5 to 7cm) wide. Refrigerate for at least 30 minutes.

When ready to bake, adjust the oven to 325°F (160°C). Line two baking sheets with parchment paper.

Arrange the logs on the baking sheets. Bake the logs until firm, 25 to 30 minutes. Remove from the oven, but leave the oven on and reduce the oven temperature to 300°F (150°C).

While still hot, transfer each log to a cutting board and cut the log crosswise into biscotti about ¾ inch (2cm) thick. Return them to the baking sheets, place them back in the oven, and bake until dry to the touch and lightly golden brown on the edges, another 8 to 10 minutes.

Let the biscotti cool on the baking sheets. Once cooled, store the biscotti in an airtight container for up to a week or in the freezer for up to a couple of months.

COLAZIONE

Maritozzi

SWEET BUNS

MAKES 15 BUNS

YOU WILL NEED

- Baking sheet
- Parchment paper
- Digital scale
- Bench scraper
- Pastry brush
- Electric mixer or whisk
- 2 piping bags
- Offset spatula

MARITOZZI

- $\frac{1}{2}$ recipe Base Brioche (page 291)
- Egg wash: 1 egg yolk whisked with 1 tablespoon heavy cream

FILLINGS

- 1 cup (250ml) heavy cream
- 2 tablespoons icing sugar, plus more for sprinkling
- $\frac{1}{2}$ cup (150g) Pastry Cream (page 301)

In 2013, our master baker Giuliano Pediconi made *maritozzi marchigiani* at the bakery, and I immediately fell in love. The cream, the sugary delicious glaze, the raisins—the sheer audacious size of these sweet buns. And back then—which is not so long ago—there wasn't anyone making them here in Canada, at least that we were aware of. And so, we began selling them when we opened Sud Forno.

However, with the rise of Instagram, customers would arrive looking for the Roman version (rather than our version from the Marche region), which is a brioche bun split open and filled with whipped cream, without glaze or raisins. The demand became so high we agreed to make them, though mostly because for the Roman version, we could use the same dough already in rotation for our bomboloni. Rest assured; these are relatively easy to make at home with a big wow factor. →

COLAZIONE

Make the maritozzi: Make the brioche dough and let it rest as directed.

Line a baking sheet with parchment paper. Divide the dough into 15 equal portions about 35g each (use a digital scale); start by dividing the dough into 3, then subdividing each third into 5 pieces. Roll each portion into a tight round bun and place on the lined baking sheet, leaving enough space between them for them to double in size. Cover loosely with plastic wrap. Allow the dough balls to rise until they double in size, 1½ to 2 hours.

Preheat the oven to 325°F (160°C).

Carefully brush the buns with the egg wash and bake until golden brown, about 20 minutes.

Meanwhile, prepare the fillings: In a medium bowl, with an electric mixer or whisk, whip the heavy cream with the icing sugar until stiff peaks form. Be careful not to overwhip the mixture.

Place the whipped cream and pastry cream in two separate piping bags and cut the tips about ¼-inch (5mm) wide. Once the maritozzi have cooled, cut them horizontally across the top but do not cut all the way through, leaving them hinged on one side so they are connected. Pipe about 1 teaspoon of pastry cream in each maritozzo and then about 1½ tablespoons of whipped cream. Use an offset spatula to smooth out the whipped cream until there is a seamless transition between bun and whipped cream. Dust with icing sugar.

NOTA BENE The frozen dough from Bomboloni (page 36) can be repurposed for this recipe. Simply remove the frozen dough balls from the freezer and place in your turned-off oven overnight, alongside a bowl of hot water—a simple proofing technique, so they are ready to be baked in the morning.

COLAZIONE

Bomboloni

ITALIAN DONUTS FILLED WITH PASTRY CREAM OR NUTELLA

MAKES 30 DONUTS

YOU WILL NEED

- 2 baking sheets
- Parchment paper
- Digital scale
- Large shallow pot, for frying
- Deep-fry thermometer
- Slotted spoon
- 2 piping bags or ziplock bags

- Base Brioche (page 291)
- Sunflower oil (about 2 quarts/2L), for deep-frying
- Granulated sugar, for coating
- 1 (7-ounce/200g) jar Nutella, for filling
- About 2 cups (650g) Pastry Cream (page 301), for filling

We started making bomboloni at our Terroni Queen Street location about twenty years ago. Historically speaking, that's a lot of donuts! My right-hand chef then—and still to this day—Giovanna Alonzi, would fry very small batches and people would just know to show up. And then, well, when we were sold out, we were sold out, which would only make the lines longer and the donut craving stronger for the next week. Remember? Back then it was a rare thing to find warm and fresh yeasted Italian donuts in downtown Toronto.

It wasn't until 2012 when Sud Forno opened, and baker Giuliano Pediconi joined the team, that we started making our bomboloni to scale. We all have fond memories of the first time he ever made the dough and the whole restaurant filled with the warm scent of vanilla, butter, and yeast. As he was frying them, he finished the cooked ones by rolling them in sugar, and we were hooked forever.

It's really the brioche dough that makes these bomboloni singular. For the filling, we've included Nutella or a simple pastry cream option. Dealer's choice. →

COLAZIONE

NOTA BENE The bomboloni dough can be frozen after being shaped into individual dough balls. The dough balls should first be frozen separately on a baking sheet, then stored in a freezer bag, so they don't stick to one another. The day you're ready to make them, remove from the freezer and place on parchment-lined baking sheets, leaving enough space between them (about 4 inches/10cm) to proof. Loosely cover them with plastic wrap and let sit until they double in size, 3½ to 4 hours, then they are ready to be fried.

Make the brioche dough and let rest as directed.

Line two baking sheets with parchment paper. Divide the dough into 30 equal portions of 35g each (use a digital scale); start by dividing the dough into 3, then subdividing each third into 10 pieces. Roll each piece of dough into a tight ball and place on the lined baking sheets, leaving enough space between them (about 4 inches/10cm) to double in size. Cover loosely with plastic wrap and let rise until doubled in size, 1½ to 2 hours.

Pour at least 2 inches (5cm) sunflower oil into a large shallow pot and heat over medium heat to 340°F (171°C). Line a tray with paper towels and place near the stove.

Using scissors, cut parchment into a square around each bombolone. Grab the top 2 corners of a parchment paper with a bombolone on it and very carefully lower it dough side down into the hot oil. Repeat with a few more, working in batches, making sure not to crowd the pot. After a couple of minutes, or as soon as the bottom side is golden brown, use the slotted spoon to carefully flip to the other side, leaving the parchment paper attached. It will detach when the oil penetrates between the dough and the paper. Discard the parchment square. As soon as the other side is golden brown, remove the bomboloni from the oil using the slotted spoon. Place them on the paper towels to drain. Carefully roll them in some granulated sugar. Everyone prefers warm donuts, so you want to work quickly here.

Place the Nutella and pastry cream in two separate piping bags and cut the tips off. Using a chopstick or a dowel, puncture a hole at the top of the bombolone. Fill each until you can see the bombolone puff up, with a scant 2 tablespoons (25g) of Nutella or pastry cream, or a bit of both if you're feeling wild, and enjoy immediately.

COLAZIONE

Cornetti

ITALIAN CROISSANTS

MAKES 14 CORNETTI

YOU WILL NEED

- Baking sheet
- Parchment paper
- Stand mixer fitted
  with the paddle
- Ruler
- Rolling pin
- Chef's knife or roller cutter
- Pastry brush

- Base Brioche (page 291)
- 2½ sticks (290g) unsalted
  butter, at room temperature
- 1 vanilla bean, split
  lengthwise
- Grated zest of 1 orange
- ½ cup (65g) all-
  purpose flour
- Egg wash: 1 egg beaten with
  1½ tablespoons whole milk
  and a pinch of fine sea salt

What's the difference between an Italian cornetto and a French croissant, you may ask? Well, a cornetto dough includes eggs, and a croissant does not. Also, a cornetto has an element of sweetness, whereas with a croissant the depth of flavour comes from the quality of the butter. No surprise there, as in general, Italian breakfasts hit much higher on the sweet side than a French breakfast. There's also the overall texture: cornetti are *morbidi* ("soft") and croissants are flakier. At Sud Forno, ours are especially soft, because we use brioche dough here, as we do for both bomboloni and maritozzi.

A happy memory for me was when our first customers would come in, stand at the bar for a cornetto and a cappuccino. I felt we were carving out a small place for the Italian breakfast experience, which is to say, a little coffee, a sweet bite, and the mandatory arguing about the previous night's football match.

For this recipe we ask that you harness your inner pastry chef.

What does that mean?

1. Work on a schedule.

2. Work in a cold space.

An ideal time to start this recipe is 2 p.m. The dough would then be ready to be refrigerated around 7 p.m. for a resting period of about 16 hours. We understand this means that, for many people, it's a weekend project. But a worthy one! To obtain the best structure, the dough must be maintained at a cool temperature so it must be worked quickly and swiftly. No one wants sticky, unmanageable dough!

Make the brioche dough and let rest as directed.

Line a baking sheet with parchment paper and lightly oil the paper. Lightly tighten the dough by pulling it along a smooth surface and shaping it into a ball. Place the dough on the lined baking sheet and loosely cover with plastic wrap. Let it proof at room temperature until doubled in size, 2 to 3 hours.

Meanwhile, in a stand mixer fitted with the paddle, cream the butter for 2 to 3 minutes. Scrape in the vanilla seeds. Add the orange zest and flour and mix until well combined, 2 to 3 minutes. Remove this blended butter from the mixer and place onto a sheet of parchment paper. Working with a spoon or a palette knife, shape the butter into an 8½ × 10¼-inch (22 × 26cm) rectangle ⅜ inch (1cm) thick. Wrap this up in the parchment sheet and refrigerate overnight.

When the brioche dough has doubled in size, press down on the plastic wrap to deflate any air and place in the refrigerator to rest overnight.

The next morning, remove the butter rectangle from the refrigerator and leave it at room temperature for 1 hour.

Slowly peel the plastic wrap (discarding it) off the dough and place the dough on a lightly floured, clean surface. Using a rolling pin, roll the dough into a rectangle 12 × 16½-inches (30 × 42cm) and about ½ inch (1.5cm) thick. →

40

COLAZIONE

When rolling, move the rolling pin from edge to edge and make sure you have just enough flour underneath, so the dough never sticks to the surface. Set the dough rectangle with a long side facing you. Remove the butter from the parchment and place it at the centre of the rectangle with a short side facing you. Now fold the rectangle of dough so both sides meet in the middle of the rectangle to cover the butter. You may need to stretch and pull the dough slightly to cover the butter rectangle completely. Dust with more flour and, using your rolling pin, elongate the rectangle to form a longer rectangle directly in front of you until it reaches ⅜-inch (1cm) thickness. Fold one end of the dough a quarter into the rectangle toward its middle and the other end to meet it. Fold this in half, flipping the longer fold over the quarter fold. You should now have 4 layers of dough. Wrap this with plastic wrap and refrigerate for 1 hour.

Remove the dough from the refrigerator, unwrap, and place it directly on a lightly floured surface with a short side facing you. Very lightly dust the dough with flour and use your rolling pin to flatten the rectangle to ⅜ inch (1cm) thick. When rolling, be firm and strong, applying even pressure from the bottom to the top of the rectangle. Fold one end of the dough a quarter into the rectangle toward its middle and bring in the other end of the rectangle to meet it. Fold this in half, flipping the longer fold over the quarter fold. You should now have 4 layers of dough. Wrap it in plastic wrap and refrigerate for 2 more hours.

Remove the dough from the refrigerator, unwrap, and place it directly on a lightly floured surface with a short side facing you. Use your rolling pin to flatten the rectangle, rolling away from you to an 8 × 10-inch (20 × 25cm) rectangle. No extra flour dusting is needed at this point. When rolling, be firm and strong, applying even pressure from the bottom to the top of the rectangle and lengthwise if necessary. Grab a ruler and use a knife to make an incision every 3½ inches (9cm) along a long edge of the rectangle. Do the same with the top of the rectangle but make an incision every 1¾ inches (4.5cm). Cut triangles by connecting the points at the base of the rectangle to the ones at the top. Once the triangles are cut, make a ⅜-inch (1cm) incision midway through the base of the triangle. To roll the cornetto, position each triangle with its base pointing toward you and tightly roll from the base to the tip while pressing outward on the base ends. The goal here is to create flaps that will protrude from the finished roll and that will then be curved together to form a crescent moon.

Place all the cornetti at least 4 inches (10cm) apart on a baking sheet lined with parchment paper. Loosely cover with plastic wrap.

PROOFING OPTIONS (CHOOSE THE OPTION THAT WORKS BEST FOR YOUR SCHEDULE):

Option 1: Proof for 3 hours, or until doubled, at room temperature and bake.

Option 2: Place unproofed dough in the fridge overnight. At 7 a.m. remove from the fridge, proof for 1 hour, then bake.

Option 3: Place in the freezer. When ready to bake, proof overnight (or for 8 to 10 hours) in your oven with the light on and a bowl of warm water.

Finally, we are ready to bake! Preheat the oven to 350°F (180°C).

Evenly brush the cornetti with the egg wash. Bake until golden brown, 18 to 22 minutes.

Remove from the oven and let cool on the pan. Enjoy as soon as possible. No one likes a stale cornetto!

VARIATIONS

CORNETTO ALLA CREMA, NUTELLA O MARMELLATA

Though these cornetti are delicious on their own, we typically serve them stuffed with Nutella, pastry cream (page 301), or jam (page 46). Place your preferred filling in a piping bag. Using a dowel or a chopstick, pierce a hole through the belly of a warm cornetto. Pipe a couple of tablespoons (30g) through the hole and enjoy!

COLAZIONE

Crostata alla marmellata di albicocche

APRICOT JAM TART

MAKES ONE 12-INCH (30CM) TART; SERVES 6

YOU WILL NEED

- 12-inch (30cm) tart tin
- Rolling pin
- Fluted pastry cutting wheel

- Basic biscotti dough (page 31)
- 1½ tablespoons unsalted butter, for the tin
- All-purpose flour, for dusting
- 1 cup (250ml) Apricot Jam (recipe follows) or any store-bought jam such as cherry or plum

Making crostata is just an excuse to flex our jam muscles at the bakery. It's as simple as that.

For those of you who haven't tried crostata but are curious: It's not a cake, it's not a cookie, it's not a crumble. We hesitate to say "tart" in English because the crust of a crostata traditionally has a much looser and drier makeup than a traditional tart crust. It's polarizing for sure, but it's also what we always ate for our after-school snack, and it's as authentically Italian as it gets. And, well, honouring that kind of education is what we see as our job at Terroni. →

Make the basic dough for the biscotti. Freeze half for another use. Divide remaining dough into 2 pieces: one weighing 14 ounces (400g) and one weighing 9 ounces (250g). Grease a 12-inch (30cm) tart tin with the butter. Lightly dust a work surface with flour. Using a rolling pin, roll the larger piece of dough out to form a round about ¼ inch (6mm) thick. Carefully place the round into the tart tin, pressing it into the edges and cutting off any dough overhang with a sharp knife. Spread the jam over the bottom of the crust.

Roll the remaining dough out on a lightly floured surface until it's about ⅛ inch (3mm) thick. Using a fluted pastry cutting wheel, cut strips about ½ inch (1.5cm) wide. Use the strips to make a lattice: Lay some strips over the jam/surface of the crostata about 1¼ inches (3cm) apart. Place another set of dough strips at an angle to the first set, but also 1¼ inches (3cm) apart. Use more dough strips to go around the circumference of the crostata. Press the ends of the dough together if more than one strip is needed to accomplish this. Refrigerate for at least 30 minutes.

Preheat the oven to 325°F (160°C).

Bake the crostata until the pastry turns light golden brown, 45 to 50 minutes.

Apricot Jam

MAKES A SCANT 2 CUPS (900G)

YOU WILL NEED

- Small ceramic saucer
- 2¼ pounds (1kg) apricots, cut into ¾-inch (2cm) pieces
- 2 cups (400g) granulated sugar
- Juice of ½ lemon, strained

Place a small ceramic saucer in the freezer. In a large saucepan or pot, combine the apricots, sugar, and lemon juice. Bring the mixture to a gentle boil over medium heat, stirring occasionally to ensure the sugar dissolves. Once it starts boiling, reduce the heat to medium-low and simmer, stirring occasionally, until the jam becomes gelatinous, 35 to 40 minutes. To test if the jam is ready, take a tablespoon of the jam and place it on the cold dish from the freezer. If you can run your finger through it easily, separating the jam, it's ready to be cooled and used.

Once the desired consistency is achieved, remove the jam from the heat, let it cool, and transfer to sterilized jars for storage or use immediately.

CONVERSATION

COLLO
CONVERSATION
QUIO✕

Bruce Mau

Bruce Mau is the cofounder and CEO of Massive Change Network (MCN), a global design consultancy based in the Chicago area. Across nearly forty years of design innovation, Bruce has worked as a designer, innovator, educator, author, and artist on a broad spectrum of projects in collaboration with the world's leading brands, organizations, universities, governments, entrepreneurs, renowned artists, and fellow optimists.

Where are you based?

Chicago, Illinois

What's your relationship to Terroni?

Terroni saved my life. I lived directly across from the first Terroni on Queen Street West. At the time that Terroni first opened, that area was something of a food desert, except for Dufflet's. So, for us, Terroni was a godsend! We were the first regular customers. We couldn't get enough of it. Practically anything that these young Italian Canadian entrepreneurs brought in, we would buy, from olive oil to serving bowls. We fell in love with Cosimo and the

whole Terroni vibe. They had so much attitude—they wouldn't cut the pizza! They had a brilliant touch for welcoming people into their culture. They loved it and they wanted everyone to love it, too.

Favourite Terroni dish (including all restaurants, Spaccio, etc.)?

It's tough to narrow it down to a single dish. I love the tuna with beans, the four seasons pizza is awesome, the sandwiches were killer for me—but the lemon pasta was a trip to the south of Italy.

Favourite Terroni memory?

I will never forget our first visit. We had been waiting for weeks for Terroni to open, watching from our apartment across the street—and then finally the day arrived! My wife, Bisi Williams, and I, almost giddy with excitement, hurried over. The shelves were still half full, the place half built, but Cosimo was there with his brilliant, beautiful, generous energy, and we could smell that we were in the right place, and that our lives had just changed for the better! We had pizzas, with wine, and then desserts—and then left with armloads of great Italian food to take home. Happy beyond belief!

Favourite Terroni location?

You know, I love Terroni everywhere, the big courthouse Terroni, uptown Summerhill Terroni—but the first one will always be the *real* Terroni for me!

Do you like it sweet or savoury?

I need both! Terroni pizza or pasta without tiramisù is somehow incomplete. The Terroni tiramisù is for me the standard definition of tiramisù—the ultimate tiramisù that all other tiramisùs will forever be measured against.

What do you like about Toronto? If based elsewhere, tell us where you live and why we should—or shouldn't—visit.

Chicago, like Toronto, is one of the greatest food cities in the world. The Taste of Chicago, an outdoor food festival that happens every summer, will blow your mind. It is the taste of the world! Chicago is home to awesome traditional food cultures and the home of true food innovators and some of the world's best restaurants. The Chicago culture of food is rich and deep and absolutely worth a trip.

But Toronto is one of the sweetest cities in the world. Terroni is very Toronto. A generous love language of food and culture. The Canadian culture is very special and more and more important in the world at this moment in history. Every time I visit, I see it more clearly and feel the generous energy that invites the world to come and be part of this great cultural experiment. If Toronto were to elect a food ambassador, it would have to be Terroni represented by Cosimo!

COLAZIONE

Panettone French Toast

SERVES 4

- 3 eggs
- ½ cup (120ml) heavy cream
- 2 tablespoons grated Parmigiano-Reggiano cheese
- ¾ teaspoon fine sea salt
- ¼ teaspoon freshly ground black pepper
- ½ loaf Panettone Classico (page 252), cut into 8 slices
- 12 very thin slices speck (about 4¼ ounces/120g)
- ¾ cup (80g) Taleggio cheese
- 2 tablespoons (30g) unsalted butter
- Canadian maple syrup, for drizzling

NOTA BENE You could also use the Pan Brioche (page 291) for this recipe.

Having a French toast recipe in an Italy-loving book doesn't really make sense . . . except it does, because we use leftover panettone for it! Usually after Christmas we would offer a sweet French toast as a dessert with *crema inglese* (crème anglaise) at all of our restaurants. In this case, we take the matter further to offer a savoury version with speck and Taleggio cheese, drizzled with maple syrup.

In a shallow bowl or pan, whisk together the eggs, cream, Parmigiano, salt, and pepper until well combined.

Cover 4 panettone slices with 3 slices of speck each and top with the Taleggio. Place the remaining 4 slices of panettone on top, sandwiching the cheese and speck between both slices.

Preheat a skillet over medium heat. Dip 2 panettone sandwiches in the egg mixture, submerging them for 30 seconds per side. Add the butter to the pan, reduce the heat to medium-low, and fry each sandwich 3 to 4 minutes per side. Repeat the process for the remaining two sandwiches. Serve while still hot with a drizzle of maple syrup.

COLAZIONE

Tartine con scarola e uova

ESCAROLE TARTS WITH POACHED EGGS

MAKES 4 INDIVIDUAL TARTS

YOU WILL NEED

- Four 4-inch (10cm) tart tins 1 inch (2.5cm) deep
- Rolling pin
- 5-inch (12.5cm) round dough cutter
- Parchment paper
- Pie weights or dried beans

PUFF PASTRY TARTS

- 1 pound (500g) Puff Pastry (page 298)
- Softened butter, for the tart tins
- Fine sea salt
- 2 cups (150g) escarole, cleaned and bottom stems removed
- 1 tablespoon extra-virgin olive oil
- 1½ tablespoons (20g) unsalted butter
- 1 garlic clove, peeled but whole
- 1 tablespoon minced oil-packed anchovy fillets
- ¼ cup (50g) finely chopped shallots
- 2 tablespoons white wine
- 2 tablespoons Taggiasca olives, pitted
- 1 tablespoon raisins
- 2 teaspoons pine nuts
- ¼ cup (80g) ricotta cheese
- ¼ cup (60ml) heavy cream
- 1 egg
- 1 tablespoon finely grated pecorino cheese
- Fine sea salt and freshly ground black pepper

This puff pastry tart is a brunch favourite for home cooks and is a recipe that has been on our Bar Centrale menu for years. What we're giving you here is a wonderful excuse to cook with escarole, a leafy green that has not been trending like kale, but one that Italian nonnas have historically had a solid handle on. With ricotta, olives, raisins, pine nuts . . . this dish has a lot going on. Make it once, and it's something I promise you'll make again.

I love it made the day after when these filling flavours have had some time together (see Nota Bene). I also love this dish in the afternoon with a white wine full of minerality and freshness, preferably Roero Arneis from Marco Porello, a wonderful producer in Italy's Aosta region. →

POACHED EGGS

- 1½ teaspoons fine sea salt
- 1 tablespoon white wine vinegar
- 4 eggs

FOR SERVING

- Fine sea salt and freshly ground black pepper
- Extra-virgin olive oil, for drizzling

COLAZIONE

Make the puff pastry and refrigerate as directed.

Make the tarts: Lightly grease four 4-inch (10cm) tart tins 1 inch (2.5cm) deep.

On a lightly floured surface, roll out the puff pastry dough to about ¼-inch (5mm) thickness. Using a 5-inch (12.5cm) round dough cutter, cut out 4 rounds. Press the pastry rounds into each tart tin, covering it completely and cutting off any extra dough. Refrigerate the tart shells for 30 minutes.

Meanwhile, preheat the oven to 375°F (190°C). Cut out parchment paper rounds about 5 inches (12.5cm) in diameter to cover the puff pastry in the tins.

Remove the tarts from the fridge, cover with the parchment rounds, and fill each tin with pie weights. Set the tart tins on a baking sheet and bake for 20 minutes. Remove the pie weights and parchment and bake for another 5 minutes without any filling. Remove the tart shells but leave the oven on.

Meanwhile, bring a large pot of salted water to a boil. Blanch the escarole for 2 minutes. Drain and rinse the leaves in very cold water. Shake dry, then roughly chop into 1-inch (2.5cm) pieces and set aside.

In a large skillet, warm the olive oil, butter, garlic, anchovies, and shallots over medium heat. Using a wooden spoon, stir the anchovies until they melt into the shallots and sauté until the garlic clove turns golden brown, 3 to 4 minutes. Increase the heat to medium-high, add the escarole, and fry for 2 to 3 minutes. Deglaze the pan with the white wine and add the olives, raisins, and pine nuts. Cook over medium heat until all the liquid is absorbed, 8 to 10 minutes. Remove from the heat and set aside to cool completely (discard the garlic clove).

In a large bowl, mix the ricotta, cream, egg, pecorino, and cooled escarole. Season to taste with salt and freshly ground pepper. Divide this mixture among the 4 tart tins.

Bake until the filling appears firm to the touch, 25 to 30 minutes.

Poach the eggs: A few minutes before serving, bring water to a boil in a medium pot and add the salt and the white wine vinegar. Crack one egg into a sieve held over the sink to drain, then gently let it slide into the simmering water. Set your timer and cook for *exactly* 3 minutes. Carefully drain the egg and set aside. Repeat the process for the remaining eggs.

Serve the tarts warm, topping each with a poached egg. Season with salt, freshly ground pepper, and a drizzle of olive oil.

NOTA BENE The puff pastry dough can be set in the pan and placed in the refrigerator overnight or frozen for up to 1 month. It can be baked directly from frozen by increasing the initial baking time by 15 to 20 minutes. Also, the filling without the egg and ricotta can be made in advance and stored in the refrigerator for up to 1 day.

COLAZIONE

Panino all'uovo

SCRAMBLED EGG SANDWICH

MAKES 1 SANDWICH

- 1 Ciabatta Bun, homemade (page 85) or store-bought
- 1 tablespoon extra-virgin olive oil
- 2 thin slices prosciutto cotto (Italian cooked ham)
- 2 eggs
- Fine sea salt and freshly ground black pepper
- 1 tablespoon (15g) unsalted butter
- 2 slices Fontina cheese
- 3 slices tomato

In 1992, when we opened Terroni on Queen Street, our customers clamored for breakfast options. Without a stove, we had to get creative. Enter the espresso machine steamer. We discovered that we could use it to scramble eggs to perfection—fluffy, healthy, and without oil or butter! We'd sandwich those scrambled eggs, along with provolone cheese, cooked ham, tomato, salt, pepper, and a drizzle of olive oil, into a panino. It became an instant hit, and while we've since diversified our menu, we still cherish our espresso machine for what it does best: brewing espresso.

Slice the bun horizontally in half. Drizzle the olive oil over each side of the roll. On the bottom half, arrange the prosciutto cotto slices.

In a small bowl, whisk the eggs and season with salt and pepper. Heat a skillet over medium heat and melt the butter. Add the whisked eggs and stir until scrambled. Spoon the scrambled eggs over the prosciutto cotto and top with the Fontina and tomato slices, seasoned with salt and pepper, while the eggs are still hot. Enjoy the sandwich immediately.

COLAZIONE

Uova al purgatorio

EGGS IN PURGATORY

SERVES 4

YOU WILL NEED

- 12-inch (30cm) pan with a lid, at least 5 inches (13cm) deep

- 4 slices Bread Crisps (page 290) or sliced fresh sourdough bread, such as Pane Pugliese (page 80)
- 4 tablespoons extra-virgin olive oil
- 1 garlic clove, smashed and peeled
- 1 small onion, finely chopped
- 4 small fresh chilies, left whole
- 2 cups (10 ounces/300g) cherry tomatoes, halved
- 1 (28-ounce/796g) can whole peeled plum tomatoes
- Fine sea salt and freshly ground black pepper
- 8 fresh basil leaves
- 8 eggs

My mother made this very often for dinner—as either a starter or a main—served with a good slice of crusty bread. We never made it *that* spicy (even though we were from Calabria), and only my dad would add more spice in the end, as his general motto in life was "the hotter, the better." Typical for a Calabrian, he would habitually carry a few fresh chilis, or have them stashed somewhere in the house, ready for whenever he needed that hit.

Make the bread crisps as directed. (If using fresh bread, just serve the slices as is.)

In a deep 12-inch (30cm) pan, warm 2 tablespoons of olive oil over medium heat. Add the garlic, onion, and chilies and cook until they turn golden, 2 to 3 minutes. Add the cherry tomatoes, increase the heat, and cook for 3 to 4 minutes, tossing them around in the pan every now and then. Crush the canned tomatoes with your hands and add them to the pan. Bring everything to a boil and cook over medium heat for about 10 minutes. Season with salt and pepper.

Reduce the heat to a simmer. Roughly tear 4 basil leaves and add them to the sauce. Crack the eggs into a bowl, make divots in the sauce, and gently lower them, one at a time, into the simmering sauce. Cover with a lid and cook until you see the egg whites firming up, 3 to 4 minutes. Uncover and season the eggs with salt and pepper.

To serve, lift the eggs gently with a large spoon and divide them among four bowls. Divide the sauce among the bowls, garnish each with one of the fried chilies from the sauce and a basil leaf, drizzle with the remaining 2 tablespoons olive oil, and serve with the bread crisps or sliced sourdough.

COLAZIONE

Frittata alla 'nduja, cipolle e fontina

FRITTATA WITH 'NDUJA, ONION, AND FONTINA

MAKES 1 LARGE FRITTATA; SERVES 6

YOU WILL NEED

- 12-inch (30cm) cast-iron skillet or other ovenproof pan
- Silicone spatula

- 3 tablespoons extra-virgin olive oil
- 1 medium onion (170g), halved and very thinly sliced
- 9 ounces (250g) potatoes, peeled and cut into $^3/_8$-inch (1cm) cubes
- 6 eggs
- 1 cup (100g) grated Parmigiano-Reggiano cheese
- 1 teaspoon minced fresh Italian parsley
- Fine sea salt and freshly ground black pepper
- 2$^1/_2$ ounces (70g) 'nduja (smoky Calabrian sausage), broken into $^3/_4$-inch (2cm) chunks (about $^1/_4$ cup)
- 1 cup (100g) grated Fontina cheese

Less than a decade ago, 'nduja was virtually unknown in North America, and even in its birthplace of Calabria, it lacked widespread popularity. However, during a memorable family vacation in Calabria, specifically in the town of Spilinga—the birthplace of 'nduja—I had the pleasure of meeting a talented chef who introduced me to the world of 'nduja. Instantly captivated by its unique flavours, I became hooked. However, upon returning to Toronto, I realized that importing 'nduja was an almost impossible task since it was virtually nonexistent in the market at that time. So, we decided to make our own at Terroni, enabling us to incorporate it into pasta dishes and pizzas. It only seemed natural to incorporate it into a frittata at Bar Centrale.

Preheat the oven to 350°F (180°C).

In a 12-inch (30cm) cast-iron skillet or other ovenproof pan, warm 1 tablespoon of olive oil over medium heat. Add the onion and cook until soft, 6 to 8 minutes. Transfer to a dish and set aside.

Bring a small pot of salted water to a boil and cook the potatoes until they have softened but are still firm, 4 to 5 minutes. Drain and let the potatoes cool for about 5 minutes.

Crack the eggs into a bowl and with a fork whisk in the Parmigiano and parsley and season with salt and pepper (be sparing with the salt because of the Parmigiano). Continue whisking for about 1 minute. Stir in the sautéed onion and blanched potatoes.

In the same skillet, heat the remaining 2 tablespoons olive oil over medium-high heat. Once hot, add the egg mixture. Distribute the 'nduja evenly over the surface of the frittata. Sprinkle the Fontina all over the surface. Reduce the heat to medium and cook for 5 minutes.

Transfer the frittata to the oven and bake until its top is firm to the touch, 15 to 20 minutes.

Remove from the oven and, using a silicone spatula, ensure that the sides are detached from the pan. Flip the frittata upside down onto a plate. This frittata is delicious served at any temperature.

59

SALSA FOCACC
IA FARINA CIAB
ATT A SOPPR
ESS ATA BUF
ALINA MOZZAR
ELLA RICOTTA O
LIO ACQUA AGL
IO OREGANO M
ORTADELLA CI
POLLA SALSICC
IA SAL E FU
NGHI A CCIU
GHE CAPPERI

PIZZA E PANE
PIZZA, FOCACCIA, PANINI

2

PIZZA E PANE

Pizza San Giorgio

PIZZA WITH BUTTON MUSHROOMS AND SOPPRESSATA

**MAKES ONE 10- TO 12-INCH
(20 TO 30CM) PIZZA; SERVES 1**

YOU WILL NEED

- Pizza stone (preferred)
  or baking sheet
- Parchment paper
- Pizza peel

- 1 ball (220g) Terroni Pizza
  Dough (page 288)
- Semola rimacinata
  (preferred) or all-purpose
  flour, for dusting
- 1/3 cup (80g) Terroni
  Tomato Base (page 294)
- 3/4 cup (80g) shredded
  mozzarella cheese
- 2/3 cup (50g) thinly sliced
  white button mushrooms
- 6 thin slices soppressata
  Calabrese
- 1/4 teaspoon red chili flakes
- Extra-virgin olive
  oil, for brushing

Semola Rimacinata

Semola rimacinata is an Italian
durum wheat flour. The word
rimacinata denotes flour that
has been milled twice. In our
bakery, we use Italian semola
rimacinata from Altamura, the
same flour that's typically used
to make Altamura bread.

**This is a tribute to my hometown of San Giorgio Morgeto,
Calabria.**

**Calabria, if you are familiar, is best known for its spicy Calabrian
soppressata. That is our claim to fame. We like our salame like
our weather. Hot! Here we added button mushrooms because
we're in Canada and its one of the only staple ingredients we
could have all year and that tastes great with a hit of spice. The
smell of this pizza is completely intoxicating. When we make
them at Terroni it's impossible for me to not snag a slice
or the whole pie.**

Make the pizza dough as directed
up through dividing the dough into
4 portions and rolling into balls, covering, and proofing for 2 to 3 hours.
(If you are making only 1 pizza,
refrigerate the dough you are not
using for up to 1 day and then continue proofing as needed.)

Preheat the oven to 500°F (260°C)
with a pizza stone or baking sheet
(lined with parchment paper) on the
bottom shelf.

Take a ball of dough and stretch the
dough into a pizza round on a lightly
floured surface (see Shaping a Pizza
Round, page 290).

Ladle the tomato sauce onto the
pizza and spread it to about 1/2 inch
(1.5cm) from the edges. Evenly distribute the mozzarella on top of the
tomato sauce. Arrange the sliced
button mushrooms evenly across the
pizza. Place the soppressata slices
on the pizza in a way that ensures
each wedge of pizza, when cut into
6, is topped with a piece of soppressata. Sprinkle the pizza with the chili
flakes to add a touch of heat.

Slide a pizza peel beneath the pizza
and swiftly transfer the pizza onto
the preheated stone (preferred) or
the baking sheet lined with parchment paper.

Bake until the crust becomes golden,
7 to 9 minutes in a domestic oven or
3 to 4 minutes in a pizza oven.

Pizza Bufalina

PIZZA WITH MOZZARELLA DI BUFALA

**MAKES ONE 10- TO 12-INCH
(20 TO 30CM) PIZZA; SERVES 1**

YOU WILL NEED

- Pizza stone (preferred) or baking sheet
- Parchment paper
- Pizza peel

- 1 ball (220g) Terroni Pizza Dough (page 288)
- Semola rimacinata (preferred) or all-purpose flour, for dusting
- ⅓ cup (80ml) Terroni Tomato Base (page 294)
- 3½ ounces (100g) mozzarella di bufala
- A couple of basil leaves
- Extra-virgin olive oil, for finishing

We started with a basic but delicious Margherita pizza at Terroni, and in the past decade our Pizza Bufalina has surpassed this staple in popularity. Buffalo mozzarella and its cousin burrata have had the same rise in popularity as Aperol and arugula. The demand has made them a contemporary staple in the "Italian" food landscape in North America. Like so often happens with Terroni goods, once we started ordering a large quantity of both these cheeses, we decided to import them ourselves. We favour Mozzarella di Bufala Campana from Caseificio La Baronia.

Make the pizza dough as directed up through dividing the dough into 4 portions, rolling into balls, covering, and proofing for 2 to 3 hours. (If you are making only 1 pizza, refrigerate the dough you are not using for up to 1 day and then continue proofing as needed.)

Preheat the oven to 500°F (260°C) with a pizza stone or baking sheet (lined with parchment paper) on the bottom shelf.

Take a ball of dough and stretch into a pizza round on a lightly floured surface (see Shaping a Pizza Round, page 290).

Ladle the tomato sauce onto the stretched pizza and spread it to about ½ inch (1.5cm) from the edges.

Slide a pizza peel beneath the pizza and swiftly transfer the pizza onto the preheated stone (preferred) or the lined baking sheet.

Bake for 5 to 6 minutes. Remove from the oven, tear the mozzarella into 1-inch (2.5cm) pieces with your hands, and distribute evenly on the pizza. Return to the oven until the crust becomes golden, 3 to 4 minutes.

Garnish with fresh basil leaves and a drizzle of extra-virgin olive oil to finish.

PIZZA E PANE

Pizza Santo Spirito

PIZZA WITH ANCHOVIES, CAPERS, AND FIOR DI LATTE

MAKES ONE 10- TO 12-INCH (20 TO 30CM) PIZZA; SERVES 1

YOU WILL NEED

- Pizza stone (preferred) or baking sheet
- Parchment paper
- Pizza peel

- 1 ball (220g) Terroni Pizza Dough (page 288)
- Semola rimacinata (preferred) or all-purpose flour, for dusting
- ⅓ cup (80g) Terroni Tomato Base (page 294)
- 3½ ounces (100g) fior di latte cheese
- 10 cherry tomatoes, halved
- 6 anchovy fillets
- 10 capers
- Extra-virgin olive oil, for brushing and drizzling

Paolo and I were trying to make an anchovy pizza even more special and so we added fresh fior di latte, cherry tomatoes, and capers. It's the perfect pizza, thanks to the sweetness of the tomatoes, the saltiness of the capers and anchovies, and the freshness of the cheese. Is it the most popular pizza? No. But it will never come off the menu!

We named it Santo Spirito after the town in Bari where my late business partner, Paolo, grew up.

Make the pizza dough as directed up through dividing the dough into 4 portions, rolling into balls, covering, and proofing for 2 to 3 hours. (If you are making only 1 pizza, refrigerate the dough you are not using for up to 1 day and then continue proofing as needed.)

Preheat the oven to 500°F (260°C) with a pizza stone or baking sheet (lined with parchment paper) on the bottom shelf.

Take a ball of dough and stretch the dough into a pizza round on a lightly floured surface (see Shaping a Pizza Round, page 290).

Ladle the tomato sauce onto the pizza and spread it to about ½ inch (1.5cm) from the edges. Tear the fior di latte into 1-inch (2.5cm) pieces using your hands and distribute the cheese evenly on the pizza along with the tomato halves. Place the anchovy fillets strategically on the pizza so that each wedge, when cut into 6, is topped with an anchovy. Sprinkle the capers evenly over the pizza.

Slide a pizza peel beneath the pizza and swiftly transfer the pizza onto the preheated stone (preferred) or the lined baking sheet.

Bake until the crust becomes golden, 7 to 9 minutes in a domestic oven or 3 to 4 minutes in a pizza oven.

Once baked, remove the pizza from the oven and drizzle it with extra-virgin olive oil as a finishing touch.

PIZZA E PANE

Ciccio farcito con verdure

WHITE PIZZA WITH GREENS

**MAKES ONE FARCITO;
SERVES 1 TO 2**

YOU WILL NEED

- Pizza stone (preferred) or baking sheet
- Parchment paper
- Pizza peel

- 1 ball (220g) Terroni Pizza Dough (page 288)
- 1½ tablespoons extra-virgin olive oil, plus more for drizzling
- 1 cup (200g) Braised Greens (page 225)
- 3½ ounces (100g) mozzarella di bufala
- Maldon salt

At Sud Forno we always made a farcito classico (stuffed Roman-style white pizza) with prosciutto, mozzarella, tomatoes, and basil, and one day while at the bakery I saw this farcito filled with a bunch of slow-cooked greens and I was like, "What the hell is that?!" It tasted great and is a somewhat healthier version and a perfect sandwich lunch option.

Make the pizza dough as directed up through dividing the dough into 4 portions, rolling into balls, covering, and proofing for 2 to 3 hours. (If you are making only 1 pizza, refrigerate the dough you are not using for up to 1 day and then continue proofing as needed.)

Preheat the oven to 500°F (260°F) with a pizza stone or baking sheet (lined with parchment paper) on the bottom shelf.

Take a ball of dough and stretch into a pizza round on a lightly floured surface (see Shaping a Pizza Round, page 290).

Drizzle with 1½ tablespoons olive oil. Slide a pizza peel beneath the pizza and then swiftly slide the pizza off it and onto the preheated stone or a baking sheet.

Bake until the crust becomes lightly golden, 4 to 6 minutes. As soon as you take it out of the oven, fold the pizza into a half-moon.

Meanwhile, reheat the greens if they are not already warm.

Stuff the greens inside the half-moon on the bottom part of the folded pizza. Tear the mozzarella di bufala over the vegetables, drizzle additional olive oil on top, and sprinkle with some Maldon salt. Cut in half and serve immediately.

Panzerotti

FRIED PIZZA POCKETS

MAKES 12 PANZEROTTI

YOU WILL NEED

- Spray bottle filled with water
- Large heavy-bottomed pot, for deep-frying
- Deep-fry thermometer
- Spider strainer or slotted spoon

- 1½ batches (1.5kg) Terroni Pizza Dough (page 288)
- 1 (14-ounce/397g) can whole peeled tomatoes
- ½ cup (50g) freshly grated Grana Padano cheese
- 2 cups (400g) roughly chopped mozzarella cheese (drained to remove excess moisture)
- 10 fresh basil leaves, chopped
- Fine sea salt and freshly ground black pepper
- Sunflower oil (about 2 quarts/2L), for deep-frying

NOTA BENE If you aren't planning to consume all 12 and want to freeze for later, it is ideal to cook all of them completely, freeze them, and then reheat them in the oven before serving. The only way you should freeze them is if you fry them first.

Friday is the best day of the week because that's when we make panzerotti at Spaccio.

Over the years, they have become a bit of an obsession with Giovanna and me, as whenever we travel to Italy, we conduct a panzerotti tour, trying the good, the bad, and the ugly (hey, even a bad panzerotto isn't that bad). With all this tasting, we knew—if we made them—we would have to go all in. They must be made fresh and fried fresh, none of this freezing nonsense. So, during the pandemic we started making panzerotti every Friday. Beyond becoming a huge hit with our customers, I think the panzerotti project is what kept us sane through that time.

Today, we make about two hundred each week. And fifteen with anchovies for the people who get it.

My son Matteo comes in and helps Gio, Luca, Ruben, and me make these, and it is the highlight of my week. Matteo follows the recipe through all the way: he works in the kitchen now and has his hands in them from the shaping to the frying. It makes me so happy that he loves the kitchen as much as I do. →

PIZZA E PANE

To get the amount of dough you need, use 1½ times the ingredients for a single batch and mix everything together. Divide the dough into 12 equal portions of 125g each. Cup your hands around each piece and roll into a nice taut ball. Place the balls on two trays dusted with flour and cover loosely with plastic wrap. Allow the dough to proof until doubled, 1½ to 2 hours, depending on the temperature of the room.

Meanwhile, drain the excess liquid from the canned tomatoes and crush them using your hands into a large bowl. Add the Grana Padano, mozzarella, and basil leaves and season with salt and pepper. Mix well and set aside.

Lightly flour a clean surface. Using your fingertips, stretch each piece of dough into a 6- to 7-inch (15 to 18cm) round. Ladle about ½ cup (120g) of filling into the centre of each round. Spray each round with a light mist of water and fold the dough over to form a half-moon. Using your fingers, press the dough around the filling to seal the seams. Dust with flour, set aside, and repeat the same process for the remaining panzerotti.

Line a baking sheet with paper towels as a landing spot for the panzerotti after frying and have near the stove. Pour 3 to 4 inches (7.5 to 10cm) sunflower oil into a large heavy pot and heat over medium heat to 360°F (182°C).

Working in batches of 1 or 2 to not crowd the pot, fry the panzerotti until golden brown all over, 3 to 4 minutes per side. Remove by using a spider strainer or slotted spoon to the paper towels, sprinkle with salt, and enjoy while warm.

PRO TIP It's important not to stretch the dough too much and not to poke the panzerotti when frying them so as not to cause any tears.

PIZZA E PANE

VARIATIONS

Anchovy-Filled Panzerotti: Make the dough and tomato filling as directed. When filling the panzerotti, add 4 anchovy fillets per panzerotto. Seal and fry as directed.

Ricotta and Salame–Filled Panzerotti: Make two different flavors of panzerotti. Use half the dough to make the tomato-filled panzerotti in the main recipe (but cut the ingredient amounts in half). Then for the other 6 panzerotti, mix together ¾ cup (210g) ricotta cheese, ½ cup (105g) cubed (⅜-inch/1cm) Genoa or finocchiona salame, and 2 tablespoons grated Parmigiano-Reggiano. Season with salt and pepper, being extra generous with the black pepper. Divide the filling evenly between each panzerotto.

PIZZA E PANE

Focaccia barese

BARI-STYLE FOCACCIA

MAKES TWO 12-INCH (30CM) ROUND LOAVES

YOU WILL NEED

- Potato ricer or sieve
- Stand mixer fitted with the dough hook
- Two 12-inch (30cm) round baking pans
- Plastic bowl scraper
- Rubber spatula

FOCACCIA

- 1 small russet potato (3½ ounces/100g)
- 2½ cups (300g) tipo "00" pizza flour
- 1¼ cups (200g) semola rimacinata
- ¾ cup (200g) Sourdough Starter (page 287) or 1⅛ teaspoons (6g) instant yeast
- 1¼ cups (300g) cold tap water
- 2 teaspoons (10g) fine sea salt
- ¼ cup (60ml) extra-virgin olive oil

ASSEMBLY

- 1 cup (200g) extra-virgin olive oil
- 2¼ pounds (1kg) cherry tomatoes, scored with a cut at their base (to make them easier to crush)
- ¾ cup (100g) pitted green olives
- 2 teaspoons (10g) fine sea salt
- 1 teaspoon dried oregano

NOTA BENE Metric measurements are more precise. If you can, please use the metric measures in this recipe!

What makes *this* focaccia the best?

It is not too high.
The bottom is crispy.
It is super oily with big cherry tomatoes.

The above qualities make this focaccia the perfect combination of crunchy, chewy with that hit of sweet from the tomato. Sounds easy . . . but it's difficult to pull off. The secret lies with the amount of oil you put on the bottom of the pan.

When we opened Terroni, we used to buy focaccia from a gentleman who had a bakery and he supplied us with focaccia the first couple of years. We then hired him to make focaccia directly in our Queen Street location, and then we found out he was stealing from us, so we had to fire him. That's the business! After that sting, we didn't make focaccia for many, many years.

A little while ago, Elena and I began to make our own at home and it started to become this battle between us! While developing the perfect recipe, we realized that even when you think you're using a lot of olive oil, it's not enough. You're basically frying this bread. We baked it in small round baking pans. After a year of playing around, we finally had, in our opinion, the perfect version. The rest, as they say, is history. The only addition we allow is mortadella!

NOTA BENE We highly recommend using sourdough in this recipe, as it adds a distinct flavour and texture. However, if you don't have sourdough starter on hand, you can simply omit it from the recipe. If you do have a starter, make sure that it has been regularly fed and maintained (see Day 7 of Sourdough Starter, page 288). If your starter is stored in the fridge, allow it to sit at room temperature for a couple of hours before incorporating it into the recipe. This will help activate the yeast and ensure optimal results.

Make the focaccia: In a small pot, boil the potato, skin on, until completely tender, about 30 minutes. Pass through a potato ricer or a sieve, discarding the skin. Allow the potato mixture to cool.

In a stand mixer fitted with the dough hook, combine the pizza flour, semola, mashed potato, sourdough starter (or yeast), and 1 cup (240g) of cold water. If you are not using sourdough, add an extra 3 tablespoons water. Mix the ingredients on medium-high speed for 4 to 5 minutes, or until the dough appears compact, elastic, and shiny. Gradually add ¼ cup (60g) more water while mixing. Reduce the mixer speed to low, add the salt, and continue mixing until the salt is fully incorporated. Increase the mixer speed to medium and slowly drizzle in the olive oil, allowing it to incorporate into the dough, another 3 to 4 minutes. The dough may feel slightly sticky. (If so, increase speed or switch from hook to paddle attachment and mix until smooth.) The long mixing process allows the gluten to develop and the dough to have structure. →

PIZZA E PANE

Remove the dough hook and cover the dough with a damp cloth, allowing it to rest for 20 minutes. Once rested, transfer the dough to a work surface. Divide the dough into 2 equal portions, each weighing 550g. Take one piece at a time and knead it into a nice round ball. Using a plastic bowl scraper, gently tighten the surface of the dough by pushing it in at its base, so it begins to dome upward, creating a taller round. The dough should have a shiny appearance without any tears.

To assemble: Pour ½ cup (100g) extra-virgin olive oil into each of two 12-inch (30cm) round baking pans, ensuring the oil is spread evenly to the borders of the pans. Place one dough ball in each pan and use your hands to spread some of the oil over the top of each ball. Cover the pans with plastic wrap and allow them to proof at room temperature for 7 to 8 hours.

Position a rack in the bottom third of the oven and preheat the oven to 450°F (230°C).

Remove the plastic wrap from the pans and flip each dough ball upside down. Lightly press the dough with your fingers, ensuring the surface of the pan is covered. Take the cherry tomatoes and gently crush them by squeezing them with your hands. Divide the crushed tomatoes over the top of the two focaccia. Repeat the process with the olives, placing them on top without pressing them into the dough. Sprinkle each focaccia with the salt and the oregano.

Bake the focaccia until they turn dark golden brown, 35 to 40 minutes.

Enjoy the focaccia right away.

VARIATION

Focaccia with Mortadella: Once the focaccia is baked, slice them in half horizontally, setting aside the top parts of the focaccia with the tomato side facing up. Layer the base of each focaccia with about 14 ounces (400g) of Mortadella di Bologna IGP (4 to 5 slices per serving) and top with the other half of the focaccia. Cut each focaccia into 8 slices to serve.

PIZZA E PANE

Pane pugliese

APULIAN BREAD

MAKES 2 LOAVES (ABOUT 1¾ POUNDS/750G) EACH

YOU WILL NEED

- Sourdough starter
- A stand mixer fitted with the dough hook
- Digital scale
- Digital thermometer
- Plastic bowl scraper
- Two 8-inch (20cm) round proofing baskets, with a cotton cloth liner
- 8- to 10-quart (8 to 10L) Dutch oven (preferred) or pizza stone and spray bottle filled with water
- A bread scoring blade or very sharp knife
- Parchment paper

SOURDOUGH REFRESHMENT

- ⅓ cup (100g) cold Sourdough Starter (page 287)
- 2 cups (250g) bread flour
- 1 cup (250g) tepid mineral water

BREAD DOUGH

- 3¾ cups (750g) semola rimacinata flour (see Note, page 62)
- 2 teaspoons honey
- 2 cups (500ml) mineral water, at room temperature (71°F/22°C)
- 1 tablespoon (15g) fine sea salt
- 2 tablespoons extra-virgin olive oil

Before we opened our own bakery, we were buying bread from a host of different bakers. It wasn't *bad*, but it was not naturally leavened and lasted only a day (and that's generous). It started to become a hassle when bread was not delivered on time, and we had customers who wanted their panini. Sometimes they even delivered old bread! And so, like many Italian restaurants before us, the time came for us to start making our own bread. But first, let me tell you a story:

In Italy, close to Rimini, there is a special rehab centre that is close to the heart of Terroni. It is called San Patrignano (sanpatrignano .org). There is a culture in Italy where people who are suffering from addiction can apply to this centre. Due to the sheer number of restaurant industry people who have gone there, many of Italy's top chefs, winemakers, bakers, and farmers give back to the centre, quite often to provide classes to those in rehab. You never know just who your teacher could be or who will drop in to lend a hand. It's incredible how inspiring this program is. Anyway, I visited the centre and one of the many aspects I *loved* was their winery. Their motto is "rebuilding the connection with nature to rebuild the man." They grow Sangiovese grapes here and to keep the work and flow going—and because I believe in these wines—we decided to import them with my wine agency Cavinona.

Anyway, one year when I was visiting them in Verona at the wine show, they had on display this beautiful bread with salumi. They told me that they made it on-site at their HQ. It's made by Giuliano Pediconi, who gives his time to teach the kids how to make the bread. So, we got in touch with Giuliano and he is an unbelievable human being who has more passion than all of us combined. He was willing to come to Toronto and make pane pugliese with us, and it became our signature loaf of bread.

He came over with his student Fabio Papa and they were this amazing duo, complete opposites. Fabio was a recovering addict, and he and Giuliano worked so beautifully together. They seemed like father and son, they had this love for each other, which was special. Coming to Canada was like a new start for both!

As Gio tells it, "I remember when we started working with them in 2012, the staff would argue over who could work with Giuliano and Fabio because they were just such amazing and deeply knowledgeable people. Giuliano still comes in once a while, for a couple of days, and works all night with the bakers. He's also *very* direct. People love and respect him because he tells you how it is. Giuliano would work these long twelve-hour shifts and I [Gio], Luca Rotatori, our head baker at Spaccio, and Fabio would just try to keep up with him. True master bakers."

Luca now heads the Bakery department, directing all of our bread and pizza-making operations. →

Refresh the sourdough: The day before you intend to make the bread dough, at around 10 a.m., place the cold sourdough starter into a clean mason jar. Add the bread flour and mineral water and stir until the mixture is well combined. Cover the jar with a cloth and allow it to rest at room temperature (71°F/22°C) until the next day.

In the morning, check the sourdough. It should have risen, developed bubbles, and have a slightly sour aroma. If the desired characteristics have not been achieved, repeat this step one more time to strengthen the leavener before proceeding with the bread-making process.

Make the bread dough: Once the sourdough is "strong" enough, we can proceed at 10 a.m. with making the bread dough.

NOTA BENE We strongly suggest weighing your ingredients in grams for this recipe.

You will need to have an active sourdough starter on hand.

AUTOLYSE

In a stand mixer fitted with the dough hook, combine the semola, honey, and room-temperature water. Mix on low speed just until the flour is combined, 7 to 8 minutes. Allow the mixture to rest in the bowl for 1 full hour. (During this hour of rest, which is the autolyse, the dough will be gaining some elasticity.)

Restart the mixer on low to medium speed for 5 minutes until the dough becomes completely smooth. Measure out 1 cup (250g) of the refreshed starter. With the mixer running, slowly add ½ cup (125g) of the starter. Add the salt and mix for 2 minutes. Gradually incorporate the remaining ½ cup (125g) starter and

continue mixing for 10 minutes on low to medium speed. If you notice that the dough is "thirsty," you may want to add 2 tablespoons water. However, keep in mind that different flours, especially hard flour, have varying abilities to absorb liquid, so use your judgment when deciding whether to add more water. The goal is to achieve a dough that is soft, smooth, malleable, and slightly tacky to the touch. Once all the ingredients are fully incorporated and the dough is smooth and elastic, stop the mixer.

BULK FERMENTATION

Transfer the dough onto a lightly floured surface. Scrape the bowl of the mixer with a scraper and lightly oil the bowl. Return the dough to the bowl, cover the top of the bowl with either plastic wrap or a damp cloth, and let sit for 1½ hours for fermentation to start (there will not be any visible changes in the dough). Make sure the temperature of the dough is maintained at 77° to 80°F (25° to 27°C). If the dough's temperature dips below 77°F (25°C), find a warmer spot and extend the bulk fermentation accordingly. Conversely, if the dough's temperature exceeds 80°F (27°C), relocate it to a cooler area and shorten the bulk fermentation period.

PRESHAPING

Transfer the dough to a work surface and divide it into 2 equal portions about 750g each. Using a plastic bowl scraper, gently tighten the dough by shaping it into taller mounds. This can be achieved by swiftly sliding the scraper beneath the dough and pushing it upward. It's important to perform this movement swiftly and with minimal actions, ensuring that the dough appears smooth and does not tear. Once divided and shaped, cover the two balls with a damp cloth and let them rest for 30 minutes before shaping.

SHAPING

Using your hands, tighten each dough ball by swiftly dragging it on the board toward you. Then round each dough ball by cupping it with your hands. Repeat this movement until each loaf has reached its tightest point without any visible rips. Coat each loaf with some extra flour to prevent sticking. Lightly dust two 8-inch (20cm) round proofing baskets with flour and place a loaf in each basket with the seam side facing up (upside down).

LEAVENING

Leave the loaves in the bread baskets at room temperature, loosely covered with plastic for 1 hour. Refrigerate overnight.

BAKING

About 1½ hours before baking, prepare two pieces of parchment paper, cutting them to the size of an 8- to 10-quart (8 to 10L) Dutch oven.

Preheat the oven to 450°F (230°C) with the Dutch oven with its lid. (Alternatively, put a pizza stone in the oven to preheat.)

Remove the loaves from the refrigerator but leave them in the proofing baskets.

When the oven is up to temp, take one piece of parchment paper and flip a loaf onto it, with the seam side down. Use a sharp blade or knife to score a cross on the bread (see Scoring Bread Loaves). Carefully remove the Dutch oven from the oven, open the lid, and gently lift the loaf on the parchment paper. Place both the parchment and the loaf inside the Dutch oven, taking precautions not to burn yourself during this step. Cover the Dutch oven with its lid and return it to the oven. (If you are using a pizza stone,

PIZZA E PANE

pull out the oven rack with the stone just enough to place the loaf on the parchment paper. Spray water on the loaf to create steam, then close the oven door. Steam is important for slowing down crust formation and increasing the volume of the bread. Using a Dutch oven is the preferred method as it creates its own steam within the cavity of the pot.)

After 20 minutes, remove the lid from the Dutch oven. Reduce the oven temperature to 400°F (200°C) and continue baking until the bread turns golden brown, another 30 minutes. Oven temperatures can vary, so keep a close eye on the bread during the final bake and adjust as necessary.

Repeat with the remaining loaf.

Allow the loaves to cool down completely before cutting into them.

Scoring Bread Loaves
Generally speaking, you should only score the skin of the bread without going too deep. If the loaf feels tight and hard, the cut can be deeper, up to $3/8$ inch (1cm) below the skin. If, however, the bread is overproofed or feels soft, the incision should be done lightly.

PIZZA E PANE

Ciabatta di Terroni

CIABATTA BUNS

MAKES 8 BUNS

YOU WILL NEED

- Digital thermometer
- Digital scale
- 1 rectangular container for proofing
- Baking sheet
- Parchment paper
- Bench scraper
- Spray bottle with water

- 1½ teaspoons instant yeast
- ⅓ cup (65g) Sourdough Starter (page 287); see Nota Bene
- 2 cups (480g) cold water (53° to 55°F/12° to 13°C)
- 5⅓ cups (650g) bread flour, plus more for dusting
- 1 tablespoon fine sea salt
- Extra-virgin olive oil, for the container

NOTA BENE We highly recommend using sourdough in this recipe, as it adds a distinct flavour and texture. However, if you don't have sourdough starter on hand, you can simply omit it from the recipe. If you do have sourdough, ensure that it has been regularly fed and maintained (see Day 7 of Sourdough Starter, page 288). If your sourdough is stored in the fridge, allow it to sit at room temperature for a couple of hours before incorporating it into the recipe. This will help activate its leavening power and ensure optimal results.

When we first opened Terroni, we had a regular panino bread that our customers were happy with, but I was never crazy about it. It wasn't light enough and the taste was rather nondescript, which in my book is . . . offensive.

But we just didn't have the bandwidth (materials, money, time, energy) to make our own then. Finally, when we opened the bakery, we went deep on ciabatta R&D. We learned that ciabatta-making requires a high level of hydration, and it can be difficult to nail the moisture level when making larger quantities. And so small-batch recipes, like the one below, yield the best quality ciabatta. This is a very Southern Italian loaf of bread, which is to say it's airy, light, and screams for mortadella and provolone picante.

In a large bowl, place the yeast, starter, and cold water (run your tap as needed to get it cold). Add the flour and salt and use a wooden spoon to mix until a soft dough forms, about 5 minutes. At this point the dough should be around 75°F (24°C). Lightly grease a rectangular container with extra-virgin olive oil, place the dough inside, and cover it with a clean damp cloth. Let it rest for 30 minutes.

After the initial rest, position the container in front of you and moisten your hands with warm water. Grab the dough from the side farthest from you and gently pull it upward, stretching it as much as possible without tearing it. Then fold the stretched portion of the dough over the rest to cover it completely. Turn the container 90 degrees and repeat this step three more times. Flip the dough upside down. Cover the container again and allow it to rest for an additional 20 minutes.

Repeat this folding process two more times, at 20-minute intervals. Once the last fold is completed, cover the dough and let it rest for 30 minutes. Swap the cloth cover for plastic film and transfer the container to the refrigerator. Allow the dough to rest there for 20 to 22 hours, during which time it should double in size.

Line a baking sheet with parchment paper. Sprinkle flour on top of the dough and use a spatula to release it from the sides of the container. Flip the container upside down onto a floured work surface. Apply more flour to the top of the dough. Using a bench scraper, divide it into 8 rectangular portions, rolling each piece in flour to ensure complete coverage. Place the buns on the lined baking sheet with the cut side facing up. Cover the buns with plastic wrap and let them rest for 1 hour.

Preheat the oven to 500°F (260°C).

Carefully flip each bun upside down and spray with water. Bake until a dark golden-brown crust forms, 20 to 25 minutes.

CONVERSATION

COLLO QUIO ×
CONVERSATION

Gianni Bardini

Former Italian Consul General in Toronto, current Italian Ambassador to Mozambique

Where are you based?

Currently in Maputo, Mozambique. Alas, far away from any Terroni restaurant.

What's your relationship to Terroni?

I am an old friend and faithful and unwavering admirer of Cosimo and assiduous visitor of his restaurants since the very beginning of the triumphal ride of Terroni.

Favourite Terroni dish (including all restaurants, Spaccio, etc.)?

On the spur of the moment—so as not to get lost in the recollection of the innumerable delicious options: Spaghetti in Canna a Mare.

Favourite Terroni memory?

Too many to single out. My common Terroni thread is friends, happiness, and fabulous and diverse culinary experiences. In short, utmost pleasure for the palate and the spirit.

Favourite Terroni location?

Maybe Queen Street, but just for sentimental reasons.

Do you like it sweet or savoury?

Having to decide, I lean toward savoury.

What do you like about Toronto? If based elsewhere, tell us where you live and why we should—or shouldn't—visit.

I come back regularly to Toronto. I particularly enjoy the unique combination of the vibrancy of downtown and the commercial areas and the kind of "up north" peace and quiet of midtown residential neighborhoods and parks. Exciting to visit but even more pleasurable to live in.

PIZZA E PANE

Panini con salsiccia e cime di rapa

SAUSAGE AND RAPINI SANDWICHES

MAKES 4 SANDWICHES

YOU WILL NEED

- Barbecue grill, griddle/grill pan, or cast-iron skillet

- 3 tablespoon extra-virgin olive oil, plus more as needed
- 1 garlic clove, smashed and peeled
- 2 large red onions, cut into ¼-inch (5mm) slices
- Fine sea salt
- 1 pound 5 ounces (600g) Terroni Sausage (page 296) or store-bought sweet Italian sausage, in casings or loose
- 1 bunch (11 ounces/320g) rapini, roughly chopped into ½-inch (1.5cm) pieces
- Freshly ground black pepper
- 4 ciabatta buns, homemade (page 85) or store-bought
- Maldon sea salt

It's wild to think that when we first opened Terroni, my dad, Vincenzo, was making all our fresh sausage himself! Probably 30 to 40 kilograms (65 to 88 pounds) per week when it was being made in my parents' basement with a hand-crank machine. Then we started to use it on everything (pizzas and pasta), so I got them an electric grinder. Then my dad started coming to Queen Street to work. And at the beginning we were making all the sausage in casings, hundreds of kilos, which took forever and was not sustainable. We naturally took some for panini, but then my dad noticed that we weren't using most of it in its casing! We now make up to 1,000 pounds (453kg) of sausage a week, machine-ground but handmade.

In a medium skillet, warm the olive oil over medium heat and add the garlic clove. Once the garlic turns golden, add the sliced onions and sauté the onions for 2 to 3 minutes. Reduce the heat to low and continue cooking until they are caramelized and soft, about 15 minutes. Taste the onions, season with salt as needed, and set them aside.

COOK THE SAUSAGES

On the grill: Preheat a barbecue grill to about 400°F (200°C). If you are using cased sausages, place them directly on the grill and cook for 5 to 6 minutes per side. You can cook bulk sausage, too, as long as you make patties that are firmly shaped. Resting them a bit in the fridge helps them stay together.

On the stovetop: If you prefer the indoors option, preheat the oven to 400°F (200°C). Place a griddle/grill pan or cast-iron skillet over medium-high heat. If you are using bulk sausage, form it into 4 patties of about 150g each. Add 1 tablespoon of olive oil to the griddle/grill pan and sear the sausages for a couple of minutes on each side. Transfer to the oven and roast until cooked through, about 10 minutes.

In the same pan you cooked the onions in, heat a fresh amount of olive oil over medium-high heat. Add the rapini and sear, then reduce the heat to medium-low and cook until softened, about 5 minutes. Season with salt and pepper.

Slice the buns in half horizontally and drizzle them with some olive oil. Toast the buns face up in the oven for 3 to 4 minutes or face down on the barbecue until they turn slightly golden.

Top each bun with some of the rapini, followed by the sausages. Add 2 to 3 tablespoons of the caramelized onions on top and a pinch of Maldon salt. Finally, cover the buns with the top half and serve immediately.

PIZZA E PANE

Panini con branzino e peperonata

SEA BASS AND RED PEPPER SANDWICHES

MAKES 4 SANDWICHES

YOU WILL NEED

- Cast-iron skillet or griddle/grill pan

- 4 Mediterranean sea bass fillets (5 ounces/140g each), skin on
- Extra-virgin olive oil as needed
- Fine sea salt and freshly ground black pepper
- 4 ciabatta buns, homemade (page 85) or store-bought
- 1 cup (250g) Piera's Stewed Peppers (page 230), at room temperature
- Pinch of Maldon salt

This sandwich was introduced for the first time in Los Angeles when we opened our location on Beverly, because people kept on requesting a fish option, instead of our nice sausage panino. Typical LA! We're not really a canned-tuna sandwich kinda place, and so we experimented with a branzino (sea bass) fillet. Back then, almost fifteen years ago, branzino wasn't as popular as it is today and so this was considered a wild idea. How things have changed!

Preheat the oven to 375°F (190°C).

Rinse the sea bass fillets under cold water and pat them dry with paper towels. Season the flesh side of the fillets with olive oil, salt, and pepper and set aside in the fridge uncovered until ready to make the sandwiches.

Heat a cast-iron skillet or griddle/grill pan over medium heat for a few minutes.

Season the sea bass fillets on the skin side with salt. Add a couple of tablespoons of olive oil to the hot pan and carefully place the fillets, skin side down, in the pan. Sear the sea bass until the skin becomes crispy and the fish can be easily flipped with a spatula, 4 to 6 minutes. Flip the fish and cook for an additional 2 minutes, then remove from the heat.

While the fish is cooking, slice the buns in half horizontally and drizzle them with some olive oil. Toast the buns open-faced in the oven until they turn slightly golden, 3 to 4 minutes.

Top each bun with some stewed peppers, followed by a sea bass fillet and a pinch of Maldon salt. Close the sandwiches and enjoy immediately.

ACCIUGHE FARI
NA ACQUA MIE
LE BURRO ZUCC
HERO SALE OLI
O VINO F    INO
CCHIO P   E P
ERONCINO MAI
S PEPE ACCIUG
HE LARDO LIEV
ITO STRACCIAT
ELL    A PISTA
C C   HI SALM
ONE LATTUGA\

APERITIVO

3

APERITIVO

Grissini

LONG THIN BREADSTICKS

MAKES ABOUT 35 GRISSINI

YOU WILL NEED

- Stand mixer fitted with the dough hook
- Digital thermometer
- Bench scraper
- A flat-bottomed tray or plate about 12 inches (30cm) across

- $4\frac{1}{4}$ cups (500g) all-purpose flour
- $1\frac{1}{4}$ cups (300ml) water
- $1\frac{3}{4}$ teaspoons (8g) instant yeast
- $1\frac{1}{2}$ teaspoons (10g) honey
- 1 tablespoon + $\frac{3}{4}$ teaspoon (15g) granulated sugar
- 1 tablespoon (15g) fine sea salt
- $1\frac{1}{2}$ tablespoons (20g) unsalted butter
- $1\frac{1}{2}$ tablespoons (20g) extra-virgin olive oil, plus more for the bowl and tray
- Sesame seeds, poppy seeds, or grated Parmigiano-Reggiano (optional)

Grissini hail from Piemonte and are really the proper Italian way to begin a meal. They are easy to make, and we do sell them at our bakeries. But the number of grissini we used to go through in the restaurant was so impossibly large that we had to scale back and only offer them on special occasions.

However, this is the perfect recipe to make at home and we encourage you to wrap the breadsticks with prosciutto while you're enjoying that first spritz of the day. →

In a stand mixer fitted with the dough hook, combine the flour, water, yeast, honey, and sugar. Mix on medium speed for about 10 minutes or until smooth. Add the salt and half of the butter and continue mixing until they are absorbed, then add the remaining butter. While the mixer is running, slowly drizzle in the olive oil and beat until all the ingredients are fully incorporated. Aim to achieve a dough temperature of around 75°F (24°C). Grease a bowl lightly with olive oil and transfer the dough to it. Cover with plastic wrap and allow the dough to rest for 20 minutes.

Transfer the dough to a work surface and shape it into a log 2¼ inches (6 to 7cm) in diameter. Lightly grease a tray or plate and place the log on it. Cover the log with plastic wrap and refrigerate for an additional 2 hours, enabling the dough to further relax and develop its flavours.

Line a baking sheet with parchment paper. Place the dough log on a work surface and use a bench scraper to cut the log into slices ⅜ inch (1cm) thick. Take each slice and roll it between your hands and the table, elongating it to a length of about 12 inches (30cm). For added variety, you can roll some of the grissini in sesame or poppy seeds, or even grated Parmigiano. Transfer to the lined baking sheet.

Cover the rolled grissini with plastic wrap and let them rise until doubled in size, for 1½ to 2 hours.

About 1 hour into this rising period, preheat the oven to 375°F (190°C).

Transfer the grissini to the oven and bake until they turn golden brown, 15 to 20 minutes. Let the grissini cool on the pan. Once cooled, store them in an airtight container. They will stay fresh for up to 3 weeks.

APERITIVO

Taralli

ROUND BREADSTICKS

MAKES ABOUT 3½ POUNDS (1.5KG) TARALLI

YOU WILL NEED

- Stand mixer fitted with the dough hook
- Baking sheet
- Parchment paper
- Spider strainer or slotted spoon

- 7½ cups (900g) all-purpose flour, plus more for dusting
- 1⅓ cups (320 ml) white wine
- ¾ cup + 1 tablespoon (200ml) extra-virgin olive oil
- 1½ tablespoons (25g) fine sea salt
- ¼ teaspoon instant yeast

Taralli are crunchy, thick breadsticks in a small round shape that pugliesi love as a snack any time of day but especially with aperitivi. Seeing as both taralli and my late business partner, Paolo, hail from Puglia, it was one of the first things we sold upon opening in 1992. All the Toronto *signore* came in to purchase them, since they were such a staple and not easy to find back then.

Warning: Making taralli at home takes quite a bit of work (make the dough, form it, boil it), BUT the homemade ones are so much tastier than the ones you can find in stores. They will keep up to 6 weeks in a dry cool place. →

99

APERITIVO

In a stand mixer fitted with the dough hook, combine the flour, wine, oil, salt, and yeast and mix on medium speed for 10 minutes until a cohesive dough forms. Cover the bowl and let the dough rest for 30 minutes.

Bring a large pot of water to a boil and preheat the oven to 375°F (190°C). Line a baking sheet with parchment paper.

Transfer the dough to a lightly floured work surface and divide into 10 equal portions. Take 1 piece and keep the rest covered with a clean kitchen towel. Using your hands, roll the piece into a log, stretching it with your hands until it reaches a diameter of about ⅜ inch (1cm). Cut the log into 4-inch (10cm) lengths, bringing the ends together and pressing them to seal. Transfer each tarallo onto a lightly floured sheet of parchment paper and keep covered. Continue the rolling out and shaping process with the remaining dough pieces.

When the water is at a rolling boil, drop a dozen taralli at a time into the pot and cook until they rise to the surface. Using a spider strainer, lift them out and transfer them to a cloth to drain and then onto the lined baking sheet.

Transfer to the oven and bake until golden, 20 to 22 minutes. Allow the taralli to cool completely on the pan before consuming.

VARIATIONS

Popular variants of taralli involve the addition of fennel seeds, rosemary, or even chili flakes. Split the dough in half and make half plain and half with one of the add-ins (reducing the amount to 1 teaspoon). Or season the entire batch.

Fennel Taralli: Add 2 teaspoons fennel seeds to the dough when mixing.

Chili Taralli: Add 2 teaspoons chili flakes to the dough when mixing.

APERITIVO

Crostini di mais

RITA'S CORN CRISPS

**MAKES ABOUT 3½ POUNDS
(1.5KG) CRISPS**

YOU WILL NEED

- Baking sheet
- Parchment paper
- Bench scraper

- 3 cups + 2 tablespoons
  (740g) warm water
- 2 teaspoons
  granulated sugar
- 1½ teaspoons (5g)
  active dry yeast
- 6⅔ cups (1kg) cornmeal,
  plus more for dusting
- 1 teaspoon fine sea salt
- ½ cup (120ml) sunflower oil

When I was a child, my mother always made *pane duro*, "hard bread." In fact, we very rarely had a soft loaf of bread at home, and I can't think of a single occurrence of it being store-bought. She would bake a loaf of bread, slice it, and rebake it slowly overnight, and it would become crispy, hard, and delicious. And this would last us a whole week. We would soak that bread in water, douse it in some olive oil, and enjoy it with dinner. But she stopped making that once she created this cornbread recipe. This bread she would cut into bite-sized crackers, and it's the perfect vessel for salami, cheese, and sun-dried tomatoes. This also happens to be one of the simplest recipes in this book.

Preheat the oven to 350°F (180°C).

In a large bowl, combine the warm water, sugar, and yeast. Allow the mixture to sit for about 5 minutes, until bubbles start to form. Add the cornmeal, salt, and oil and mix the ingredients with your hands for about 5 minutes, until the mixture has a sandy texture that is not sticky. If needed, add extra cornmeal to achieve the desired consistency— think packed sand. The mixture may not fully come together, and that's okay. Cover the bowl with plastic wrap and let it rest in a warm place for 20 minutes.

Line a baking sheet with parchment paper. Spread the cornmeal mixture evenly in the lined pan, pressing it to a thickness of about ¼ inch (5 to 7mm) to form a large flat cornbread.

Bake until the cornbread is firm and dry to the touch, about 20 minutes. Remove from the oven and reduce the oven temperature to 200°F (90°C).

Let the cornbread cool slightly, 4 to 5 minutes, then using your hands or a bench scraper, cut the cornbread into small pieces, shaping them into squares or parallelograms about 2 inches (5cm) across.

Return to the oven and bake until they are completely dry and crisp, about 2 hours.

Let cool completely before eating. The crisps will keep for up to 1 week.

APERITIVO

Pane e acciughe

BREAD AND ANCHOVIES

SERVES 4

- ½ loaf Pane Pugliese (page 80) or similar type of bread (13 ounces/375g), cut into 8 (¾-inch/2cm) slices
- ¼ cup (60ml) extra-virgin olive oil
- ¾ cup (175g) cold best-quality unsalted butter
- 16 oil-packed Cantabrian anchovy fillets (105g)
- Freshly ground black pepper

Being an anchovy lover, I used to eat Rita's Corn Crisps (page 103) with anchovy fillets and chunks of Parmigiano. Then I tried the combination with butter somewhere in Italy and knew I needed to put it on the menu. The important thing is to use cold good-quality butter on a beautifully toasted piece of bread with a cured anchovy fillet (in olive oil). It's the perfect aperitivo snack.

Preheat the oven to 400°F (200°C).

Remove the crusts from the sliced bread and arrange on a baking sheet. Drizzle with the olive oil and toast in the oven until crispy and golden, 4 to 5 minutes.

Cut the cold butter into slices about ¼ inch (5mm) thick and spread them over each slice to cover the surface. Divide the anchovy fillets equally on each slice, add pepper, and serve.

APERITIVO

Gnocco fritto

FRIED DOUGH POCKETS

SERVES 8 TO 10

YOU WILL NEED

- Stand mixer fitted with the dough hook
- Deep-fry thermometer
- Deep heavy-bottomed pot for deep-frying
- Rolling pin
- Bench scraper
- Spider strainer

- 4¼ cups (500g) bread flour, plus more for dusting
- 1 cup + 2 teaspoons (250g) cold water
- ¼ cup (50g) Sourdough Starter (page 287; optional); see Nota Bene
- 2 teaspoons (15g) honey
- 1¼ teaspoons (4g) instant yeast
- 4 tablespoons (50g) cold lard
- 2 teaspoons (10g) fine sea salt
- Extra-virgin olive oil, for the bowl and tray
- Sunflower oil or other oil (about 2 quarts/2L), for deep-frying

NOTA BENE Using sourdough in this recipe adds a distinct flavour and texture. However, if you don't have starter on hand, you can simply omit it from the recipe and add 2 tablespoons (30g) water. If you do have starter, ensure that it has been regularly fed and maintained. If your starter is stored in the fridge, allow it to sit at room temperature for a couple of hours before incorporating it into the recipe. This will help activate the leavening agent and ensure optimal results.

It was around 2007 when we put these fried pockets on the Terroni menu—and we haven't looked back. This recipe is a crowd-pleaser, but is a tad more challenging as we make it the traditional way with lard. It is *very* rewarding! You can add various toppings such as cheeses, prosciutto, salami, and mortadella. This is typically enjoyed after work before dinner, but due to the labour involved, it also makes a great lunch or dinner. (We recommend making this and serving it with a nice platter of salumi and some Lambrusco.)

In a stand mixer fitted with the dough hook, combine the flour, cold water, sourdough starter (if using), honey, and yeast. Mix on medium speed until the dough is smooth and not sticky, 10 to 15 minutes.

Continuing at medium speed, add 2 tablespoons of lard and the salt. Once absorbed, add the remaining lard and mix until a smooth dough is formed. If the dough looks too sticky, work it by hand on a lightly floured surface, then shape it into a ball. Aim to finish at a temperature of around 70°F (21°C).

Lightly grease a bowl with some olive oil, place the dough inside, cover it with plastic wrap, and set it to rise at room temperature for 30 minutes. If the dough temperature looks like it will go higher than 72°F (22°C), reduce the rest time to only 20 minutes. On the other hand, if the temperature is lower than 68°F (20°C), extend the rest time to 40 minutes.

Transfer the dough to a work surface and shape it into a log. Lightly grease a tray and place the log onto it. Cover the log with plastic wrap and refrigerate for a minimum of 2 hours and up to 8 hours.

Pour 3 inches (7.5cm) of sunflower oil into a deep heavy pot and heat over medium heat to 375°F (190°C). Line a tray with paper towels and place near the stove.

Meanwhile, place the dough on a lightly floured surface and divide into 3 equal portions. Use a rolling pin to roll the dough to a ¹⁄₁₆-inch (2 to 4mm) thickness. Cut the dough into 2¼-inch (6cm) squares.

Working in batches of a few at a time, drop the squares into the hot oil, taking care not to overcrowd the pot. Once they become inflated, flip them over for an even fry until golden, 3 to 4 minutes. Using a spider strainer, carefully remove them from the oil and place on the paper towels to drain.

Gnocco fritto is something to be enjoyed warm so get them on a cutting board with your favourite salame and mozzarella and serve immediately.

APERITIVO

Bombolini salati

FRIED MINI PANINI

MAKES 16

YOU WILL NEED

- Baking sheet
- Parchment paper
- Deep heavy pan, for deep-frying
- Slotted spoon

- ¼ recipe Base Brioche (page 291)
- Sunflower oil (3 quarts/3L), for deep-frying
- Fine sea salt

Make the brioche dough as directed, but quarter all the ingredient amounts. Let the dough rest for 20 to 30 minutes.

Line a baking sheet with parchment paper. Divide the dough into ½-ounce (15g) pieces each, roll each one into a tight ball, and place on the lined baking sheet, leaving enough space between them for them to double. Cover loosely with plastic wrap and let rise until doubled in size, 1½ to 2 hours.

Line a tray with paper towels and place near the stove. Pour 3 inches (7.5cm) of oil into a deep heavy pot and bring it to 340°F (170°C). Using scissors, cut a square around each bomboline placed on the parchment paper. Grab the top 2 corners of the parchment paper with the bomboline on it and very carefully lower it dough side down into the hot oil. After a couple of minutes, or as soon

as the bottom side is golden brown, carefully flip to the other side, leaving the parchment paper attached. It will detach when the oil penetrates between the dough and the paper. As soon as the other side is golden brown, remove the bombolone from the oil using a slotted spoon. Place them on the paper towels to drain. After 1 minute, carefully sprinkle them with some salt.

FILLINGS

Bombolini alla Vecchia: Cut 4 fried bombolini horizontally but not completely, leaving a hinge between the two parts. Dividing evenly, layer each one with 4 thin slices (100g) mortadella, ¼ cup (50g) Stracciatella cheese, and ¼ cup (30g) coarsely chopped pistachios.

Bombolini Stile Parma: Cut 4 fried bombolini horizontally but not completely, leaving a hinge between the two parts. Dividing evenly, layer with 4 thin slices (60g) prosciutto di Parma, ¼ cup (20g) shaved Parmigiano-Reggiano cheese, and ½ cup (10g) arugula.

This recipe is a testament to the versatility of brioche dough. It seemed a natural step after making sweet bombolini. We had this amazing pastry that could go either way, sweet or savoury, and so we began experimenting with different fillings. We've included our top 4 favourite options here: Alla Vecchia (mortadella and Stracciatella cheese), Stile Parma (Prosciutto, Parma cheese, and arugula), Norvegese (smoked salmon, capers, mascarpone), and Calabrese (soppressata, artichoke, and pecorino cheese).

Bombolini alla Norvegese: Cut 4 fried bombolini horizontally but not completely, leaving a hinge between the two parts. Dividing evenly, layer on 4 tablespoons (40g) mascarpone, 2 tablespoons capers, ¼ cup (30g) thinly sliced shallots, and 4 small slices (60g) smoked salmon. Garnish with some freshly ground black pepper. Finish each with a small Boston lettuce leaf.

Bombolini alla Calabrese: Cut 4 fried bombolini horizontally but not completely, leaving a hinge between the two parts. Dividing evenly, layer on 8 thin slices (40g) soppressata, ¼ cup (20g) finely grated pecorino cheese, and ¼ cup (40g) coarsely chopped pickled artichoke (or other preferred pickled vegetable).

APERITIVO

Salatini di pasta sfoglia

SAVOURY PUFF PASTRY SNACKS

SERVES 6

YOU WILL NEED

- Digital scale
- Rolling pin
- 2-inch (5cm) round
  pastry cutter
- Pastry brush

PUFF PASTRY BASE

- 700g Puff Pastry
  (page 298), refrigerated
- All-purpose flour,
  for dusting
- Egg wash: 2 egg yolks
  beaten with 1 tablespoon
  water and a pinch of salt

Make the pastry base: Make the puff pastry dough and chill as directed. Weigh out 700g of dough and save the remainder for another use.

On a lightly floured surface, roll the dough out into a rectangle about 15 × 12-inches (30 × 40cm) and about ¼ inch (5mm) thick. Divide it into 3 equal rectangles 5 × 12 inches (13 × 30cm), place on parchment paper on a baking sheet, and refrigerate for 10 minutes.

Preheat the oven to 350°F (180°C).

Salatini is essentially a name for a platter of salty snacks. This is what is put on the table during aperitivo hour in Italy. At Terroni, all of our salty snacks were really born of necessity when we began catering in earnest. It wasn't practical to make our pizzas for catering jobs, so we started making small puff pastries that were easier on our kitchen logistically speaking as well as easier to serve in a catered-event setting. (This also was a way to repurpose our main dough, without needing to invent a new base dough.) We are offering three options below: little pizzas, a Gorgonzola/honey and walnut option, and asparagus with speck and Taleggio.

PIZZETTE

- ⅓ cup (80ml) Terroni
  Tomato Base (page 294)
- 3½ ounces (100g) fior
  di latte cheese, cubed
  (about ½ cup)
- Fine sea salt and freshly
  ground pepper
- Extra-virgin olive oil
- ¼ cup (25g) finely
  grated Parmigiano-
  Reggiano cheese
- 8 small fresh basil leaves

Line a baking sheet with parchment paper. Place one pastry dough rectangle on a cutting board and use a 2-inch (5cm) round pastry cutter to cut as many dough rounds as possible. Lightly brush with the egg wash. On each round, place 1 tablespoon of tomato sauce, 1 tablespoon of fior di latte, and season with salt and pepper and a drizzle of olive oil. Place them on the lined baking sheet and refrigerate. Gather the puff pastry scraps, cut them into smaller pieces, brush with egg wash, roll them in the Parmigiano, sprinkle with salt, and add them to the baking sheet to bake with the rest. When ready to bake, sprinkle the pizzette with the basil.

TASCHINA

- ½ cup (85g) crumbled
  Gorgonzola cheese
- 2 fresh figs, cut
  into quarters
- ¼ cup (30g) coarsely
  chopped walnuts
- Honey, for drizzling

Place a second puff pastry rectangle on a lightly floured surface. Cut it into 8 equal squares. Lightly brush with the egg wash. Place about 1 teaspoon Gorgonzola cheese at the centre of each one, and top with a quartered fig and a couple pieces of walnuts. Grab two opposite corners of each square and bring them together, forming a triangle, sealing its sides by pressing down on them. Score each triangle belly by making an incision about ¾ inch (2cm) in length. Lightly brush the exterior with more egg wash. Add them to the baking sheet in the fridge. →

111

APERITIVO

DANESE SALATA

- 8 asparagus spears, trimmed and cut into 2-inch (5cm) pieces
- 8 slices (85g) speck
- ½ cup (60g) thinly sliced Taleggio cheese

Group the asparagus pieces into 8 small bundles. Lay each bundle on a slice of speck, top with 1 teaspoon Taleggio, and wrap the speck around the asparagus and Taleggio. Set the last puff pastry rectangle on a lightly floured surface. Cut it into 8 equal squares. Lightly brush with the egg wash. Place the speck/asparagus bundle at the centre of each square. Grab one corner of each square and bring it toward its middle and then grab the opposing corner and bring it to the middle to overlap the other. Using the palm of your hand, gently press on the top, where they come together. Lightly brush with the egg wash and add to the baking sheet in the fridge to rest for 30 minutes.

Transfer to the oven and bake until golden, 15 to 20 minutes. Drizzle honey on the Gorgonzola ones and serve immediately.

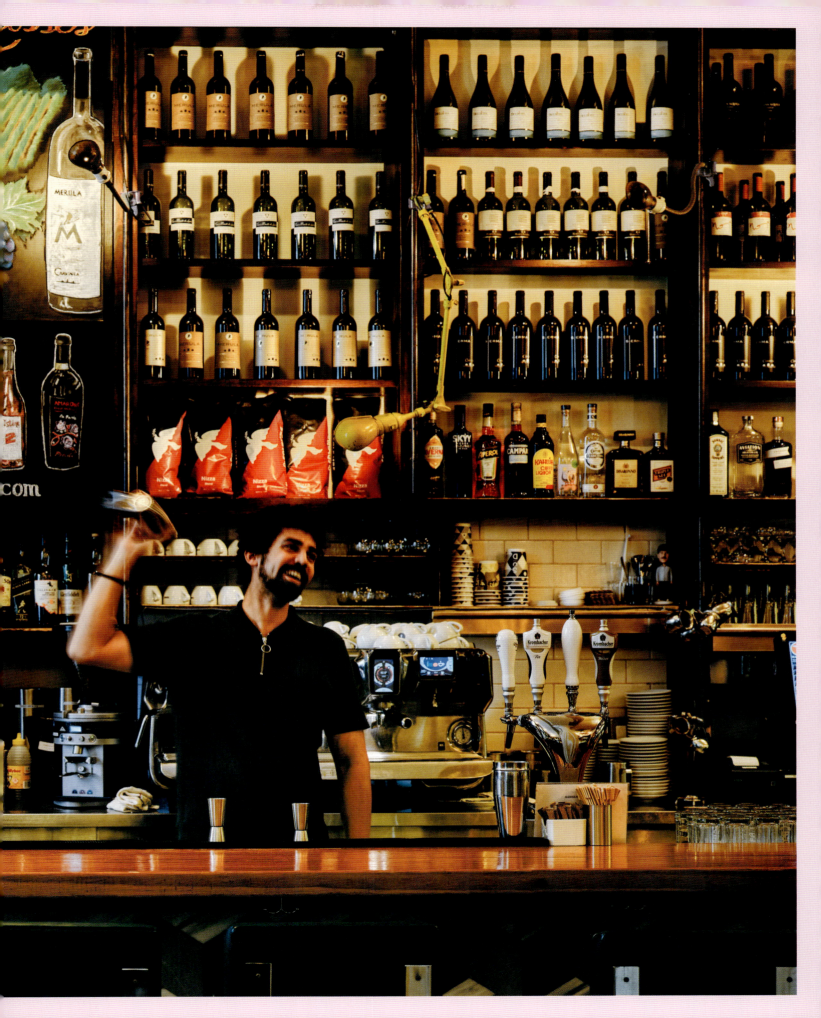

APERITIVO

Panettone gastronomico

STUFFED SAVOURY BRIOCHE

SERVES 8 TO 10

YOU WILL NEED

- Plastic bowl scraper
- A paper panettone mold, 6¼ inches (16cm) in diameter and 5¼ inches (13cm) in height or ovenproof stock pot of the same size
- Egg slicer (optional)
- Four wooden or steel skewers at least 12 inches (30cm) long

- Base Brioche (page 291)
- ²/₃ cup (150g) mayonnaise
- 14 slices salame finocchiona (3 ounces/85g)
- ¼ cup (40g) Crotonese cheese shavings
- 6 Boston lettuce leaves
- ³/₄ cup (180ml) extra-virgin olive oil
- 8 slices cooked ham (3 ounces/85g)
- 8 slices Fontina cheese (3 ounces/85g)
- 2 hard-boiled eggs, cut into thin slices
- Maldon salt
- Freshly ground black pepper
- 12 slices prosciutto di Parma (4¼ ounces/120g)
- 6 slices fior di latte cheese (6½ ounces/180g)
- 10 fresh basil leaves

We were trying to create something special and festive that people could come in and pick up for a great holiday party. Something high impact. And I suppose at the time of brainstorming we were surrounded by a couple hundred panettone, and so we thought, "Why don't we make a delicious ham-y version of this Lombardian giant that people can eat during aperitivo hour?"

So we started by promoting it as a New Year's Eve party snack in the bakery. I always thought it was going to be a bit of an oddball, hard sell, but people love it and call for it each December (as it's made to order). Each layer has a different filling: salame finocchiona, Fontina, prosciutto di Parma, fior di latte . . . I suggest once you nail the recipe below, you start experimenting with different cheeses or salumi to try. If you find a winner, please come into one of our bakeries and let us know. Just maybe we'll put it on next year's menu! →

115

APERITIVO

Make the brioche dough and let rest as directed.

Transfer the dough to a work surface. Using the plastic bowl scraper, gently tighten the dough into a taller mound, pushing it upward by sliding the scraper swiftly beneath the dough. Try to do this movement as swiftly as possible, using only a couple of moves. It should look shiny and not ripped. Cover with plastic wrap and rest for 30 minutes more.

Repeat the shaping step above. Place the dough into a paper panettone mold (6¼ inches × 5¼ inches) or a small Dutch oven greased and lined with parchment paper. Cover with plastic wrap and place in the oven with the light on (but oven off). Let rise until doubled in size, 2 to 3 hours.

Remove from the oven and remove plastic wrap. Preheat the oven to 325°F (160°C).

Place the panettone in its mold on a baking sheet and into the oven. Bake until the core temperature reaches 208°F (98°C), about 50 minutes.

Let the panettone cool completely before removing from the mold. Once cool, wrap it with plastic and store in the fridge. (The panettone can be stuffed up to 3 days after it is made and is easier to slice after a day in the refrigerator.)

Begin by slicing the panettone into horizontal slices, aiming for a thickness of about ½ inch (1.5cm). Set aside the top of the panettone. Spread about ½ tablespoon of mayonnaise in the centre of a plate. Place the first panettone slice flatly on top of the mayo to keep it in place. Next, spread 2½ tablespoons of mayo on this slice and layer with half of the salami, half of the Crotonese cheese, and half of the lettuce.

For the next layer, drizzle 1 tablespoon of olive oil on a slice of panettone and position it, olive oil side down, on the lettuce. Take another slice of panettone and place it on top of the sandwiched slices. Spread 2½ tablespoons of mayonnaise on this slice and add half of the cooked ham and half of the Fontina cheese. Distribute the egg over the Fontina and season with a sprinkle of Maldon salt and black pepper. Drizzle 1 tablespoon of olive oil on the fourth slice of panettone and place it on the egg, with the olive oil side facing down.

Proceed to add the fifth slice of panettone, drizzling it with 1 tablespoon of olive oil. Add half of the prosciutto, half of the fior di latte cheese, and season with Maldon salt, black pepper, and half of the basil leaves. Drizzle 1 tablespoon of olive oil on the sixth slice of panettone and place it on the basil, with the olive oil side facing down. Repeat the above steps, continuing to rebuild

the panettone with 6 more stuffed disks, using the top of the panettone (set aside at the beginning) as the last disk.

To ensure stability, take wooden skewers and insert one through each quarter of the panettone, from top to bottom. Use a bread knife to cut through the panettone from top to bottom, dividing it into 4 equal quarters. Wrap the panettone in plastic and refrigerate until ready to serve. Prior to serving, remove the skewers to allow guests to enjoy the various delightful little sandwiches.

4

COCKTAILS

We are a wine-oriented restaurant. In order for a cocktail to make it onto the menu, our criteria are strictly:

1. Italian ingredients as much as possible;
2. can't be too sweet;
3. must be delicious!

The Right Spritz

MAKES 1 COCKTAIL

What makes it "right"? This is a fresh, less sweet take on what's known as a *negroni sbagliato*, which translates to "the wrong negroni." This cocktail uses a refreshing Dolomiti rhubarb bitter that is rounded out by the sweetness of the classic vermouth from Torino (imported by Cavinona) making it very "right," and very *alta italia* (northern Italian). Both of these elements make the selection of sparkling wine more forgiving, as in you can pair with any sparkling wine of your choice.

YOU WILL NEED

- Mixing glass
- Ice
- Bar spoon
- Rocks glass

- 1½ ounces (45 ml) Doladira aperitivo
- 1 ounce (30 ml) sweet vermouth (we like Bordiga)
- 1 ounce (30 ml) sparkling wine
- Orange slice, for garnish

Add the Doladira and the vermouth to a mixing glass with ice. Using a bar spoon, stir well. Pour into an ice-filled rocks glass. Top it up with sparkling wine and add an orange slice as a garnish.

Sfumato

MAKES 1 COCKTAIL

I love mezcal and especially how it jibes with Montenegro. The combination of these two spirits in this cocktail really hits a note with me. Two mezcals that you will always find on my home bar are Mezcal Verde Amaras and Profesor Mezcal Espadín.

YOU WILL NEED

- Shaker
- Ice
- Champagne coupe glass

- ¾ ounce (25 ml) Aperol
- ¾ ounce (25 ml) mezcal
- ¾ ounce (25 ml) Amaro Montenegro
- ¾ ounce (25 ml) fresh lime juice
- Dried lime wheel, for garnish

In an ice-filled cocktail shaker, combine the Aperol, mezcal, Amaro Montenegro, and lime juice. Shake vigorously. Double strain into a chilled coupe glass. Garnish with a dried lime wheel.

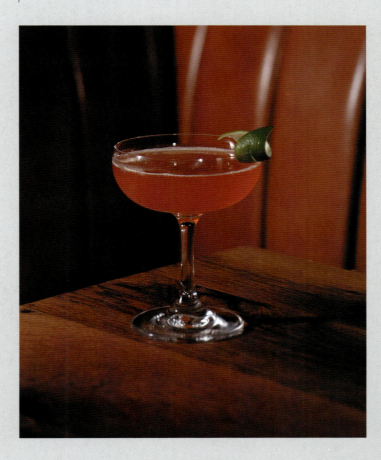

COCKTAILS

Calita

MAKES 1 COCKTAIL

This is my favourite cocktail. Again, I love mezcal, and when paired with Campari and the acidity of the lime, it really comes together. Don't be thrown off by the amaretto; this is really NOT a sweet cocktail.

YOU WILL NEED

- Shaker
- Ice
- Champagne coupe glass

- 1 ounce (30 ml) Campari
- ¾ ounce (25 ml) mezcal
- ½ ounce (15ml) amaretto
- ¼ ounce (7.5 ml) Maraschino
- 1 ounce (30 ml) fresh lime juice
- Dried lime wheel, for garnish

In an ice-filled cocktail shaker, combine the Campari, mezcal, amaretto, Maraschino, and lime juice. Shake vigorously. Double strain into a chilled coupe. Garnish with a dried lime wheel.

La Coccola

MAKES 1 COCKTAIL

This cocktail is spirit-forward, concentrated, and delicious after dinner if you're in need of a medicinal, digestive treat.

YOU WILL NEED

- Shaker
- Ice
- Coupe glass

- 1 ounce (30ml) Vecchia Romagna brandy
- ½ ounce (15ml) Fernet Branca
- ½ ounce (15ml) Frangelico
- ½ ounce (15ml) simple syrup
- Mint leaf, for garnish

In an ice-filled cocktail shaker, combine the brandy, Fernet, Frangelico, and simply syrup. Shake vigorously. Double strain over fresh ice into a coupe. Garnish with a fresh mint leaf.

Terroni Sour

MAKES 1 COCKTAIL

A crowd-pleaser for thirty years now.

YOU WILL NEED

- Shaker
- Ice
- Rocks glass

- 1½ ounces (45ml) bourbon
- ½ ounce (15ml) amaretto
- 1 ounce (30ml) fresh lemon juice
- Dried lemon wheel, for garnish
- 1 Amarena cherry, for garnish

In an ice-filled cocktail shaker, combine the bourbon, amaretto, and lemon juice. Shake vigorously. Double strain over fresh ice into a rocks glass. Garnish with a dried lemon wheel and cherry.

Sempre in vacanza
Always on Holiday

MAKES 1 COCKTAIL

The name kind of says it all. Because of that pineapple, the rum, and the lime, this cocktail will take you out of the Canadian winter and onto the beach . . . at least in your mind.

YOU WILL NEED

- Shaker
- Ice
- Coupe glass

- 1 ounce (30ml) rum
- ½ ounce (15ml) Campari
- ½ ounce (15ml) Amaro Lucano
- ½ ounce (15ml) fresh lime juice
- 1 ounce (30ml) pineapple juice
- Dried pineapple slice, for garnish

In an ice-filled cocktail shaker, combine the rum, Campari, Amaro Lucano, lime juice, and pineapple juice. Shake vigorously. Double strain into a chilled coupe. Garnish with a dried pineapple slice.

Buon per te
Good for You

MAKES 1 COCKTAIL

One of the only honourable ways to drink limoncello.

YOU WILL NEED

- Shaker
- Ice
- Stemless wineglass

- 1 ounce (30ml) gin
- ½ ounce (15ml) limoncello
- 2 ounces (60ml) grapefruit juice
- ½ ounce (15ml) ginger syrup
- Splash of soda water
- Dried grapefruit slice, for garnish

In an ice-filled cocktail shaker, combine the gin, limoncello, grapefruit juice, and ginger syrup. Shake vigorously. Double strain into a stemless glass over fresh ice. Top it up with soda water. Garnish with a dried grapefruit slice.

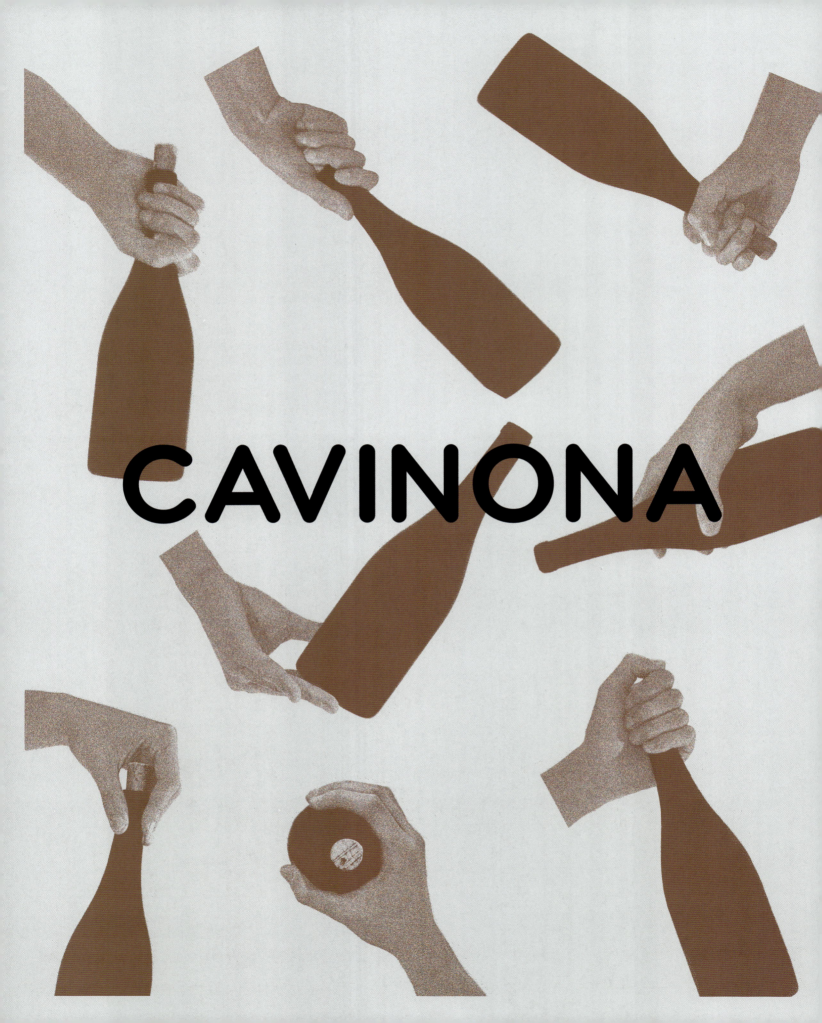

Introducing Italy by the Glass

In 2006 I started Cavinona Wine Agency with my wife, Elena. And I should say for the record that Cavinona actually *belongs* to Elena.

When we first began this business, Terroni was not a place where guests came to drink a beautiful bottle of wine. Not because we didn't *want* to offer beautiful wines, but because we did not have *access to them*.

Obviously spending so much time in Italy, I was frustrated I couldn't find my favourite varietals in Ontario.

We wanted Etna wines like Nerello Mascalese, Nero D'Avola, and Frappato from Sicily. We wanted Tintilia from Basilicata. Susumaniello and Nero di Troia from Puglia. We were looking (and to this day always looking) for more interesting Nebbioli from Alto Piemonte and Val d'Aosta (alpine wines), like Carema. From Lombardia Sforzato, Sassella, Grumello (all made with Nebbiolo grapes). We were on a super hunt for Franciacorta, which DID NOT exist in Ontario.

So, we did the same thing as with every other product we wanted but could not find: We found a way (a very admin-heavy way) of bringing in the products ourselves. It's how we began with food products at Terroni and, hey, why would it be different with wine?

My family and I are wine drinkers, and the world of storytelling about Italy through wine is something that has always inspired me. So, we became wine importers.

Ironically, we started importing with a Lagrein wine, a steely red wine from Alto Adige, the northern Italian region just below Austria (also known as "Sud" Tyrol). I say ironically as you quite literally cannot get further from what it means to be *terroni* than Alto Adige, a region that has a lot more in common with Vienna than, say, Napoli. But Abbazia di Novacella, the Lagrein producer, was one of the first winemakers to give us a chance to sell his product in Ontario. And considering we had no one in our portfolio and basically were bullshitting our way to understanding what an importer does, they took a big risk. But it paid off. Little by little we began adding producers to our portfolio.

At first it was just me and our long-time friend and Terroni employee Karilynn Watson placing orders. Eventually my sister Anna joined and she is leading Cavinona today, eighteen years later, with a great staff. We bring in well over one hundred producers now, from all over Italy.

I'm shocked at how many wine agencies there are in Toronto alone now. And it's a tough business. But for us in 2006, well, we had three restaurants, and so we were selling a decent volume through our own means of distribution. That has always been one of the keys to our success. Another key is perseverance. And I mean that in two aspects:

Perseverance with producers—I visited Giuseppe Rinaldi, one of the most sought-after producers in Piemonte, three times in a span of two years (our first vintage was from 2013) before he gave me a first order of a measly twenty-four bottles. Just last year I received a slightly less measly forty-eight bottles. On a larger scale, there are people like Ferrando, who in northern Piemonte makes Carema, and Ermes Pavese from Val d'Aosta, who works with the Prie Blanc grape.

For Ferrando, every year we went to Vin Italy (the wine fair every April held in Verona) he was our first stop. At the beginning it was always a "NO, we don't have wine to sell you." After two to three years of this, they started recognizing our faces and learned that we were buyers and sellers, and cared deeply about the products we chose to carry.

We explained that, as the final sellers, when we carry the wines, we tell their story to our staff and our customers.

There's a stronger connection than what you get from selling to an agent who sells from a price list. Eventually he gave me five cases of the white label and three of the black.

For Ermes Pavese, it's a similar story. They were always kind of close to each other in the pavilion, so for us they were a one-two stop. They never stayed at the show the whole time, so we always wanted to hit them up first. At the beginning, Ermes only sold us twenty-five cases, and today we get around one hundred cases. It's one of my favourite northern Italian white wines that we carry: a mere 20 kilometers (12½ miles) from Monte Bianco (Mont Blanc). Keep in mind: We could sell more, but they just don't have it.

And perseverance with paperwork with the monopoly, which in Ontario is the LCBO (Liquor Control Board).

When we began, we were known to keep our prices down and our margins honest. We're still known for that and I'm always on the lookout for a great value wine with an interesting story and personality behind it. As our producer list grew, it became important to me that our customers started getting to know them personally. I wanted them to meet the faces behind the wines they loved. So, since 2006 we've been inviting our producers, our customers, and staff to spend a cold November Sunday afternoon talking and tasting wines. We wanted to create a beautiful event where everyone could meet. They could taste the wines, try some food, and ask as many questions as desired. Throughout the year I constantly bump into people who thank me for hosting this event, because it's so special to them to meet the actual producers and participate in the Cavinona Wine Event.

Cavinona brings me joy first and foremost because I get to share these wines with people in the restaurants.

Just being able to introduce wines that most people couldn't have enjoyed in Ontario makes Cavinona worth it to me. Of course I also love to visit the producers in the context of their vineyards and share their stories.

OLIO PANGRAT
TATO FUNGHI P
ARMIGIANO RU
COLA BA   LS
AMICO CA   LA
MARI CAPPERI B
ASILICO SCALO
GNO PEPE ACET
O SA   LE CEC
I RIC   OTTA P
ISELLI CRESCIO
NE TONNO FAGI
OLI POMODORO

5

ANTIPASTI, APRISTOMACO E INSALATE

STARTERS, OPENERS, AND SALADS

ANTIPASTI, APRISTOMACO E INSALATE

Funghi assoluti

BAKED OYSTER MUSHROOM SALAD

SERVES 4

YOU WILL NEED

- baking sheet
- parchment paper

- ½ garlic clove, minced
- ½ cup (120ml) extra-virgin olive oil
- 1¼ pounds (560g) oyster mushrooms
- Fine sea salt
- ¾ cup (80g) dried bread crumbs
- ¾ cup (80g) grated Parmigiano-Reggiano cheese
- 7 ounces (200g) arugula
- ⅓ cup (80ml) balsamic vinegar

This is a signature Terroni dish. It stood out back then and still does thirty years later. It was created in a funny way. Elena, my wife, and Paolo, my late partner, are both from Bari, Puglia. They always had inside jokes going on, speaking in their home dialect. (In Barese dialect, *assoluti* means "on their own"—as in mushrooms served on their own.) Back in 1993, after making pizza and panini, we started experimenting with different dishes that were slightly more elevated but still had the casual feel that people associated with Terroni. We decided to make funghi assoluti because it was something they used to have back in Puglia. We used oyster mushrooms, baked in the oven with bread crumbs, and they wanted to serve it like that. But I wasn't convinced people would understand it, funghi assoluti as an appetizer. It didn't feel like a thing Torontonians would embrace . . . even *I* thought it was a bit odd! So, I added the arugula, put the mushrooms on top, added Parmigiano, balsamic, and olive oil, and turned it into a salad.

I think customers love it because of the taste and texture: the crispiness the Parmigiano and bread crumbs provide in contrast to the toothiness of mushrooms. Even mushroom-haters love this salad.

Preheat the oven to 500°F (260°C). Line a baking sheet with parchment paper.

In a small bowl, whisk the garlic into the olive oil. Lightly grease the parchment paper with about one-third of the garlic-infused oil.

Break down any large pieces of the oyster mushrooms into smaller, bite-sized pieces using your hands. Leave the smaller mushrooms as they are and spread all the mushrooms evenly on the prepared baking sheet. Drizzle the mushrooms with one-third of the garlic oil and season with salt. Sprinkle all the bread crumbs and half of the Parmigiano over the mushrooms.

Bake the mushrooms until they become crispy and turn a golden-brown colour, 10 to 12 minutes.

While the mushrooms are baking, arrange the arugula in the centre of a serving platter.

Place the mushrooms on top of the arugula. Drizzle with the remaining garlic-infused oil and the balsamic vinegar. Sprinkle the remaining grated Parmigiano over all.

Serve the salad immediately and enjoy the delicious combination of crispy oyster mushrooms and fresh arugula.

ANTIPASTI, APRISTOMACO E INSALATE

Calamari alla griglia

GRILLED CALAMARI

SERVES 4

YOU WILL NEED

- Barbecue grill, griddle/grill pan, or a cast-iron skillet
- Tongs

- 1 3/4 pounds (750g) calamari (6 or 7 squid), tubes and tentacles cleaned
- 1/2 cup (120ml) + 2 tablespoons extra-virgin olive oil
- Fine sea salt and freshly ground black pepper
- 3 medium vine tomatoes (9 1/2 ounces/270g) cut into 3/4-inch (2cm) cubes
- 12 fresh basil leaves, cut into strips
- 1 1/2 teaspoons capers
- 1 small shallot (2 ounces/30g), finely diced
- 5 1/2 ounces (160g) mixed greens
- 3 tablespoons balsamic vinegar

NOTA BENE If you are using whole frozen squid you need about 3 pounds (1.4kg); thaw it completely in the refrigerator before cleaning and using. If you are using fresh calamari you will need about 2 1/4 pounds (1kg). Cleaned weight should be 1 3/4 pounds (750g).

This dish was created at the second Terroni at Victoria Street in 1994. Selven, one of our cooks who has been working for us for almost thirty years, came up with this dish. He showed me this way of grilling the calamari, then adding some fresh tomatoes, red onion, and capers on a bed of mixed greens. It's one of those salads that we always think should maybe change, but it has become such a popular staple that we don't touch it!

Preheat a barbecue grill to 400°F (200°C). Or if cooking indoors, when it's time to cook, preheat a griddle/grill pan or large cast-iron skillet on the stovetop.

Clean your sink and fill it with cold water. Or use a large pot and fill it with cold water. Place the squid in the water for 5 minutes, shaking them every once in a while, to remove any sand, then place them in a colander to drain and then pat dry.

Rinse the tubes inside and out ensuring they are completely clear and empty. Pat dry. Lay one tube horizontally on a cutting board. Starting on one side, cut into the tube vertically almost to the top, but do not cut through. Continue to make cuts at 1/4-inch (6mm) intervals as you would a paper frill. Repeat with the remaining tubes. Place each tube in the colander as you prepare the rest. Rinse once more with cold running water, pat dry, and transfer to a bowl. Add the tentacles to the bowl along with 4 tablespoons of olive oil, season with salt and pepper, and mix well.

In a medium bowl, combine the tomatoes, basil, capers, and shallot. Season with salt, pepper, and 3 tablespoons of olive oil. Arrange the mixed greens in the centre of a serving platter. Add the diced tomato mixture to the middle.

Toss the calamari one last time in the bowl. Use tongs to place on the grill (or on the griddle pan) and cook for 2 to 3 minutes per side.

In a small bowl, whisk together the balsamic vinegar and the remaining olive oil until emulsified. Add the grilled calamari, season with salt and pepper, and toss. Place on the bed of tomatoes and greens and serve immediately.

ANTIPASTI, APRISTOMACO E INSALATE

Farinata con insalata di barbabietole

CHICKPEA PANCAKE WITH BEET SALAD

SERVES 4

YOU WILL NEED

- Whisk
- Baking sheet
- Parchment paper
- 14-inch (36cm) round baking pan or unperforated pizza pan
- Large serving platter (about 15 inches/38cm)

FARINATA BATTER

- 2 cups (200g) chickpea flour
- 2 tablespoons + 1 teaspoon extra-virgin olive oil
- 1 teaspoon fine sea salt
- Freshly ground black pepper

ROASTED BEETS

- $1\frac{1}{4}$ pounds (550g) heirloom baby beets (10 to 12)
- Fine sea salt and freshly ground black pepper
- Extra-virgin olive oil, for drizzling

FARINATA

- $2\frac{1}{2}$ tablespoons extra-virgin olive oil
- Maldon salt

SALAD

- 2 tablespoons extra-virgin olive oil
- 1 tablespoon balsamic vinegar
- $1\frac{1}{2}$ teaspoons orange juice
- 1 teaspoon honey
- Fine sea salt and freshly ground black pepper
- $1\frac{1}{2}$ tablespoons grated ricotta salata
- 10 fresh mint leaves, roughly chopped
- A generous handful of watercress
- $2\frac{1}{2}$ tablespoons pistachios, toasted
- 15 to 20 pea shoots

One of the most famous dishes out of Liguria on Italy's west coast, this is an extremely simple and rustic recipe using chickpea flour, water, salt, and olive oil. From Genova up to the border of France, you'll find this on any hardworking Ligurian menu (along with pesto, of course).

You'll usually see this baked in a round cast-iron pan and served with a little sea salt. It's best enjoyed piping hot and eaten like you would a slice of pizza on the street. It's oily, crispy, soft, and the perfect snack on the run. Here we incorporate it into a salad, since selling just a single slice wasn't sexy enough, but it still maintains its delicious simplicity. →

NOTA BENE This recipe requires a resting period of 12 hours.

ANTIPASTI, APRISTOMACO E INSALATE

Make the farinata batter: Place the chickpea flour in a bowl. Whisking constantly, gradually add 4 cups plus 3 tablespoons (1L) water until the flour is completely incorporated and there are no clumps remaining. Once the mixture is smooth, whisk vigorously and skim off any foam that forms on the surface. Repeat this process for a total of three times. Season the batter by mixing in the olive oil, salt, and a few grinds of pepper. Allow the mixture to rest overnight or for 12 hours at room temperature. The batter can last up to 36 hours, but must be kept in the fridge if the resting period is more than 12 hours.

Meanwhile, roast the beets: Preheat the oven to 375°F (190°C). Line a baking sheet with parchment paper.

Trim the tops and bottoms of the beets and wash them under running water. Dry the beets using a paper towel and place them on the baking sheet lined with parchment paper. Season the beets with salt, pepper, and a drizzle of olive oil.

Roast the beets until a knife can easily pierce through them, 35 to 40 minutes.

When cool enough to handle, peel the beets and set aside until you are ready to prepare the salad. (If not used immediately, refrigerate them for the next day.)

When ready to bake the farinata: Preheat the oven to 425°F (220°C). Grease a 14-inch (36cm) round baking pan and line it with parchment paper. Evenly spread the olive oil on the parchment paper.

Use a whisk to stir the farinata batter for 3 to 4 minutes, ensuring that everything that has settled is lifted from the bottom and that the mixture is smooth. Taste the mixture for seasoning. Pour the whole mixture into the greased baking pan and sprinkle with Maldon salt.

Bake until the farinata turns golden and crispy, 20 to 25 minutes.

Meanwhile, finish the salad: In a small bowl, whisk together the olive oil, balsamic vinegar, orange juice, and honey and season with salt and pepper. Whisk for 1 to 2 minutes until well combined. Set the dressing aside.

Cut the beets into quarters and place them in a bowl. Add the ricotta salata, mint leaves, watercress, and half of the pistachios. Pour the dressing over the salad ingredients and gently toss everything together. Taste the salad and season with salt and pepper to your liking.

Once the farinata is ready and crispy, remove it from the baking pan and transfer it to a serving platter. Cut the farinata into 4 equal parts. Give the beet salad one final toss, then place it in the middle of the farinata. Garnish the salad with pea shoots and sprinkle the remaining pistachios on top. Serve and enjoy!

ANTIPASTI, APRISTOMACO E INSALATE

Nizzarda

ITALIAN NIÇOISE

SERVES 1

YOU WILL NEED

- Spider strainer

SALAD

- 1 egg
- Fine sea salt
- 3 ounces (85g) baby potatoes or fingerlings (3 or 4)
- 10 green beans, trimmed
- 5 cherry tomatoes, halved
- 1½ teaspoons very thinly sliced shallots
- Freshly ground black pepper
- A fistful of arugula (1 ounce/30g)
- 8 Taggiasca olives
- 1 (80g) can Italian tuna in olive oil, drained
- Fine sea salt
- 4 to 5 anchovy fillets

DRESSING

- 1 tablespoon extra-virgin olive oil
- 1½ teaspoons red wine vinegar
- Fine sea salt and freshly ground black pepper

The origins of the Nizzarda very likely go back to being an Italian take on the French Niçoise.

You can imagine the amount of pasta we eat in the Terroni family, and so this salad is really a digestive godsend when we want a break from the sugar and carbs, which is almost never. This is my go-to salad—I enjoy it a couple of times a week for lunch. It'll fill you up and provide you with all the nutrition you need. The anchovies are just a bonus! You can double this recipe to make a side salad for 4.

Place the egg in a small pot filled with cold water. Bring the water to a boil and let it cook for 7 minutes. Remove the egg from the pot and cool it under cold running water.

Meanwhile, bring another small pot of salted water to a boil. Set up a bowl of ice and water and place near the stove. Add the potatoes to the boiling water and cook until they are tender enough to be easily pierced with a fork, 10 to 12 minutes. Use a spider strainer to scoop the potatoes them from the boiling water to the ice bath.

In the same pot of boiling water, cook the green beans until they are crisp-tender, 2 to 3 minutes. Drain and immediately cool them in the ice bath along with the potatoes.

Once the potatoes and green beans have cooled, drain them. Cut the potatoes into quarters and set them aside. Peel and rinse the boiled egg under water and set aside.

Make the dressing: In a small bowl, whisk together the olive oil, vinegar, and salt and pepper to taste for a minute, until emulsified.

Assemble the salad: In a large bowl, combine the quartered potatoes, green beans, cherry tomatoes, and sliced shallots. Pour the prepared dressing over the vegetables, add some freshly ground pepper, and gently toss.

Arrange the arugula in a mound in the centre of a serving bowl and mound the tossed vegetables on top, drizzling any remaining dressing over the top. Arrange the olives on top of the vegetables. Scoop the tuna on top of the olives and vegetables, being careful not to break it up too much. Cut the boiled egg into quarters, season with salt and pepper, and place one piece on each half of the salad. Finally, place the anchovy fillets flat on top of the tuna and serve with another drizzle of olive oil, if you like.

ANTIPASTI, APRISTOMACO E INSALATE

Mozzarella in carrozza

FRIED MOZZARELLA SANDWICHES

SERVES 4

YOU WILL NEED

- Small heavy-bottomed pot, for deep-frying
- Deep-fry thermometer
- Spider strainer or slotted spoon

- 1 pound (500g) Mozzarella di Bufala Campana DOP
- 8 slices (3 ounces/85g each) brioche, homemade (page 291) or store-bought
- 18 anchovy fillets (2 ounces/60g)
- Fine sea salt and freshly ground black pepper
- Pinch of dried oregano
- 2 tablespoons extra-virgin olive oil
- 5 eggs
- ¾ cup (90g) all-purpose flour
- 1¾ cups (200g) dried bread crumbs
- 2 cups (100g) panko crumbs
- Sunflower oil (about 2 quarts/2L), for deep-frying

NOTA BENE It's important to use a spider or slotted spoon to turn the sandwiches during frying to prevent them from sticking together or breaking apart.

In Italy, when you buy fresh mozzarella, you eat it *fresh*, usually on the same day. You don't even put it in the fridge because the cold will ruin it. If you store the fresh cheese in the water, it will protect it, but the day after, it's just not as good. So that's why mozzarella in carrozza was invented.

Remove the mozzarella from its liquid and squeeze out any excess water. Cut it into ⅜- to ½-inch (1 to 1.5cm) slices and place these on paper towels on a tray to further drain the liquid.

Place 4 slices of brioche flat on a surface and divide the mozzarella slices evenly on them, making sure to cover the surface of each slice of brioche but also stay inside its margins. Dividing evenly, top with the anchovies. Season everything with salt, pepper, and oregano and drizzle with the olive oil.

Close each sandwich with the remaining brioche. Using your hand, gently press down onto each sandwich to compact it and ensure everything stays together. Cut the crust off each, turning it into a square. Divide each square sandwich into 4 pieces, either by cutting them into 4 triangles or 4 squares.

Prepare a dredging station in three shallow bowls: Crack the eggs into one, season with salt and pepper, and whisk until combined. Place the flour in the second bowl. In the third, mix the bread crumbs and panko crumbs. Start by dipping all the sandwiches in the flour bowl, shaking off any excess and placing them on a tray. Take each flour-dipped sandwich and fully dip it into the egg bowl. Shake out any excess egg and evenly dip it into the bread crumb bowl. Once again, shake off any excess. Place on a tray to rest in the refrigerator for 30 minutes. Repeat the egg and bread crumb panko dipping process one more time.

Pour 3 inches (7.5cm) sunflower oil into a small heavy-bottomed pot and heat over medium to high heat until it reaches 335°F (170°C).

Line a tray with paper towels and place near the stove. Add the mini sandwiches to the hot oil and fry for 3 to 4 minutes, turning them with a spider strainer from time to time, until golden brown and crisp. Once done, transfer to the paper towels to drain. Season with salt and serve hot.

139

ANTIPASTI, APRISTOMACO E INSALATE

Fave e cicoria

FAVA BEAN PURÉE AND DANDELION

SERVES 6

YOU WILL NEED

- Immersion blender
  or food processor

FOR THE FAVA BEAN PURÉE

- 2 cups (14 ounces/400g)
  dried peeled fava beans
- 1 cup (180g) diced potatoes
- 1 fresh bay leaf
- 1 tablespoon fine sea salt
- 3 tablespoons extra-
  virgin olive oil

FOR THE DANDELION

- Fine sea salt
- 12 cups (400g) dandelion
  leaves, coarsely chopped
  into 2-inch (5cm) pieces
- ¼ cup (60ml) extra-
  virgin olive oil
- 1 garlic clove, smashed
  and peeled

GARNISH

- 1 tablespoon (15g)
  slivered shallots
- 1 fresh chili pepper, sliced
- Extra-virgin olive oil
- Bread Crisps (page 290)

This is a very simple dish, one of my favourites: purée of fava beans with *cicoria* (dandelion). I remember very vividly the first time I had it: It was in a restaurant in the heart of Bari, a typical modest restaurant where one would go for lunch. You must use split fava beans, meaning with no skin on them. Simply boil them with some potatoes until they almost come apart and then you purée the mixture with lots of olive oil. The fava bean purée should have the consistency of mashed potatoes. And just like mashed potatoes, people like different consistencies. Add water as you see fit. I personally don't like the purée to be too dense. And for the cicoria, you blanch them, boil them, and put them on top, and drizzle more EVOO.

Make the fava bean purée: Wash the fava beans by placing them in a sieve and running cold water over them.

In a large pot, combine the fava beans and potatoes with cold water to cover by about 2 inches (5cm). Gently bring to a boil. Add the bay leaf and salt, reduce the heat to medium-low, and cook, skimming the foam off the top at regular intervals, until tender and the favas start coming apart on their own, about 45 minutes.

Drain, discard the bay leaf, and return the mixture to the pot. Add the olive oil and purée with an immersion blender until smooth, adding water if needed to achieve your preferred consistency. (Alternatively, do this in a food processor.) Adjust the seasoning to taste.

Prepare the dandelion: Set up a large bowl of ice and water and place near the sink. In a medium pot, bring 5 quarts (5L) water and 1 tablespoon fine sea salt to a boil. Add the dandelion to the boiling water and blanch for 2 to 3 minutes. Drain the greens and submerge into the icy water. Once cooled, drain.

In a large skillet, heat the olive oil and garlic over medium heat and sauté until the garlic becomes golden, about 1 minute. Add the drained dandelion and sauté, seasoning with salt, until soft, 5 to 6 minutes.

Serve by spooning some of the fava bean purée onto the centre of a plate, adding about ¼ cup of the sautéed dandelion and garnishing with the shallot, chili pepper, and a drizzle of olive oil. Enjoy with some bread crisps.

This is the perfect winter lunch with a warming glass of vino rosso. I love it with Primitivo from Carvinea, a wonderful producer from Puglia *(who happens to be my father-in-law, Beppe).*

PARMIGIANO REGGIANO PECORINO OLIO SALE PEPE ALLORO LENTICCHIE NDUJA VINO CASTAGNE GUANCIALE BIETOLA FAGIOLI CIPOLLE PORRI SEDANO ZUCCHINE ZUCCA CAVOLFIORE

ZUPPE
SOUPS

6

ZUPPE

Minestrone

VEGETABLE SOUP

SERVES 8 TO 10

- ½ cup (100g) dried borlotti beans
- 1 cup + 2 tablespoons (270ml) extra-virgin olive oil, plus more for drizzling
- 2 cups (200g) finely diced red onions
- 1 bay leaf
- Fine sea salt and freshly ground black pepper
- 1 cup (100g) very thinly sliced leeks (1/16-inch/2mm rounds), white and light-green parts only
- 1 cup (100g) diced peeled carrots
- 2 cups diced (200g) celery
- 1 cup (100g) cubed peeled potatoes (3/4-inch/2cm cubes)
- 1 cup (100g) cubed zucchini (3/4-inch/ 2cm cubes)
- 1 cup (100g) cubed peeled winter squash (3/4-inch [2cm] cubes)
- 1 cup (100g) small cauliflower florets and stems cut into 3/8-inch (1cm) pieces
- 1 cup (100g) small broccoli florets and stems cut into 3/8-inch (1cm) pieces
- 1 bunch (7 ounces/200g) black kale (aka lacinato kale)
- 1 garlic clove, minced
- 3½ ounces (100g) green beans, trimmed
- 1½ cups (7 ounces/200g) cherry tomatoes, halved
- Bread Crisps (page 290)
- Grated Parmigiano-Reggiano or Pecorino Romano cheese, for serving

NOTA BENE This recipe makes a large batch because it freezes well. All the amounts listed can be modified to reduce waste. For instance, if your zucchini weighs 5¼ ounces (150g), you can use the whole amount instead of just 3½ ounces (100g).

Minestrone is a controversial topic. Everyone thinks they make the best one and there are so many ways of making it. And the discussion goes on and on: with beans or without, with pasta or without, etc. Giovanna was charged with the task of creating Terroni's minestrone and all our other soups. Everyone thought she was an old nonna (she was twenty-two), because the soups she created tasted rich and wholesome. You will need a very large pot to make this.

Minestrone is one of those dishes that doesn't need to be taken too seriously. If a vegetable is not available, it doesn't matter. If you have pasta or legumes at home, throw them in. It does also depend on the season, of course.

Soak the beans in water to cover for 12 hours or overnight. Drain.

In a large pot, heat 3 tablespoons of olive oil over medium heat. Add half of the chopped onions and sauté until the onions are softened and starting to colour, about 4 minutes. Add the soaked beans, bay leaf, and cold water to cover by 2 inches (5cm). Bring to a boil, cover, reduce to a simmer, and cook until the beans are tender, about 1 hour. Remove from the heat, season with salt and pepper, and set aside. (Do not drain.)

In a separate heavy-bottomed pot, heat ¾ cup (180ml) of olive oil over medium heat. Add the remaining onions and all the leeks. Sauté until they become soft and translucent, a good 3 to 4 minutes. Add the carrots, celery, and potatoes and cook, stirring often, an additional 5 minutes.

Add cold water to cover the vegetables by 1 inch (2.5cm) and bring to a boil over medium heat. Reduce to a simmer and add the zucchini, squash, cauliflower, and broccoli. Add more cold water to cover by 1 inch (2.5cm). Bring to a boil, then reduce to a simmer, cover, and cook for 35 minutes.

Meanwhile, prepare a cold-water bath in your sink and soak the kale for 5 to 10 minutes, periodically

shaking it in the water. Remove it from the water and rinse it under running water for a couple of minutes. Place each leaf on a cutting board, trim away about 1 inch (2.5cm) from the bottom of the stem, and chop it into 1-inch (2.5cm) pieces.

In a large skillet, heat 3 tablespoons of olive oil over medium heat. Add the garlic and cook until golden, about 1 minute. Add the chopped kale and fry until wilted, 4 to 5 minutes, stirring it with a wooden spoon. Season with salt and set aside.

Set up a large bowl of ice and water and set near the sink. In a small pot of boiling water, cook the green beans for 2 to 3 minutes. Drain and transfer to the ice bath. Once cooled, drain the green beans and set aside.

When the soup has been simmering for 30 minutes, add the cooked borlotti beans along with their cooking broth, the fried kale, green beans, and cherry tomatoes. Gently bring everything to a boil, then simmer for 5 minutes. Taste the soup and adjust the seasoning with salt and pepper to your liking.

Serve the soup hot, along with bread crisps, a generous dusting of grated Parmigiano or Romano, and a plentiful drizzle of olive oil.

144

Pasta e fagioli

PASTA AND BEANS

SERVES 4 TO 6

YOU WILL NEED

- Large soup pot
- Immersion blender

- 2 cups (14 ounces/400g) dried white kidney beans
- 6 tablespoons extra-virgin olive oil
- 1$\frac{1}{2}$ tablespoons minced garlic
- 1$\frac{1}{2}$ cups (220g) chopped red onion
- $\frac{3}{4}$ cup (80g) chopped celery
- $\frac{3}{4}$ cup (80g) chopped carrots
- 1 red chili pepper, roughly chopped
- 1 fresh bay leaf
- 1 cup (200g) canned plum tomatoes, milled or crushed by hand
- 1 cup (120g) cubed peeled potatoes
- 3$\frac{1}{2}$ tablespoons (50g) unsalted butter
- $\frac{3}{4}$ cup (3$\frac{1}{2}$ ounces/100g) thin strips of sliced prosciutto
- Fine sea salt and freshly ground black pepper
- 1$\frac{3}{4}$ cups (10$\frac{1}{2}$ ounces/300g) dried tubetti pasta, or 2 cups (14 ounces/400g) fresh pasta, such as maltagliati
- 4 tablespoons grated Parmigiano-Reggiano cheese

One really can't have a restaurant called Terroni without serving *pasta e fagioli*. It's a very typical dish of the south, also known as a *cucina povera* (poor kitchen) dish since the ingredients are cheap and abundant.

We would go through tons of prosciutto in the restaurants and end up with all the end pieces of the prosciutto and were trying to figure out what to do with them, so we added them to the soup. The skin we added together with the beans to add extra flavour, and we cut up the meaty bits to add at the end for garnish. We would import all types of legumes from Puglia and people would come in winter just to have this soup at the bar.

In a large bowl, soak the beans in water to cover overnight. Drain and rinse.

In a large soup pot, heat 4 tablespoons of olive oil over medium heat. Add the garlic, onion, celery, carrots, chili pepper, and bay leaf and sauté the ingredients until they become fragrant and have softened slightly, about 5 minutes. Add the beans to the pot and continue sautéing for an additional 3 to 5 minutes.

Add 7$\frac{1}{2}$ cups (1.8L) water and the tomatoes, gently bringing everything to a boil. Once boiling, add the potatoes, reduce the heat to a simmer, and cook until the beans are fully cooked through and tender, about 1$\frac{1}{2}$ hours.

Ladle 2 cups (500ml) of the soup into a bowl. Use an immersion blender to purée the soup in the bowl until it reaches a smooth and creamy consistency. Return the puréed base to the pot, stirring it back into the soup until incorporated.

In a skillet, heat the remaining 2 tablespoons olive oil and the butter over medium-high heat. Add the prosciutto and sauté until it becomes crispy and golden, 2 to 3 minutes. Transfer the cooked prosciutto to the pot, mixing it into the soup. Taste the soup and adjust the salt and pepper according to your preference.

Meanwhile, in a medium pot, bring salted water to a boil. Add the pasta and cook according to the package directions. Drain the pasta and add it to the soup base, combining it well.

To serve, ladle the soup with the pasta into individual serving bowls. Finish each dish by generously sprinkling grated Parmigiano over the top.

ZUPPE

Zuppa di lenticchie e 'nduja

LENTIL SOUP WITH 'NDUJA

SERVES 6 TO 8

YOU WILL NEED

- Large pot

- 2 cups (400g) brown lentils, preferably from Pantelleria or similar type
- $\frac{1}{3}$ cup (80ml) + 2 tablespoons extra-virgin olive oil, plus more to finish
- 1 garlic clove, smashed and peeled
- 1 cup (100g) thinly sliced leeks ($\frac{1}{16}$-inch/2mm rounds), white and light-green parts only
- 7 ounces (200g) 'nduja or other good-quality smoky sausage meat
- $\frac{1}{4}$ cup (60ml) dry white wine
- 9 ounces (250g) potatoes, peeled and cut into $\frac{3}{8}$-inch (1cm) cubes
- $\frac{3}{4}$ cup ($3\frac{1}{2}$ ounces/100g) finely chopped celery
- $3\frac{1}{2}$ ounces (100g) carrots, finely chopped
- 1 fresh bay leaf
- Freshly ground black pepper
- 1 generous cup (5 ounces/150g) halved cherry tomatoes
- Fine sea salt
- 1 tablespoon minced fresh Italian parsley
- Bread Crisps (page 290)

I love lentils, and all my kids love them, too, even my son who doesn't like to eat any other legumes! This dish is a one-pot wonder. Simply chuck all the ingredients into a pot and it becomes this incredibly nourishing dish. You don't have to soak the lentils, which makes it a great weekday meal (i.e., very little prep time). At home, we serve it as a side with sausage or a nice piece of halibut.

Thoroughly rinse the lentils. In a large pot, combine the olive oil and crushed garlic clove. Sauté over medium heat until the garlic becomes golden, about 5 minutes. Add the leeks and 'nduja, breaking up the latter with a wooden spoon, and cook until the leeks become tender, 8 to 10 minutes.

Deglaze the pot with the wine, scraping the bottom to remove any browned bits. Add the potatoes and cook for 7 minutes so they absorb the smokiness of the 'nduja and gain some colour. Add the celery, carrots, lentils, and 8 cups (2L) water, and bring the mixture to a boil over medium heat. Reduce the heat to medium-low, add the bay leaf, and a pinch of black pepper. Cover and simmer for 30 minutes.

Add the cherry tomatoes (and more water if a thinner soup is desired) and continue cooking for an additional 10 minutes over medium-low heat. Season the soup with salt and pepper to taste and stir in the parsley.

Serve the hot soup with a drizzle of extra-virgin olive oil and a few bread crisps per person. This soup can also be frozen.

Verdura di Mamma Rita

COSIMO'S MOM'S WHITE BEAN AND CHARD STEW

SERVES 6 TO 8

YOU WILL NEED

- Bowl
- Colander
- Medium pot
- Large sauté pan

BEANS

- 1½ cups (10 ounces/280g) dried navy beans
- 1 tablespoon extra-virgin olive oil
- 1 garlic clove
- 1 small sprig rosemary
- Water
- Fine sea salt and freshly ground black pepper

SWISS CHARD

- 1 bunch (1¼ pounds/550g) Swiss chard
- 2 tablespoons extra-virgin olive oil
- 1 garlic clove, smashed and peeled
- 1 chili pepper
- Fine sea salt

FOR SERVING

- Extra-virgin olive oil, for drizzling
- Rita's Corn Crisps (page 103), Bread Crisps (page 290), or sliced bread

When I was growing up, my mother served this dish as a primo or side dish. We decided to include it in our menu as people absolutely loved it because it is hearty, healthy, and can be made with any leafy green vegetable. Add some chili and good olive oil and enjoy it with Bread Crisps (page 290). And it's vegan!

Cook the beans: Soak the beans in a bowl of cold water for 12 hours. Drain in a colander, and rinse.

In a medium pot, combine the beans, olive oil, garlic, and rosemary. Add cold water to cover by about 1 inch (2.5cm). Bring the water to a boil. Reduce to a simmer, cover, and cook until the beans are just tender, 50 minutes to 1 hour. Remove from the heat and season the beans with salt and pepper. Set aside.

Prepare the Swiss chard: Prepare a cold-water bath in your sink and place the Swiss chard in it for 5 to 10 minutes, gently shaking it in the water at intervals. After soaking, remove the Swiss chard from the water and rinse it under running water for a couple of minutes. Trim about 1 inch (2.5cm) from the bottom of the chard stems. Chop the remaining stems and leaves into 1-inch (2.5cm) pieces.

In a large sauté pan, heat the olive oil over medium heat. Add the garlic and chili and cook until the garlic turns golden, about 1 minute. Add the chard and season with salt. Cover the pan and cook over medium-low heat until tender, about 5 minutes.

Add the cooked beans along with their cooking broth to the pan. Cook over medium-low heat for an additional 15 minutes to meld all the flavors. Taste and adjust the seasoning with salt if needed. Remove the pan from the heat, cover, and let it sit for 5 to 10 minutes.

To serve, drizzle the dish with a generous amount of olive oil and accompany it with corn crisps, bread crisps, or fresh bread.

ZUPPE

Zuppa di castagne

CHESTNUT SOUP

SERVES 6 TO 8

YOU WILL NEED

- Skimmer
- Immersion blender, regular blender, or food processor

- ¼ cup (60ml) extra-virgin olive oil, plus more for drizzling
- 7 ounces (200g) guanciale, skin removed and cut into ⅜ × ½-inch (1 × 1.5cm) strips (about 2 cups)
- 1 cup (100g) sliced leeks (¼-inch/5mm rounds), white part only
- 1 sprig rosemary
- 7 ounces (200g) potatoes, peeled and cut into ¾-inch (2cm) cubes
- 3 cups (1 pound/500g) peeled roasted chestnuts (see Note)
- 6 cups (1.5L) whole milk
- Fine sea salt
- 1 fresh bay leaf
- Freshly ground black pepper
- Pinch of ground cinnamon
- Pinch of ground nutmeg
- ¼ cup (60ml) heavy cream
- Bread Crisps (page 290)

Another Terroni classic, this dish recalls Milano in autumn when you see fresh chestnuts on all the menus of the classic osterie and trattorie. (If you wish to make a Milanese smile, simply send them a box of glazed chestnuts from Galli; it's like a secret handshake among northern Italians.)

For all the chestnut skeptics out there: This soup is piled with guanciale and is really a gateway dish to chestnut appreciation.

Line a plate with paper towels and place near the stove. In a medium pot, heat the olive oil over medium heat. Once the oil is hot, increase the heat to high and add the guanciale strips. Fry them until they become crisp, 1 to 2 minutes. Use a skimmer to remove the crispy guanciale from the pot and set it aside on the paper towels.

Reduce the heat under the pot to medium and add the leeks and rosemary. Cook, stirring occasionally, until the leeks are soft and translucent, 8 to 10 minutes.

Add the potatoes and continue cooking for an additional 5 minutes. Add the chestnuts, milk, 1¼ cups (300ml) water, and a generous pinch of salt. Bring everything to a boil over medium heat. Reduce the heat to a simmer, add the bay leaf and a good grind of pepper, cover, and simmer for 50 minutes to 1 hour to allow all the flavours to mingle and give depth to the soup.

Add the cinnamon, nutmeg, and cream and continue cooking over low heat for 10 more minutes. Discard the bay leaf and rosemary sprig. Using an immersion blender, carefully purée the soup until it becomes very smooth and creamy in texture. (If you don't have an immersion blender, you can transfer the soup in batches to a regular blender or food processor and blend to achieve the desired consistency.) Taste and adjust seasoning with salt and pepper as needed.

Serve topped with the crispy guanciale strips and a drizzle of some extra-virgin olive oil (about 1 teaspoon per serving). Serve the bread crisps on the side.

NOTE ON CHESTNUTS

Fresh Chestnuts:

If using fresh, start with about 1¾ pounds (800g). Rinse the chestnuts and score them horizontally across their belly through the shell (2 to 3mm deep). Soak the chestnuts in hot water for at least 2 hours. In a pot of lightly salted boiling water, blanch the chestnuts for about 5 minutes, until the shells start to open and the insides of the chestnuts are exposed. Drain. Preheat the oven to 450°F (230°C). Season the chestnuts with extra-virgin olive oil and salt and roast them on a baking sheet for about 20 minutes. Transfer the chestnuts to a clean kitchen towel, wrap, and let them rest until just cool enough to handle (but still hot), then peel back the shells to remove them along with the inner chestnut skin.

Cleaned and Steamed Chestnuts:

Look for vacuum-packed chestnuts at your favourite greengrocer, typically sold in 3-ounce (100g) pouches. Preheat the oven to 450°F (230°C), season with extra-virgin olive oil and salt, and roast the chestnut flesh until dark golden brown, 30 to 35 minutes. We love toasting a few even more over a flame (a gas stove flame works) to give the soup a real *caldarroste* (roasted chestnuts) flavour.

Vellutata di finocchio

CREAM OF FENNEL SOUP

SERVES 6 TO 8

YOU WILL NEED

- Large pot
- Blender

- 2 pounds (900g) fennel
  (we know, this is A LOT of
  fennel. It's the main player.)
- ¼ cup (60ml) extra-
  virgin olive oil, plus
  more for drizzling
- ½ cup (120g)
  minced shallots
- 1½ cups (250g) cubed
  peeled potatoes
  (¾-inch/2cm cubes)
- 1¾ cups (420ml) vegetable
  stock or water
- 1 bay leaf
- Fine sea salt and freshly
  ground black pepper
- ½ cup (50g) finely grated
  Parmigiano-Reggiano
  cheese (optional)

Like you, perhaps, I was quite suspicious about the notion of fennel soup, but it turned out to be delicious. It's super simple and comes together very quickly. The key to this soup is lots of Parmigiano-Reggiano and olive oil! It goes through this transformation of raw fennel into a very smooth, light, delicious dish. Especially good for those cold Canadian nights. We serve this at the restaurant seasonally. We also sell it in jars in our retail spots.

Remove the root end and green stalks and fronds of the fennel (save for making stock). Roughly chop the fennel into ¾-inch (2cm) cubes. Reserve the fennel fronds for garnish.

In a large pot, heat the olive oil over medium heat. Add the shallots and sauté until they become soft and translucent, 6 to 8 minutes.

Add the chopped fennel and potatoes and continue sautéing for an additional 10 minutes allow the veg to gain colour and depth.

Pour in the stock and add the bay leaf to the pot. Bring everything to a boil. Reduce the heat to a simmer, cover, and simmer until the fennel and potatoes soften, about 20 minutes.

Discard the bay leaf and transfer the contents to a blender. Blend the ingredients until the soup becomes smooth and creamy in texture. You may need to do this in batches depending on the size of your blender. Taste and adjust the seasoning with salt and pepper if necessary.

To serve, ladle the creamy fennel and potato soup into bowls. Finish each serving with a drizzle of olive oil. If desired, top with some grated Parmigiano-Reggiano and some of the reserved fennel fronds, chopped.

I love drinking Sangiovese from San Patrignano with this.

CECI AGLIO OL
IO SAL E RO
SMARI NO P
REZZEMOLO FU
NGHI SALSICCI
A VINO PISELL
I PARMIGIANO P
REZZEMOLO Z
UCHHINI POMO
DO RO MOZZ
AR ELLA PE
PE LIMONE CA
PPERI SPINACI

PRIMI
FIRST COURSES

7

PRIMI

Ciceri e tria

TRIA WITH CHICKPEAS

SERVES 4 TO 6

YOU WILL NEED

- Pasta machine, stand mixer with a pasta attachment, or rolling pin
- Deep heavy-bottomed pot, for deep-frying
- Deep-fry thermometer
- Spider strainer or slotted spoon

CHICKPEAS

- 1 cup (7 ounces/200g) dried chickpeas
- 1 tablespoon + 1 teaspoon extra-virgin olive oil
- 1 garlic clove, smashed and peeled
- 1 sprig rosemary
- 1 bay leaf
- Fine sea salt and freshly ground black pepper

TRIA PASTA

- Fresh Semola Rimacinata Pasta (page 293)
- Semola flour, for dusting
- Sunflower oil (about 2 quarts/2L), for deep-frying

SAUCE

- 3 tablespoons extra-virgin olive oil, plus more for drizzling
- ¾ cup (7 ounces/200g) finely diced white onion
- 1 garlic clove, smashed and peeled
- 1 sprig rosemary
- 1 fresh chili, left whole
- Generous 1 cup (150g) halved cherry tomatoes
- Fine sea salt

This is a dish I stumbled upon when travelling to Lecce, Puglia, with my wife. We were wandering the streets and decided to stop in at a little restaurant for lunch. They had Ciceri e Tria on the menu, and I had no idea what it was, so I ordered it and it was delicious. Pasta and chickpeas, but with a crunchy part. I thought, "This is unbelievable, why doesn't everybody know about this dish?" I loved it so much that we named an osteria we opened in 2008 in Toronto Ciceri e Tria. The *tria* refers to the fact that two-thirds of the pasta that makes up this dish is fried. It's one of those simple dishes that has few ingredients, but they all count and make it so special. It's also a very comforting dish for winter.

The dish was always fixed on the menu even though the rest of the menu changed from day to day. The recipe for the dish is inscribed in the sides of the head table of the restaurant (featured in our photo). Gio used to make "tria" pasta by hand at this table, but it was too tall for her. One day my dad, Vince (aka Geppetto), swung in after parking illegally on Victoria Street and delivered a beautiful wooden stool for Gio to stand on so she could reach more easily. The kicker was that he designed it and made it so it would fit perfectly in a little alcove under the table.

Osteria Ciceri e Tria, the restaurant, has since then morphed into La Bettola, but its spirit lives on as today we still feature this dish as a special in the Terroni locations.

NOTA BENE You will need to start this recipe the day before to soak the chickpeas.

Cook the chickpeas: Soak the chickpeas in cold water to cover for 12 hours. Drain and rinse.

In a pot, combine the chickpeas, olive oil, garlic, rosemary, and bay leaf. Add cold water to cover by 2 inches (5cm). Bring to a boil. Reduce to a simmer, cover, and cook until tender, 45 minutes to 1 hour.

Remove from the heat and season with salt and pepper. Set aside. (These flavourful chickpeas can be prepared ahead of time and stored in the refrigerator or freezer in their cooking broth until needed. Drain before using.) →

I like Montefalco Rosso, Antonelli (Umbria) with this dish.

Make the tria pasta: Prepare the dough as directed up to the end of the resting period. If using a rolling pin, dust your work surface with semola flour. Using a pasta machine or a rolling pin, roll the dough to a thickness of $\frac{1}{8}$ to $\frac{1}{16}$ inch (3 to 2mm). Allow the rolled-out dough to rest for 10 to 15 minutes until dry to the touch. Cut the dough into little rectangles or parallelograms about $\frac{3}{4}$ × 2 inches (2 × 5cm). Measure out two-thirds of the pasta to be fried. (Set aside the remainder to be boiled later.)

Line a tray with paper towels and place near the stove. Pour 2 inches (5cm) sunflower oil into a heavy-bottomed medium pot and heat over medium-high heat to 356°F (180°C).

Working in batches, add the pasta to be fried to the hot oil and cook until dark golden, 2 to 3 minutes. Use a spider or slotted spoon to remove the fried tria from the oil and place them on the paper towels to drain.

Bring a large pot of salted water to a boil for the reserved fresh pasta.

Make the sauce: In a saucepan, heat the olive oil over medium heat. Add the onion, garlic clove, rosemary, and fresh chili. Sauté until the garlic becomes golden and the onion turns soft and yellow, 3 to 4 minutes. (Discard the garlic clove.) Add the cherry tomatoes, season with salt, and cook for another 2 to 3 minutes, stirring with a wooden spoon. Stir the drained chickpeas into the sauce, bring to a boil, and then reduce the heat to a simmer.

Add the reserved fresh pasta to the boiling salted water and cook for 3 to 4 minutes. Drain and add to the pot with the chickpeas. Stir the pasta into the chickpeas and cook for an additional 1 to 2 minutes.

Portion the pasta onto each plate and top each dish with some of the fried tria and a drizzle of extra-virgin olive oil.

CONVERSATION

COLLO QUIO x
CONVERSATION

Jessica Allen

Television host and writer

Where are you based?

As of 2021, Hamilton. But I still work in Toronto and lived there for nearly twenty-five years.

What's your relationship to Terroni?

I got a job at Terroni in 1998. I washed dishes and made coffee. Eventually I started serving and then I was a floor manager. After a decade, I got a job at a magazine. It seemed like a smart move for an aspiring writer. But I couldn't bear to leave the restaurant entirely, so I held on to my Friday night managing shift for a couple of years. During this time, I also worked closely with Elena on the Terroni magazine. I was editor-in-chief to her publisher! I'm proud of the issues we put out together and am amazed at how the publication continues to grow.

In many ways, I grew up at—and with—Terroni. It was like a second home. I made lifelong friends, and I learned so much about food and wine. I'm in awe of not only how Terroni has grown, but how so many people continue to grow with it. Seeing children of staff members with whom I used to work all grown up and now serving me espresso doesn't just make me feel old. It warms me right up.

What a time we had. It was magical. Today, when I go sit at the bar of Queen Street, or visit a Sud Forno or a Spaccio, I get a little ache in my heart. Not a bad kind, although it's tinged with melancholy. I think I miss being on the other side of the counter.

Favourite Terroni dish (including all restaurants, Spaccio, etc.)?

This is like asking a parent who their favourite child is. It's simply not fair. And it changes every day! But fine: A San Giorgio pizza or a Ciccio or Garganelli Geppetto or a Pappardelle Iosa or a Nizzarda. But does Fabio still do the Tagliatelle Fabbietto when artichokes are in season? I think it had mint, pecorino, and prosciutto in it, too. Good Lord, it's divine!

Favourite Terroni memory?

The staff Christmas parties in the late '90s are memorable—and not just because I'm embarrassed about the inappropriate joke involving a glass of milk I routinely performed.

I remember a chaotic night at Queen Street, before any major renovations. I was washing dishes and had a stack of eight clean and hot pizza plates ready to put back on the shelf. Only my hands were soapy, and I dropped them. It was like time stopped. It even felt like the music paused. Every customer stopped eating. I looked down the length of the counter to the pizza station and there was Cosi paused in the middle of spinning dough. He looked at me, shook his head, smiled, and then the music played again.

I think my favourite memory involves a now legendary story that I wasn't even around to witness. A little backstory: Legendary Terroni pizzaiolo Dave Mattachioni was obsessed with Bruce Springsteen. He played his music exclusively when he worked. If we tried to change it, he'd change it back to Bruce. Dave even named his first child—Baby Basilio "Bruce" Mattachioni—after The Boss. And then, one Saturday afternoon in the late 2000s, Bruce Springsteen comes into Terroni on Queen. Only Dave wasn't there. He was working at the uptown Terroni, which was slammed. His phone was blowing up. The new place was packed and the young apprentices weren't strong enough to be left on their own. So, while Bruce ate his meal—a Margherita pizza—with his family, Dave did what most of us couldn't: He continued to do his job. Years later, Dave told me he almost cried that afternoon. He bolted after his shift to try and meet Bruce, but it was rush hour. After drinking an espresso and paying the bill, Bruce had left maybe ten minutes before Dave finally arrived. As time has gone by, the pain has lessened for Dave. Still, he just really wished he could've told Bruce how important his music had been to the success of the restaurant.

But mostly, my favourite memory is a feeling that you couldn't plan for or predict: those nights when the restaurant was packed, the music was just right, diners were eating and laughing, and every staff member was multitasking ten things in unison with *sprezzatura*. It was like a choreographed dance that couldn't be taught. You just had to be there.

Favourite Terroni location?

Terroni Queen Street

Do you like it sweet or savoury?

Savoury—unless it's something Giovanna has just baked.

What do you like about Toronto? If based elsewhere, tell us where you live and why we should—or shouldn't—visit.

Listen, even though I made the move to Hamilton a couple of years ago, I will admit that Toronto cannot be beat by most cities anywhere on Earth for the sheer variety of quality international food. But I still think you should visit Hamilton. Less than an hour from Toronto, you'll find beaches, conservation areas, an incredible arboretum and botanical garden, great art galleries, gorgeous historical homes, and both long-established and new restaurants. I'm begging you: Please bring Terroni here. I'll help on weekends!

Pappardelle alla iosa

"PASTA MAYHEM": SAUSAGE, PEAS, AND MUSHROOMS

SERVES 4

YOU WILL NEED

- Ladle

- 4½ tablespoons extra-virgin olive oil
- 2 garlic cloves, minced
- 1 pound (455g) Terroni Sausage (page 296) or store-bought hot Italian sausage, casings removed
- ½ cup (120ml) white wine
- 5 ounces (150g) oyster mushrooms, shredded (2 cups)
- 5 ounces (150g) button mushrooms, thinly sliced (2 cups)
- Fine sea salt
- ⅓ cup (50g) peas
- 1¼ pounds (500g) store-bought fresh pappardelle, or 1½ recipes Fresh Egg Pasta (page 292) cut into pappardelle
- ½ cup (50g) finely grated Parmigiano-Reggiano cheese
- 2 tablespoons minced fresh parsley

This dish came together because we love pappardelle and my father was making sausage. We added the mushrooms because it just worked well together. And for the name "iosa," I can thank my wife, Elena, because she comes up with the best names: "When Cosi showed me this dish and the list of ingredients, I thought 'Wow, this is quite a bit of ingredients!' I had to think of a friend of mine who lives in Bari, who would always shout *'la iosa!'* when something wildly busy was happening—this roughly translates to 'a lot of movement, chaos.' So, when I saw this long list of ingredients, I thought, these are pappardelle alla iosa."

Bring a large pot of water to a boil for the pasta.

Meanwhile, in a large skillet, heat 2 tablespoons of olive oil and half the garlic over medium heat and cook until the garlic becomes golden. Increase the heat to high, add the sausage, and use a wooden spoon to stir and break up the sausage into big chunks. Cook until it turns golden brown and starts to become visibly crispy, 8 to 10 minutes.

Deglaze the pan with the white wine. Transfer the fried sausage to a bowl and set aside.

In the same pan, warm another 2 tablespoons of olive oil over medium heat. Add the remaining garlic and cook until the garlic starts to brown. Add the mushrooms and continue cooking until the mushrooms turn a lovely golden brown and the oyster mushrooms begin to crisp up, 3 to 4 minutes.

Return the sausage to the pan along with half a ladle of boiling water and reduce the heat to a simmer.

Meanwhile, salt the boiling water and blanch the peas for about 2 minutes. With a slotted spoon, scoop the peas out of the water and add them to the pan with the sausage and mushrooms.

Add the pappardelle to the boiling water and cook for 4 to 5 minutes, or 2 minutes less than the package directions. Reserving some of the pasta water, drain the pasta.

Increase the heat under the pan with the sausage and add the drained pappardelle directly to the pan. Toss the pasta in the pan for 1 to 2 minutes. Add the Parmigiano and a little more pasta water if needed to achieve the desired consistency while constantly tossing the pasta.

Finally, sprinkle in the parsley and give the dish one last toss to incorporate all the flavours.

I would enjoy a glass of Nebbiolo here. I love the wines of Brandini.

PRIMI

Rigatoni arcobaleno

"RAINBOW RIGATONI": ZUCCHINI, CHERRY TOMATOES, AND BUFFALO MOZZARELLA

SERVES 4

- Fine sea salt
- 3 tablespoons extra-virgin olive oil, plus more for drizzling
- ½ cup (120g) minced shallots
- 1 pound (450g) zucchini (about 2 medium), cut into ⅛-inch (2 to 3mm) rounds
- 2 cups (300g) halved cherry tomatoes
- ⅔ cup (150g) hand-crushed canned peeled plum tomatoes
- Freshly ground black pepper
- 1 pound (500g) rigatoni
- ½ cup (50g) finely grated Parmigiano-Reggiano cheese
- 1 (9-ounce/250g) ball mozzarella di bufala
- 8 fresh basil leaves
- Extra Parmigiano-Reggiano cheese, for garnish

When we started, it was hard to find buffalo mozzarella and since we always wanted to use it at its freshest when we had it, this recipe was a good way to show it off. It's a very nice, fresh dish with tomatoes, zucchini, and basil. We also had it often as a staff meal with fior di latte instead of buffalo mozzarella.

At the restaurant it also turned out to be a go-to dish for many kids, next to the Gnocchi alla Simi (page 184). My daughter Sofia has loved this dish her whole life. Whenever she'd be at the resto with her friends for her birthdays she got to make the menu and all her friends had to have arcobaleno whether they liked it or not.

Bring a large pot of salted water to a boil for the pasta.

Meanwhile, in a large skillet, warm the olive oil over medium-low heat. Add the shallots and sauté until they become translucent, 3 to 5 minutes. Increase the heat to high, add the zucchini, and fry until the zucchini becomes slightly browned and tender, 2 to 3 minutes. Keep tossing the pan to evenly cook the zucchini.

Add the cherry tomatoes and toss them for an additional minute. Pour in the crushed plum tomatoes and bring everything to a boil. Season the sauce with salt and pepper, then reduce the heat to a simmer.

Add the rigatoni to the boiling water and cook to al dente 2 minutes shy of the package direction. Drain the rigatoni and add to the sauce, constantly tossing the pasta for a couple of minutes to coat it evenly. As you do this, add the Parmigiano and tear half of the mozzarella di bufala into the pan. Remove the pan from the heat and tear 4 basil leaves into the sauce and stir.

Divide the pasta onto four plates and top each dish with the remaining mozzarella di bufala, which you can tear with your hands. Garnish each plate with fresh basil, extra Parmigiano, and finish with a drizzle of extra-virgin olive oil.

I like this with Outis Rosso Etna, Ciro Biondi.

Spaghetti al limone

SPAGHETTI WITH LEMON SAUCE

SERVES 4

YOU WILL NEED

- Spider strainer or tongs
- Fine sea salt
- 12 ounces (350g) dried spaghetti or 1 pound (500g) fresh spaghetti
- 1½ tablespoons extra-virgin olive oil
- 1 shallot, minced
- 2 tablespoons capers
- 6 ounces (180g) baby spinach
- Grated zest and juice of 1 lemon
- ¼ cup (30g) freshly grated Parmigiano-Reggiano cheese
- 6 tablespoons (85g) unsalted butter
- ½ cup (60g) Parmigiano-Reggiano shavings

This recipe hails from 2000, when we opened Terroni Balmoral. Pasta with lemon was something I didn't know growing up, but it was immediately a huge hit at the restaurant and hasn't left the menu since. With the spinach, the lemon, the salty capers, and the Parmesan shavings, it's the perfect summer pasta. It's all about the balance between the cheese and citrus: That hit of acid is what makes it delicious—and lighter than you imagine.

My daughter Olivia is the ultimate judge of this dish. Her palate is bang on with this every time and she keeps us all in line with this (and everything else as well . . .).

Bring a large pot of salted water to a boil. Add the pasta and cook to 2 minutes shy of the package directions.

Meanwhile, in a large skillet, heat the olive oil over medium-high heat. Add the shallot and capers and sauté until soft, 2 to 3 minutes. Stir in the baby spinach and ¼ cup (60ml) of pasta water and remove from the heat. Add the lemon juice to the pan.

As soon as the pasta is 2 minutes away from being fully cooked, increase the heat under the skillet, and, using tongs or a spider strainer, transfer the pasta directly into the pan. Add the grated Parmigiano and continue to cook the pasta, tossing it for 2 to 3 minutes, adding the butter and the lemon zest a little at a time.

Divide the pasta onto four plates and garnish each with the shaved Parmigiano-Reggiano. Serve immediately.

This is a tough one winewise. My experience over the years taught me that nothing beats Fiano di Avellino, a white wine from Campania. A producer I love is Ciro Piccariello.

PRIMI

Ravioli di Zio Paperone

DUCK CONFIT RAVIOLI

SERVES 8

YOU WILL NEED

- Cheesecloth
- Butcher twine
- 5-quart (5L) Dutch oven
- Immersion blender
- Piping bag
- Baking sheet
- Parchment paper
- Rolling pin or pasta machine

DUCK CONFIT

- 17 ounces (500g) fatty duck legs
- Fine sea salt and freshly ground black pepper
- 1 whole clove
- ½ star anise
- ¼ cinnamon stick
- 1 sage leaf
- ¼ teaspoon peppercorns
- 2 cups (17 ounces/500g) duck fat

RAVIOLI FILLING

- 1 tablespoon + 1 teaspoon extra-virgin olive oil
- ½ cup (100g) finely chopped white onion
- ¼ cup (50g) sliced leeks (¹⁄₁₆-inch/2mm rounds), white part only
- 1 garlic clove, finely chopped
- 1 cup (100g) cubed peeled butternut squash (³⁄₄-inch/2cm cubes)
- 2 tablespoons rum
- ⅓ cup (50g) cubed dried figs (³⁄₈-inch/1cm cubes)
- Fine sea salt and freshly ground black pepper
- ½ cup (50g) grated Parmigiano-Reggiano cheese
- 1 egg yolk

The only reason this pasta recipe is in the book is because Meredith wanted it. *Punto e basta!*

This dish basically happened by mistake. Duck was very exotic to us at Terroni, but someone pitched the idea of a ravioli stuffed with duck confit and actually made them—and it was delicious. Turns out people loved this recipe, so it stuck. (For those non-Italians, Zio Paperone is Italian for Scrooge McDuck.)

RAVIOLI DOUGH

- Spinach Pasta (page 292)
- Flour, for dusting

BUTTER AND SAGE SAUCE

- 2 sticks + 2 tablespoons (9 ounces/250g) unsalted butter
- 10 to 12 small to medium fresh sage leaves
- ½ cup (50g) finely grated Parmigiano-Reggiano cheese

NOTA BENE The duck confit takes about 21 hours of which only about 40 minutes are active; it can be made well in advance.

Make the duck confit: Season the duck legs with salt and pepper. Lay them flat on a tray and refrigerate overnight or for at least 12 hours. Afterward rinse the duck legs well under cold water and pat them dry using paper towels.

Preheat the oven to 250°F (120°C).

In a 4-inch (10cm) square of cheesecloth, assemble the clove, star anise, cinnamon stick, sage, and peppercorns. Bundle it up and tie it securely with butcher twine.

In a small saucepan, heat the duck fat over medium-low heat until it melts. Pour the melted duck fat into a 5-quart (5L) Dutch oven, then add the duck legs and the bouquet garni, ensuring that the legs are fully immersed in the fat.

Cover and bake for 8 hours.

Once the duck legs are cooked, remove them from the Dutch oven and drain the fat, saving it in a jar for later use (such as a substitute for butter or oil). Pull all the meat off the duck legs and roughly mince with a knife. Set aside. →

This dish is MADE for wine and you can go in many directions. A simple but delicious choice would be Chianti Classico by Istine.

168

PRIMI

Make the ravioli filling: In a small pot, heat the olive oil over medium heat. Add the onion, leeks, and garlic and cook until they soften, 10 to 12 minutes.

Add the squash and cook for an additional 5 minutes. Pour in the rum to deglaze the pan. Add 1¼ cups (300 ml) water, bring to a boil, add the figs, season with salt and pepper, cover, and cook over medium-low heat for 20 minutes.

Use an immersion blender to purée the mixture completely. Set it aside to cool.

In a bowl, combine the duck confit, cooled fig purée, the Parmigiano, and egg yolk. Mix everything together using your hands until you have a uniform consistency. Season with salt and pepper to taste, aiming for a slightly saltier finish than usual. Transfer the filling to a piping bag.

Make the ravioli dough: Make the dough and let it rest as directed. Line a baking sheet with parchment paper and lightly dust the paper with flour. Use a rolling pin or pasta machine to roll the dough until it becomes very thin and you can see your hand through it (¹⁄₁₆ inch/2mm). Cut the dough into several long rectangular strips, about 4 inches (10cm) wide.

Set a strip with a long side facing you. Using the piping bag, pipe about 1 tablespoon of filling about ½ inch (1.5cm) up from the bottom edge of the strip, spacing them about 1 inch (2.5cm) apart. Fold each strip in half along its length, bringing the top part of the strip together with the bottom, over the filling and sealing them with your fingers. Press around the filling to form a belly and cut around the ravioli to create rectangles. Place them on the lined baking sheet. (The ravioli can be refrigerated for 4 to 5 hours or frozen for up to 1 month.)

When you're ready to cook the ravioli, bring a large pot of salted water to a boil.

Meanwhile, make the butter and sage sauce: In a skillet, melt the butter with the sage leaves over medium-high heat.

Add the ravioli to the boiling water for 2 to 3 minutes for fresh, or 4 to 5 minutes if they are frozen. Drain the ravioli, transfer to the butter sauce, and cook for an additional minute. Add the grated Parmigiano and serve immediately.

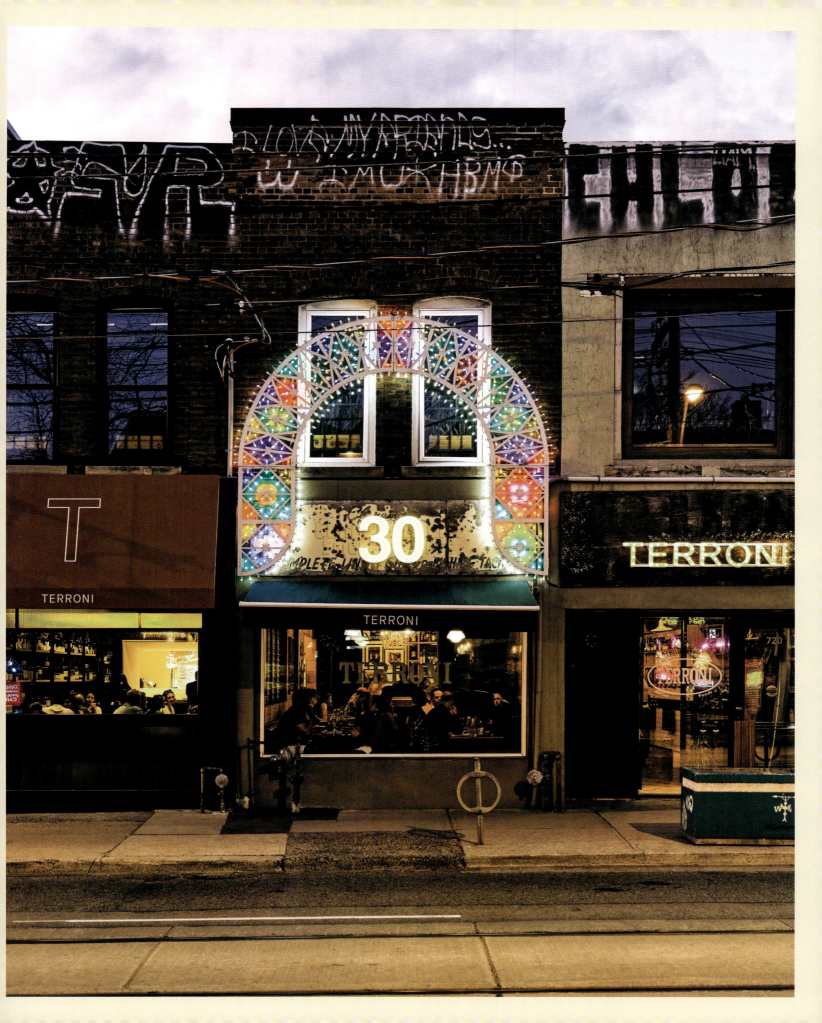

PRIMI

Sugo della domenica

COSIMO'S SUNDAY SAUCE WITH RIGATONI

SERVES 8 TO 10

YOU WILL NEED

- Large Dutch oven or similar pot
- Food mill with fine disk (see Nota Bene)
- Ladle

- 4 (28-ounce/794g) cans whole peeled tomatoes
- 4½ pounds (2kg) bone-in beef short ribs
- Fine sea salt and freshly ground black pepper
- 6 tablespoons extra-virgin olive oil
- 2¾ cups (300g) finely diced white onions
- ½ cup (120ml) white wine
- 2¼ pounds (1kg) rigatoni or paccheri

NOTA BENE If you do not have a food mill, no stress. Simply crush the tomatoes with your freshly washed hands on a clean work surface.

I grew up with this sauce, with its smell. It's all about the smell. When I was a kid, I would wake up every Sunday to the smell of my mom making Sunday sauce. And as you get older, and you're perhaps a little hungover, you think, "Thank God, Mom's making the sauce." The whole house is taken over by the smell of the sauce.

Fast-forward to when I had my own house and family. I personally like to use short ribs, but my mom used to make it with all kinds of cuts. I just love short ribs because they braise perfectly and turn out super tender.

Now, I start my Sunday by listening to classical music or something dramatic, like Italian opera. I play it on speakers on low to slowly get the house moving. Dramatic I know, what can I say, I'm Calabrese. I grab the biggest pot that I have at home, some olive oil, and I start by searing some short ribs. I like the pieces to be thick and meaty, at least 3 inches (7.5cm). After they are super golden brown, I take them out, add the onions, and sauté those. Deglaze with white wine, return the ribs to the pot, add the tomato, and let the whole thing simmer for at least 5 hours. This is one of those recipes where you make a lot! It's not something you make for two people. Afterward you end up with the deep red/brown sauce, you pick up the spoon, taste, and the flavour is just there! By the time all the kids wake up, they can smell it and they all try to dip bread in it. We usually have it for dinner with rigatoni or paccheri. →

Winewise? Well, it's Sunday, which means we are bringing out the big guns. I would open a nice Barolo here, perhaps by a winemaker like Ettore Germano.

PRIMI

Set a food mill with a fine disk (see Nota Bene) over a bowl or pot. Gradually ladle the canned tomatoes through the mill, churning to create a smooth sauce. Set the tomato sauce aside.

Cut the short ribs so that each piece has a bone. Season the ribs with salt and a dash of pepper.

In a Dutch oven, heat the olive oil over medium-high heat. Add the short ribs and sear them on all sides until they turn a rich golden brown, 5 to 7 minutes. Remove them from the pot. Add the onions, reduce the heat to medium, and sauté until they become very soft, 8 to 10 minutes.

Increase the heat again and return the short ribs to the pot. Sauté them for an additional 3 to 4 minutes. Deglaze the pot with the white wine. Add the milled tomatoes to the pot and a generous pinch of salt. Bring everything to a boil over medium heat, then reduce the heat to the minimum setting. Cover the pot with a lid but leave a slight opening by propping the lid on a wooden spoon. Allow the dish to simmer, stirring periodically, until the sauce has reduced and taken on a rich brownish-red colour, 5 to 6 hours. Season the sauce with salt to taste.

When you're ready to make the pasta, bring a large pot of salted water to a boil. Add the pasta and cook to 3 to 4 minutes shy of the package directions. Reserving about 1 cup (250ml) of the pasta cooking water, drain the pasta and return it to the pot.

Ladle 8 to 10 ladles of the tomato sauce (depending on your preferred sauciness) onto the pasta. Stir the sauce into the pasta using a wooden spoon over medium-low heat and add a bit of the reserved cooking water if needed to achieve the desired doneness of the pasta.

To serve, portion the pasta into individual bowls and top each serving with a short rib.

PRIMI

Calamarata al sugo di polpo

CALAMARATA WITH OCTOPUS SAUCE

SERVES 4

- 1 (2 3/4-pound/1.2kg) octopus, fresh or frozen
- 1/2 cup (120ml) extra-virgin olive oil, plus more for drizzling
- 1 1/2 (28-ounce/794g) cans whole peeled tomatoes, milled or crushed by hand
- 2 garlic cloves, peeled but whole
- 1 fresh chili pepper, roughly chopped
- 1 small bunch of parsley, roughly chopped
- Fine sea salt and freshly ground black pepper
- 1 pound (500g) calamarata pasta

How to Clean an Octopus

Prepare a cold-water bath in your sink and place the fresh octopus in it. Let it soak for 5 to 10 minutes, gently swirling it in the water to loosen any residual grit or sand. This step helps ensure the octopus is thoroughly cleaned.

After soaking, transfer the octopus to a colander and rinse it under cold running water. Place the octopus on a large cutting board and, using your fingers or a paring knife, carefully pinch and cut out the eyes from the head. Next, make a small incision at the base of the head to create an opening. Gently flip the head inside out to expose its inner cavity and discard any innards. Once cleaned, carefully flip the head back to its original position.

Find the beak, which is a tough and translucent part located at the centre where the tentacles meet. Slightly cut the area to expose the beak and then carefully enlarge the opening to extract it from the octopus and discard.

Calamarata is a thick ring-shaped pasta that hails from Napoli. Often people will use squid ink to dye it black, so it evokes calamari. Here we serve it with fresh octopus and tomato sauce. (Fresh octopus is next to impossible to find here in Toronto. We use high-quality Spanish octopus.)

I remember cooking this dish many, many years ago on a summer night in Toronto at Paolo's house. I cooked the whole octopus with a lot of olive oil over low heat for a little less than an hour. The key is to never open the lid! The idea was to use this as a test run for placing this dish as a secondo on the Terroni menu, with nothing else, just the octopus. But that night, the octopus shrank so much that I panicked and served it with pasta. What a wonderful mistake! The result is a delicious seafood sauce that gets soaked up with those hearty calamarata noodles.

Clean the octopus, if needed (see How to Clean an Octopus).

In a large pot, combine the octopus, olive oil, tomatoes, garlic, chili, and parsley and bring to a boil over medium-low heat. Cover and cook until the octopus is tender and infused with the flavours of the sauce, about 50 minutes. Season with salt and pepper. Turn off the heat and let the octopus rest in the sauce, covered, for 1 hour.

When ready to serve, gently reheat the octopus. Once the sauce is warm, carefully remove the octopus from the pot and separate the tentacles for easier serving. If you wish, you can cut the tentacles into big pieces at least 1 inch (2.5cm) long or you can keep the octopus whole for a dramatic centrepiece. Keep the octopus warm while you finish the dish.

Bring a large pot of salted water to a boil for the pasta.

Add the calamarata pasta and cook to 4 minutes shy of the package directions. Drain the pasta and add to the pot with the octopus sauce, mixing to coat the pasta thoroughly.

Cook the pasta in the sauce until it reaches the desired al dente texture, for another 3 to 4 minutes.

To serve, either top each individual portion of calamarata with a whole tentacle or tentacle pieces, or arrange the pasta and whole octopus on a large platter. Finish with a drizzle of extra-virgin olive oil.

I love Etna Bianco from Graci here. The perfect glass for summer.

PRIMI

Orecchiette con cime di rapa

ORECCHIETTE WITH RAPINI

SERVES 4

- Fine sea salt
- 1½ pounds (800g) rapini, leaves and florets picked from stems, stems roughly chopped
- 14 ounces (400g) homemade Orecchiette (page 293), or 12 ounces (350g) dried orecchiette
- 6 tablespoons extra-virgin olive oil, plus more for drizzling
- 2 garlic cloves, smashed and peeled
- 1 fresh chili pepper, roughly chopped
- 3 tablespoons finely chopped anchovy fillets
- 2 tablespoons homemade bread crumbs

I'll just come out and say: I am the master of this dish. And there is only one way to make it.

And the "light bulb" moment of this recipe is that it's all made in one pot (with a little side pan for the olive oil and anchovies). You bring some salted water to a boil, throw in your chopped rapini, and once it comes up to a boil again, you add your orecchiette. To another saucepan or pot, you add your nice amount of olive oil and whole garlic. Let it brown and take it out. I never like to cut garlic into small pieces since it's often overpowering. I like to just infuse the oil with its aroma. Let it cool down a little bit and add your anchovies and break them up. Then you have this beautiful olive oil and anchovy sauce. Once the pasta is ready, drain it and the rapini in a colander over the sink and shake vigorously. Your first thought will be, "Oh my god, I overcooked the greens," but this is what we want. The whole pasta will be coated in little pieces of rapini and it becomes almost like its own sauce. In the meantime, I reheat my olive oil and anchovy sauce and slowly toss the pasta and greens in this savoury oil. I like to serve it in a nice ceramic bowl directly at the table. Serve with extra toasted bread crumbs, if you like.

Bring a large pot of salted water to a boil.

Add the chopped rapini stems and cook for 2 minutes while the water comes back to a boil. When the water is boiling again, add the pasta and the rapini leaves and florets and cook to a little shy of al dente according to the package directions.

In a large skillet, warm the olive oil over medium heat. Add the garlic, chili, and anchovies and stir with a wooden spoon until the anchovies dissolve in the oil. Remove the garlic when golden brown. Add the bread crumbs, toasting them in the oil until they become crispy. Remove from the heat and set aside.

Drain the pasta and rapini into a colander set over the sink. Shake vigorously to coat the pasta with the rapini and add directly to the skillet. Using a wooden spoon, toss and mix them well with the oil. Serve in pasta bowls with an extra drizzle of olive oil.

I am recommending two wine options here. For a white I would suggest Timorasso from Piemonte. For a red I would go with something fresh like Cerasuolo d'Abbruzzo from Cataldi Madonna.

PRIMI

Garganelli Geppetto

GEPPETTO'S SAUSAGE AND DANDELION GARGANELLI

SERVES 4

- Fine sea salt
- 1 bunch (10 ounces/300g) dandelion greens
- 6 tablespoons extra-virgin olive oil
- 2 garlic cloves, smashed and peeled
- 1 fresh red chili pepper (optional), left whole
- 1 pound to 1 pound 5 ounces (450 to 600g) loose Terroni Sausage (page 296) or store-bought sweet Italian sausage, casings removed
- ½ cup (120ml) dry white wine
- 1 pound (500g) garganelli, rigatoni, or penne
- 1 cup (100g) freshly grated Parmigiano-Reggiano cheese
- 1 cup (100g) cubed or shredded Fontina cheese
- Freshly ground black pepper

This dish is moreish, so we like a well-balanced Tuscan red, like a Rosso di Montalcino from Tricerchi.

Geppetto was the nickname given to my father (his real name was Vincenzo) because he was a cabinetmaker and worked with wood. You might think, "What does this have to do with pasta?" Well, he started making sausage for us after he retired. He did anything and everything he could to help me when I started the business. Culturally, that was implanted in his DNA. He came here as an immigrant and he, his family, and his friends helped one another any way they could. He was a cabinetmaker, so anytime anyone needed anything built he was their man. He built all the shelves at Queen Street. He built Balmoral completely. It was natural for him to also pass on food traditions; making sausage and salame was a ritual he had with his Italian friends here. When we needed to make sausages for the restaurants, he took that challenge full on. This recipe uses our house-made Terroni sausage, dandelion, and Fontina, and is a white pasta, meaning: no tomato sauce. First, we tried it with rigatoni but, after speed-dating other pastas, discovered that garganelli was the better fit.

Bring a large pot of salted water to a boil.

Prepare a cold-water bath in your sink. Soak the dandelion greens in the cold water for 5 to 10 minutes, periodically shaking them to loosen any debris. After soaking, remove the greens from the water and rinse them thoroughly under running water for a couple of minutes. Place the bunch of greens on a cutting board and trim about 1 inch (2.5cm) from the bottom of the stems. Chop all the greens into 1-inch (2.5cm) pieces.

In a large skillet, heat 2 tablespoons of olive oil, 1 garlic clove, and the chili (if using) over medium heat. Increase the heat to high and add the sausage. Use a wooden spoon or potato masher to break the sausage into smaller pieces. Stir and cook the sausage until it starts to brown, 2 to 3 minutes. Reduce the heat to medium and continue cooking until the sausage turns golden brown and becomes visibly crispy, 8 to 10 minutes.

Pour in the white wine, stirring to deglaze the pan and scrape up any browned bits from the bottom. Transfer the sausage to a bowl and set aside.

In the same pan, heat 2 tablespoons of olive oil and the second garlic clove over medium heat. Once the garlic turns golden, add the chopped dandelion greens to the pan. Cover the pan and cook the greens for 2 minutes. Season the greens with salt and add the sausage.

Add the garganelli to the boiling water and cook to 3 minutes shy of the package directions. Reserving about ¼ cup (60ml) of the pasta water, drain the pasta and add to the pan with the greens and sausage. Toss everything together, stirring well and adding some of the reserved pasta water to create a creamy and cohesive sauce.

Sprinkle in the grated Parmigiano, tossing until it mixes well with the other ingredients. Add the Fontina and continue tossing until it is fully combined, using a bit more pasta water if needed to achieve the desired consistency.

Drizzle the dish with the remaining 2 tablespoons of olive oil and give it a final taste test, adjusting the seasoning with salt and freshly ground black pepper as needed. Serve immediately.

PRIMI

Gnocchi alla Simi

GNOCCHI WITH TOMATO SAUCE AND FRESH RICOTTA

SERVES 6

YOU WILL NEED

- Fine sieve, potato ricer, or food mill
- Ridged wooden gnocchi board or fork
- Baking sheet
- Parchment paper
- Spider strainer

GNOCCHI

- 2¼ pounds (1kg) russet potatoes
- 2½ cups (300g) tipo "00" flour, plus more for dusting
- 1 egg, lightly beaten
- Fine sea salt

SIMI SAUCE

- 2 tablespoons extra-virgin olive oil, plus more for drizzling
- 1 garlic clove, smashed and peeled
- 1½ (28-ounce/794g) cans whole peeled tomatoes, milled or crushed by hand
- Fine sea salt
- ½ cup (50g) freshly grated Parmigiano-Reggiano cheese
- 8 fresh basil leaves
- ¾ cup (180g) fresh ricotta cheese

This dish is named after my firstborn daughter, Simona, because when she was small, she would eat it all the time. It was one of those things you play around with. I'm guessing we probably made a lot of gnocchi al pomodoro and I happened to have ricotta at home and added it to the dish on top. Initially, it was just a kids' pasta dish, but it was so good, so we started to serve it at the restaurant as well. It was a huge success! If you don't want to make gnocchi, supplement with quite literally any pasta on your shelves.

Make the gnocchi: In a large pot, combine the potatoes with cold water to cover by 2 inches (5cm). Bring to a boil and cook uncovered until a fork can easily pierce through them, about 50 minutes.

Drain the potatoes and peel them while they are still warm. Use a fine sieve, food mill, or a potato ricer to mill the potatoes onto a work surface.

Add the flour, egg, and a scant 1 teaspoon salt to the milled potatoes and gently mix everything together using your hands. Be careful not to overmix; you only need to combine the ingredients until a soft dough forms.

Line a baking sheet with parchment paper and dust the paper with flour. Divide the dough into 12 portions. Roll the dough into ropes about 1¼ inches (3cm) thick, using only a minimal amount of flour to prevent sticking. Cut each rope into little pieces measuring 1¼ inches (3cm) in length. To give the gnocchi their characteristic ridges, roll each piece using a wooden gnocchi board or on the tines of a fork. Place the formed gnocchi on the lined pan and refrigerate until you are ready to use them. Do not store in the fridge for longer than 5 hours or your gnocchi will be doughy and gummy. Alternatively, you can freeze the gnocchi for up to 1 month.

Bring a large pot of salted water to a boil for the gnocchi.

Meanwhile, make the Simi sauce: In a saucepan or skillet, heat the olive oil over medium heat and add the garlic. Sauté the garlic until it turns golden in colour. Add the milled tomatoes and bring to a boil. Reduce the heat and let them simmer for about 10 minutes. Season the sauce with salt to taste and continue to simmer.

Once the salted water is vigorously boiling, add the gnocchi and cook until they rise to the surface, 2 to 3 minutes. Drain the gnocchi and add them to the tomato sauce. Stir them gently with a wooden spoon and cook for an additional 1 to 2 minutes. Add the Parmigiano and 4 of the basil leaves to the sauce.

To serve, spoon the gnocchi into bowls and top each portion with a dollop of fresh ricotta. Drizzle some olive oil over the dish and garnish with the remaining fresh basil leaves.

GAMBERETTI T
RIGL IE ACCI
UGH E SARD
INE POLPO CAL
AMARI CIPOLL
A AGLIO ARANC
IA OLIO ARANC
IA CAROTA SED
ANO LIMONE AL
LORO S PIGO
LA PO MOD
ORINI SCAMOR
ZA RADICCHIO

SECONDI
SECOND COURSES

8

SECONDI

Frittura di pesce e frutti di mare

FRIED SEAFOOD

SERVES 4

YOU WILL NEED

- Deep heavy-bottomed pot, for deep-frying
- Deep-fry thermometer
- Large sieve
- Spider strainer

- 4 whole calamari, cleaned, tentacles and tubes separated (see Nota Bene)
- 16 heads-on shrimp
- 4 whole red mullets, fresh anchovies, or sardines, cleaned and heads removed
- Sunflower oil (about 4 quarts/4L), for deep-frying
- 1¾ cups (300g) semola rimacinata flour (see Note, page 62)
- Fine sea salt
- Lemon wedges, for serving

NOTA BENE We suggest you buy cleaned calamari at your trusted fishmongers.

A beautiful thing about frittura di pesce is that you can almost use whatever fish you want (except tuna!), and any white fish works beautifully. We use calamari, shrimp, and anchovies or red mullet, and we serve them with lemon. That's it. No tartar sauce. If you want a sauce with this, you belong to the group of people who try to order a steak well-done—you're in the wrong restaurant and will be offered a pizza. (We're not kidding, it happens all the time!)

Mastering calamari fritti in a restaurant comes down to one thing: changing your oil every day! More important, at home: fresh oil, yes, be very careful around hot oil, always use a spider-style strainer, and always, always, wear a shirt and pants.

Line a large tray with paper towels. Rinse the calamari tubes well and cut crosswise into rings about 1¼ inches (3cm) wide. Place on the paper towels to dry. Rinse the tentacles well and place them on the paper towels to dry.

Wash the shrimp thoroughly under cold running water and remove the heads, legs, shells, and tails (if desired). Use a paring knife to cut and remove the vein, rinse once again, and place on the paper towels to dry.

Place the fish on a cutting board and run your knife along the backbone from head to tail. Continue cutting through the bone and out through the belly. Flip the fish and repeat the process on the other side. Wash the fillets and lay them on the paper towels to dry slightly.

Line a second large tray with paper towels and place near the stove. Pour 4 inches (10cm) sunflower oil into a large deep pot and heat over medium-high heat to 360°F (180°C).

Place the semola flour in a bowl and toss the calamari in the flour. Working in batches to not overcrowd the pot, take some of the calamari, place them in a large sieve, and shake off any excess flour. Add them to the hot oil and deep-fry until golden and crisp, 3 to 4 minutes. Drain and place on the paper towels to drain and season with salt.

Continue this process, frying the seafood in small amounts, taking care not to overcrowd the pot and changing the paper towel when necessary to ensure the frittura remains crisp and not overly oily.

Serve immediately, with lemon wedges.

It may sound strange, but we suggest an alpine wine for this seafood dish: Blanc de Morgex from Ermes Pavese. This Prié Blanc grape cuts like a knife.

SECONDI

Polpo scottato

SEARED OCTOPUS

SERVES 4

YOU WILL NEED

- Cast-iron skillet

OCTOPUS

- 1 (3-pound/1.4kg) octopus
- 2 tablespoons extra-virgin olive oil
- ½ red onion
- 2 garlic cloves, peeled but whole
- 1 carrot
- 1 celery stalk
- ½ orange
- ½ lemon
- 1 bay leaf
- Ice cubes
- ¼ cup (60ml) red wine vinegar
- Fine sea salt and freshly ground black pepper

SALAD

- 4 tablespoons extra-virgin olive oil, plus more for drizzling
- 12 fingerling or baby potatoes, boiled and cut into ½-inch (1.5cm) pieces
- 1½ cups (200g) cherry tomatoes, halved
- Pinch of dried oregano
- ½ cup (80g) Leccino olives
- Fine sea salt and freshly ground black pepper
- 5 ounces (150g) arugula

This dish reminds me a lot of Puglia, because that's where I saw, for the first time, fishermen smacking octopus *hard* against a rock, and I asked Elena, my wife, what the hell they were doing!? She looked at me like I was an alien. "What do you mean, you don't know what they are doing? They are tenderizing the *polpo*!" Since then, I have consumed a lot of octopus and have gained a fair amount of knowledge in this area.

When I introduced octopus back home, the first challenge was where to source the octopus from and what suppliers. Could it be frozen? How do we stabilize market price? Whenever we can now, we buy it fresh. But we've also found great-quality frozen octopus from Spain, and we encourage you to still make this dish if you find a good frozen option.

Prepare the octopus: Clean the octopus (see How to Clean an Octopus, page 179).

In a large pot, combine the olive oil, onion, garlic, carrot, celery, orange, lemon, and bay leaf. Set over medium-high heat and sauté for 3 to 5 minutes. Cover with cold water and ice (ratio of 5:1, water to ice). Add the cleaned octopus and gently bring to a boil. Reduce the heat, add the vinegar, cover, and simmer for 40 minutes. Remove the pot from the heat and allow the octopus to cool in the cooking liquid.

Remove the octopus from its cooking liquid. Remove the head and separate the tentacles from one another. Dry them on paper towels and season with salt and pepper.

Make the salad: In a cast-iron skillet, heat 1 tablespoon olive oil over medium-high heat. Add the potatoes and cook for 4 to 5 minutes. Remove from the pan and set aside.

Add 2 tablespoons of olive oil to the pan and sear the octopus pieces for 3 to 4 minutes per side, until crispy. Remove from the pan and set aside.

Add the cherry tomatoes, oregano, olives, and the remaining 1 tablespoon of olive oil and toss in the pan for 1 minute. Return the fingerling potatoes to the pan. Season everything with salt and pepper.

Divide the arugula onto four plates and divide the cherry tomato mixture evenly onto the four plates. Top each plate with 2 tentacles and finish with a drizzle of olive oil.

This dish is great served warm with a glass of Falanghina from Fattoria la Rivolta, Campania.

SECONDI

Pesce al cartoccio

SEAFOOD IN PARCHMENT PACKETS

MAKES 4 PACKETS

YOU WILL NEED

- Parchment paper
- Butcher twine

SEAFOOD

- 4 fillets (about 4 ounces/125g each) sea bass, sea bream, or snapper
- Fine sea salt and freshly ground black pepper
- Extra-virgin olive oil
- 1 pound (450g) mussels
- 4 squid tubes, tentacles included, cleaned (see Nota Bene)
- 16 heads-on shrimp

PACKETS

- 1½ cups (200g) cherry tomatoes, halved
- 2 garlic cloves, julienned
- 1 lemon, cut crosswise into 8 slices
- 4 small chilies
- 1 tablespoon minced fresh Italian parsley
- 8 fresh basil leaves
- ½ cup (120ml) dry white wine
- Extra-virgin olive oil, for drizzling
- Maldon salt

NOTA BENE For ease of preparation, have your fishmonger give a thorough cleaning of all of your seafood. If that's not possible follow the recipe instructions for cleaning.

I like this with Grillo, Terre di Giurfo.

This is a stunning dish that impresses any guest you have, and it's simple to make.

Gio introduced it the first time at the osteria and really wowed me. We would use a branzino fillet, calamari, shrimp, mussels, tomatoes, and olive oil and tightly wrap it all in this beautiful little package. Fifteen minutes later it's ready to be served in its little parcel. People would rip it open, and the aromatic steam would fill the room—it's fresh, easy, and healthy since it's steamed in its own juices. Serve it alongside a refreshing green salad.

Preheat the oven to 425°F (220°C).

Prepare the seafood: Rinse the fish under cold water and gently pat dry with a paper towel. Season with salt, pepper, and a drizzle of olive oil. Set aside on a plate and refrigerate until needed.

Rinse the mussels in a colander with fresh water, removing any visible debris like seaweed or sand. Place them in a bowl and refrigerate until needed.

Ensure your sink is clean and fill it with cold water. Immerse the squid in the water for 5 minutes, occasionally shaking them to eliminate any sand. Transfer the squid to a colander to drain. Thoroughly rinse the tubes inside and out. Place them on the cutting board and slice into rings, each about 1¼ inches (3cm) wide. Rinse the rings, pat them dry, and season with salt, pepper, and a drizzle of olive oil. Refrigerate until needed.

Rinse the shrimp meticulously under cold running water, removing the heads, legs, and shells (leave the tails on if desired). Use a paring knife to cut and remove the vein. Rinse the shrimp again, pat them dry, and season with salt, pepper, and olive oil and set aside in the refrigerator until ready to assemble.

Assemble the packets: Cut out 8 parchment paper rectangles, each measuring 16 × 12 inches (40 × 30cm). Take 2 parchment rectangles and layer them on top of each other on a cutting board for a double layer of parchment. Position a sea bass fillet at the centre of the rectangle, parallel to its length, then add one-quarter of the squid rings and some tentacles (100g), 4 shrimp, one-quarter of the mussels, one-quarter of the tomatoes, one-quarter of the garlic, 2 lemon slices, 1 chili, a sprinkle of parsley, and 1 basil leaf. Fold a long side of the parchment over the fish and then fold the short ends in, enveloping it like a present. Gently unfold the parchment so that it forms a safe cradle before you add a splash of white wine. Fold the longer edges of the paper together over the fish. Fold them downward in ¾-inch (2cm) folds, forming an accordion pattern and keeping close to the fish. Secure the other ends of the parchment with a twist, and tie using butcher twine. Repeat to make three more packets. Set the packets on a baking sheet.

Bake until the mussels have fully opened, 15 to 18 minutes. You can slightly open one parcel in the middle to confirm.

Meanwhile, cut the remaining basil leaves into a chiffonade.

Gently unfold the parchment in the centre, adding an extra drizzle of olive oil, a pinch of Maldon salt, and some basil chiffonade.

Baccalà

MAMMA RITA'S SALTED COD

SERVES 4 TO 6

- 1 pound 2 ounces (500g) salted cod
- 2 tablespoons extra-virgin olive oil, plus more for drizzling
- ¾ cup (200g) minced yellow onion
- 1½ cups (390g) coarsely diced tomatoes
- ¼ cup (60g) black olives
- Fresh basil, roughly chopped
- Chili flakes (optional)
- Pane Pugliese (optional; page 80) or a similar store-bought bread

NOTA BENE This recipe takes 3 to 4 days depending on how long it takes you to rehydrate the cod. Active cooking time is only 30 minutes. Alternatively you can purchase already rehydrated cod.

This recipe is from my mother, Rita. She loved to cook it on special occasions or on Good Friday. A lot of these recipes that come from my mother or my family are simple dishes, which makes them the ideal recipes for this book. A lot of people are a bit scared of cooking fish but baccalà is super forgiving: It's fatty and does not get dry, and you can cook the hell out of it. You can even prepare it in advance and leave it for later. It's a surprisingly hearty, filling dish. When we were children, our favourite part was probably the dipping of bread in the leftover sauce.

Place the cod in a large deep bowl, cover with 4 quarts (4L) cold water, and let sit for 24 hours. Drain and rinse. Repeat this soaking and rinsing process three times. After that, you should taste a bit of the cod to assess saltiness. If you still find it too salty, you can repeat the process a fourth time.

In a large saucepan, heat the olive oil over medium heat. Add the onion, cover, and cook for 4 to 5 minutes. Add the tomatoes, cover, and cook for another 2 to 3 minutes. Uncover and mash the tomatoes and onion using a fork, until it becomes a uniform pulp.

Add the cod, ¾ cup (180ml) water, and the olives. Cover and cook over medium-low heat until the cod is tender and some of the tomato juices have evaporated, about 20 minutes.

Add the basil and a drizzle of olive oil. Mamma Rita does not add salt since she finds the recipe is salty enough from the olives and the cod. She also recommends adding some chili flakes and serving it with lots of bread for dipping.

SECONDI

Parmigiana di Titina

TITINA'S EGGPLANT PARMIGIANA

SERVES 8 TO 10

YOU WILL NEED

- Deep heavy-bottomed pot, for deep-frying
- Deep-fry thermometer
- Casserole dish about 10 × 14 inches (25 × 35cm)

- 4½ pounds (2kg) Sicilian or Italian eggplant (4 to 5 eggplants), cut into slices ¼ inch-(5mm) thick (lengthwise for Italian, crosswise for Sicilian)
- Fine sea salt
- Double batch Terroni Tomato Base (page 294)
- 1 pound 5 ounces (600g) fior di latte or fresh mozzarella cheese (drained to remove some moisture)
- Sunflower oil (about 3 quarts/3L), for deep-frying
- 5 eggs
- About 4 cups (500g) all-purpose flour
- Extra-virgin olive oil or butter, for the casserole dish
- 2 cups (200g) finely grated Parmigiano-Reggiano cheese
- 3 cups (300g) finely grated smoked scamorza cheese
- 15 to 20 fresh basil leaves, plus a few more for garnish

Eggplant Parmigiana can be difficult to pair with wine, but I love it with Aglianico del Vulture from Grifalco.

This is another dish close to my heart. Paolo's mother would always make this for us when we visited Puglia. We would eat it cold, warm, at any temperature; she would seemingly always have it on hand in her kitchen. They had a house by the sea and the kids would just come in and out of the kitchen and grab some parmigiana. It's very simple, but so delicious. It took a while until we introduced it to the restaurants, because we weren't sure how to position it—as an appetizer, main, secondo ... When we finally did, it was Elena's mom, Titina, who came to the Terroni Queen location to show Giovanna how to make her Neapolitan version. We put it on as a secondo, and it's one of our biggest hits, especially with vegetarians. Some people have tried to bake it, to avoid the frying part, but no, the only true way to make this dish is to fry the eggplant, *punto e basta!*

Layer the sliced eggplant in a colander, seasoning each layer generously with salt. Place the colander over a bowl, cover it with plastic wrap, and use a weight to help the eggplant release its bitter juices. You can use plastic storage containers filled with water as weights for this purpose. Allow the eggplant to sit for 1½ to 2 hours while the bitterness is drawn out.

Meanwhile, in a pot, cook the tomato base over medium-low heat until the sauce reduces to nearly half its volume, stirring often with a spoon, about 45 minutes.

In the meantime, cut the fior di latte into ⅜-inch (1cm) dice and place in a small colander over a bowl to drain any excess liquid.

Rinse the eggplant under cold water and pat it completely dry with paper towels.

Line a baking sheet with paper towels and set a wire rack over it. Pour 3 inches (7.5cm) sunflower oil into a deep heavy-bottomed pot (oil should not reach higher than halfway) and heat over medium heat to 360°F (180°C).

Set up a dredging station in two bowls: In one bowl, quickly whisk the eggs with 2 tablespoons water and a pinch of salt. Place the flour in the second bowl. Dip each piece of eggplant in the egg mixture, shaking off any excess, and then coat it in the flour by dabbing it in the bowl.

Working in batches, deep-fry the eggplant until golden, 3 to 4 minutes. Place the fried eggplant on the wire rack to drain.

Preheat the oven to 350°F (180°C).

Grease a 10 × 14-inch (25 × 35cm) casserole dish with a bit of olive oil. Ladle a bit of the tomato sauce into the casserole dish to cover the bottom. Add a layer of the fried eggplant, cover it with tomato sauce, and then add about one-quarter of the fior di latte, ½ cup (50g) grated Parmigiano, ¾ cup (75g) grated scamorza, and 4 to 5 torn basil leaves. Repeat this layering until all the eggplant is used up.

Bake until the top turns golden brown and bubbling, 40 to 45 minutes.

Let it sit for 10 to 15 minutes before serving it still hot. Alternatively, you can let it cool to room temperature before serving.

SECONDI

Porchetta di Terroni

PORK ROAST

SERVES 10 TO 12

YOU WILL NEED

- A very large pot
- A large container for brining
- Butcher twine
- Large roasting pan
- Digital thermometer

BRINE

- 9 quarts (9L) water
- 2 tablespoons black peppercorns
- 2 garlic cloves, peeled but whole
- 1¾ cups (350g) fine sea salt
- ¾ cup (150g) granulated sugar
- 2 cups (500ml) apple cider vinegar
- 10 bay leaves
- 3 tablespoons juniper berries, lightly crushed
- 2 tablespoons fresh rosemary leaves

PORK SHOULDER

- 10- to 12-pound (5kg) boneless pork shoulder, skin on
- 1 tablespoon freshly ground black pepper
- 1 teaspoon fennel seeds
- 5 garlic cloves, minced
- 10 fresh bay leaves, roughly chopped
- 2 sprigs rosemary, leaves picked and roughly chopped
- 1 sprig sage, roughly chopped
- ¼ cup (60ml) extra-virgin olive oil
- ¼ cup (60ml) duck fat
- Fine sea salt

FOR SERVING

- Ciabatta Buns (page 85)
- Sautéed Rapini (page 229)

Giovanna, my right hand at Terroni, is the queen behind our porchetta.

"We started making traditional porchetta for special parties and events. It was always so well received that we wanted to share it with our guests more often. When we opened the osteria, we used to have *sabato animale* where I'd take a whole animal, often a little pig, and make a menu using all the parts of the animal. Of course, in the case of the pig, this included a porchetta. We served it plain and simple on a bun with Maldon salt and it was, in everyone's opinion, 'the best thing ever!' And so, when Sud Forno opened on Queen Street (a few years later), we just started making this version of porchetta every Saturday: We roast it overnight, put it on display at noon, and carve at it until it's gone! We've now upped our sabato porchetta game, because our head baker Luca makes *rosetta panini* (the traditional Roman buns) and we serve the porchetta with caramelized onions and rapini on this freshly baked bun and it's insanely delicious." →

NOTA BENE The pork shoulder roast or *spalla di maiale porchettata* recipe we're offering here is our adaptation of a traditional porchetta: It's easier to execute and it hits all the spots while still being packed full of flavour and killer crackling. The herbs we use are few and typical; the secret lies in the amount of salt and pepper used in the brine.

If you have leftover porchetta, tightly wrap it with plastic wrap and refrigerate it. It will last up to 5 days in the fridge. You can thinly slice it and pan-fry it with caramelized onions and chili flakes for a delicious sandwich or you can add eggs to it for a decadent breakfast. It also makes a great addition to a bean stew or soup.

For this dish, skip the wine and enjoy a nice cold beer instead.

SECONDI

Make the brine: In a large pot, combine 2 quarts (2L) of water, the peppercorns, garlic, salt, sugar, vinegar, bay leaves, juniper berries, and rosemary and bring to a boil. Cool off by adding the remaining 7 quarts (7L) of water. Transfer to a large container capable of fitting the pork shoulder.

Prepare the pork shoulder: Place the pork shoulder on a cutting board skin side up and use a sharp knife to score the skin across the width of the meat, without going too deeply in, about ⅜ inch (1 cm). Take the knife in the opposite direction to score a grid over the skin. Flip the meat over and, using a knife, pierce some holes roughly throughout the shoulder all the way to the skin to allow the brine to penetrate the meat. Place the pork shoulder in the brine and place in the refrigerator for 24 hours.

The next day, in a dry skillet, toast the black pepper and fennel seeds over medium heat. In a bowl, mix together the garlic, bay leaves, rosemary, and sage.

Remove the pork shoulder from the brine and dry it well. Cut it open horizontally to flatten it but keep it in one piece (like butterflying). Massage the olive oil and duck fat all over the shoulder, being sure to cover the insides of any holes you might encounter as well as the skin side. Place the shoulder skin side down and open it up. Season generously with salt and the black pepper/fennel mixture. Spread the garlic/herb mixture evenly on the inside and close the shoulder by folding it back into its original shape. Tie tightly with butcher twine and season the outside of the shoulder with additional salt. Place the pork shoulder skin side up in a large roasting pan and leave uncovered in the refrigerator for 24 hours.

Preheat the oven to 300°F (150°C).

Slow-roast the shoulder until it reaches 140°F (60°C) in the centre, 3 to 4 hours.

Increase the oven temperature to 500°F (260°C) and roast until the skin becomes golden and crispy and crackling forms all over the skin, about 5 minutes. Keep a close eye on it, as it burns very quickly.

Let rest for 15 to 20 minutes and serve with ciabatta buns and rapini.

SECONDI

Salsiccia e patate

TERRONI SAUSAGE WITH POTATOES

SERVES 4

The key to this dish is the quality of the sausage. Rely on your trusty butcher and make this dish.

YOU WILL NEED

- Baking sheet
- Parchment paper

- 1¾ pounds (800g) Yukon Gold potatoes
- 1 cup (200g) canned plum tomatoes
- 1 white onion (7 ounces/200g), cut into wedges ⅜ inch (1cm) thick
- ¼ cup (60ml) extra-virgin olive oil, plus more for drizzling
- Fine sea salt and freshly ground black pepper
- 2 sprigs rosemary
- 1 pound 5 ounces (600g) Terroni Sausage (page 296) or store-bought sweet Italian sausages in casing

Preheat the oven to 400°F (200°C). Line a baking sheet with parchment paper.

Peel the potatoes and cut them into 1¼- to 1½-inch (3 to 4cm) cubes, adding them to a bowl with cold water as you work so they don't oxidize.

Drain the potatoes and place them in a large bowl. Crush the canned tomatoes with your hands as you add them to the bowl. Add the onion and olive oil and season with salt and pepper. Tear 1 sprig of the rosemary with your hands, add it to the bowl, and mix well. Spread the potato mix on the lined pan. Arrange sausages over the potatoes, then drizzle it all with olive oil.

Roast until the potatoes are cooked through and are a bit crisp on the edges, 35 to 40 minutes, stirring the potatoes and turning the sausages two or three times during cooking. Tear the second sprig of rosemary over top, to garnish.

SECONDI

Semicalda di Terroni

SAUSAGE, BEAN, AND RADICCHIO STEW

SERVES 4 TO 6

A Terroni original! The idea? To create a nice, warm dish that showcases beans and isn't a side dish. We also always have a lot of sausage on hand, so from a practical perspective that also was going to be part of the equation. The dish is served *semicalda* or lukewarm, both a practical consideration in a busy restaurant but also a lovely temperature at which to enjoy the dish. And the beautiful radicchio leaf served as its vessel.

BEANS

- 1½ cups (280g) dried navy beans (see Nota Bene)
- 1 tablespoon extra-virgin olive oil
- 1 garlic clove, peeled but whole
- 1 sprig rosemary
- Fine sea salt and freshly ground black pepper

SAUSAGE

- 2 heads radicchio
- 3 tablespoons extra-virgin olive oil, plus more to finish
- 1 small red onion, minced
- Fine sea salt and freshly ground black pepper
- 1 garlic clove, smashed and peeled
- 1 red chili
- 14 ounces (400g) loose Terroni Sausage (page 296) or store-bought sweet Italian sausage, casings removed
- ½ cup (120ml) white wine
- ⅓ cup (80g) shaved Parmigiano-Reggiano cheese
- 2 teaspoons aged balsamic vinegar
- Maldon salt
- Bread Crisps (page 290)

NOTA BENE You can use 3 cups canned white navy beans (1 pound 7 ounces/ 650g) instead, seasoned to taste.

Cook the beans: In a large bowl, combine the beans and water to cover. Soak for 12 hours, then drain and rinse them.

In a small pot, combine the beans with the olive oil, garlic, and rosemary. Add cold water to cover by 2 inches (5cm). Bring to a boil. Reduce to a simmer, cover, and cook until the beans are tender, about 40 minutes. Remove from the heat, season with salt and pepper, and set aside.

Prepare the sausage: Pull off 6 to 8 whole leaves from the radicchio. Immerse these in cold water to keep them crunchy. Tear the remaining radicchio into 2-inch (5cm) pieces with your hands.

In a skillet, heat 1 tablespoon of olive oil over medium-high heat. Add the onion and sauté until it becomes soft, 3 to 4 minutes. Add the torn radicchio pieces and fry them over high heat for 1 to 2 minutes until wilted. Season with salt and pepper and set aside.

In a second large skillet, heat the remaining 2 tablespoons of olive oil over medium heat. Add the garlic and chili and sauté until the garlic turns golden, 8 to 10 minutes. Add the sausage and cook, stirring often with a wooden spoon and breaking it apart with a potato masher if necessary, until browning and forming a golden crust, 8 to 10 minutes. Deglaze the pan with the white wine. Add the cooked beans and continue

to cook over medium-low heat until most of the liquid has evaporated, resulting in a stew-like consistency rather than a soup, 15 to 20 minutes.

Stir in the sautéed radicchio and taste the stew, adjusting the seasoning if needed.

Take the whole radicchio leaves out of the water, shaking off any excess liquid, and arrange 1 to 2 leaves per plate with the inside facing upward, creating a bowl-like presentation. Ladle the bean and sausage stew inside each leaf. Drizzle with olive oil and add some shavings of Parmigiano to each serving. Finish with a drizzle of aged balsamic vinegar, some Maldon salt, and serve with the bread crisps.

We love Pinot Nero from Abbazia di Novacella with this stew!

SECONDI

Polpette

MEATBALLS

MAKES ABOUT 35 MEATBALLS; SERVES 8 TO 10

YOU WILL NEED

- Food processor or stand mixer fitted with a meat grinder attachment
- Baking sheet
- Parchment paper
- Digital thermometer

MEATBALLS

- $3/4$ cup (100g) cubed white bread, such as Pane Pugliese (page 80) or similar, crusts removed
- $3/4$ cup (180ml) milk
- 1 pound (450g) beef blade, cut into 1- to 2-inch (2.5 to 5cm) cubes and ground
- 3 ounces (90g) mortadella, diced and then ground
- 3 ounces (90g) Prosciutto di Parma, diced and then ground
- 1 cup (100g) finely grated Parmigiano-Reggiano cheese
- $1/3$ cup (30g) finely grated Pecorino Romano cheese
- 1 egg, lightly whisked
- 1 garlic clove, minced
- 2 tablespoons minced fresh Italian parsley
- $1/2$ teaspoon fine sea salt
- Freshly ground black pepper
- 2 cups (160g) fine dried bread crumbs

This recipe is peculiar because although meatballs are traditionally made as an example of *cucina di recupero*—or a dish made from leftovers—due to the inclusion of all the cured meats and cheeses, this is actually a fairly expensive recipe! Having said that, this is our favourite meatball recipe to make at home; it is rich, savoury, and very satisfying. →

TO FINISH

- $1/2$ cup (120ml) extra-virgin olive oil
- $3/4$ cup (200g) minced white onion
- $2^1/2$ quarts (about 2.5L) Classic Tomato Sauce (page 294)
- Fine sea salt and freshly ground black pepper

NOTA BENE This may seem like a lot of meatballs. If you're not having 8 hungry people over for dinner, make the full recipe anyway, because the cooked meatballs will freeze very well in their sauce for several weeks.

If you have a stand mixer fitted with the meat grinder attachment, you can use this to grind the prosciutto and mortadella; if you don't, you can use a food processor to mince the mortadella and prosciutto before mixing it by hand with the ground beef. Alternatively, you can ask your friendly butcher to grind all three meats together for you.

A simple wine for simple meatballs: Sangiovese Superiore, Fattoria Zerbina.

SECONDI

Make the meatballs: Place the cubed bread in a small bowl and cover with the milk. Let stand for at least 20 minutes.

Preheat the oven to 450°F (230°C). Line a baking sheet with parchment paper.

Using your hands, knead the bread in the milk until it blends into it.

In a large bowl, combine the ground beef, mortadella, prosciutto, Parmigiano, Romano, egg, garlic, parsley, the soaked bread/milk mixture, the salt, and pepper to taste. Using your hands, mix everything until well combined, 5 to 6 minutes.

Scoop 2 tablespoons (30g) of the meat mixture into your hands, shape it into a meatball by rounding it between your palms, and place the ball on the prepared baking sheet. Repeat with the remaining meat mixture.

Pour the bread crumbs into a bowl, roll the meatballs in the bread crumbs, and return them to the prepared baking sheet. (Discard any unused bread crumbs.)

Bake until golden and crisp, 15 to 20 minutes. If you plan on eating or trying a meatball before it's been cooked in the tomato sauce, ensure that a core temperature of at least 165°F (74°C) has been reached.

Meanwhile, to finish: In a large saucepan, heat the olive oil over medium heat. Add the onion and cook until the onion is soft and golden, 4 to 5 minutes. Add the tomato sauce and gently bring to a boil. Then reduce to a simmer.

Once the meatballs are out of the oven, gently add them to the sauce one by one, bring everything to a boil, and simmer for 45 minutes.

Taste the sauce, adjust the seasoning with salt and pepper, and serve. You can make this a complete meal by adding cooked pasta to the sauce.

COLLOQUIO×

CONVERSATION

Nicholas Carlino "Nicolino"

General Manager: The Clove Club, London, United Kingdom

Where are you based?

London, UK

What's your relationship to Terroni?

When I was a teenager my neighbour Max was a manager at Queen Street. He asked if I wanted a job when I finished exams after my first year of university: "Want a job? It's a good job . . . actually, it's a shitty job, but you get tips." I started washing dishes at Queen Street and it was the best job I've ever had; due in most part to the people I met, but also, the dishwasher was responsible for making espresso, helping with take-out orders, and much to Vince's chagrin, unofficial DJ (the CD carousel was beside the sink). I stayed for fifteen years, working my way up to senior management across many of the locations. As the company grew, so did I.

Favourite Terroni dish (including all restaurants, Spaccio, etc.)?

Mangiabun!

Favourite Terroni memory?

Too many to count, but one that sticks out for obvious reasons: I met my wife there (and I know I'm not alone in the Terroni nuptials department). Mel was a host, and I was a surly bartender. The rest is history.

Favourite Terroni location?

They're all special. I really enjoyed my time at La Bettola; it had a unique focus and twist on the classic Terroni model. But really, Queen Street raised me, I spent more time in that building and with those people; it was more than family.

Do you like it sweet or savoury?

Savoury!

What do you like about Toronto? If based elsewhere, tell us where you live and why we should—or shouldn't—visit.

I love Toronto. Its culinary diversity never ceases to amaze me. Standards of service, flavours, and quality are unparalleled. I moved to London five years ago with the dream of working in Michelin fine dining (it had yet to exist in Canada). Terroni was not "fine dining," but their ethos of commitment to their product and the respect of their peers I carry with me every day. I'm now the general manager at The Clove Club, a Michelin two-star restaurant in London. The UK's highest-rated restaurant on The World's 50 Best list. Something I never could have achieved without the time I spent with Cosi and Anna and Vince, and everyone else. Come and visit!

SECONDI

Brasciole di manzo

BRAISED BEEF ROULADE

SERVES 4 TO 6

YOU WILL NEED

- Meat tenderizer
- Wooden toothpicks
- Large pot with lid
  for braising

BRASCIOLE

- 16 thin beef scaloppine
  (about 3 ounces/85g each)
- 1 garlic clove, minced
- ¼ cup (30g) minced
  fresh Italian parsley
- 1½ cups (150g) finely
  grated pecorino cheese
- Freshly ground
  black pepper
- 16 slices lardo or pancetta
  (about 6½ ounces/180g)
- ⅔ cup (160ml) extra-
  virgin olive oil
- 1 white onion,
  finely chopped
- 2 fresh bay leaves
- ¾ cup (180ml) white wine
- 3 quarts (about 3L) Terroni
  Tomato Base (page 294)
- Fine sea salt

FOR SERVING

- 1 pound 5 ounces (600g)
  homemade Orecchiette
  (page 293) or 17 ounces
  (500g) dried orecchiette
- 1 tablespoon ricotta
  squanta or forte (optional;
  see Nota Bene)
- Grated cacioricotta or
  pecorino (optional), about
  1 tablespoon per portion

NOTA BENE Ricotta squanta or forte is a traditional soft cheese from Puglia made from milk fermented with bacteria and yeast.

Traditionally in Italy, brasciole were made with horse meat. In braised form, one does not really notice the flavour of horse. It has always been considered a poor man's dish because the meat gets pounded, braised, and then filled with pecorino to enhance the flavour.

Similar to the Sunday Sauce (page 174) or the Meatballs (page 206), this recipe has meat braised in tomato sauce for hours. What's great about these dishes is that they can serve as a primo and a secondo at the same time. You can serve the sauce with pasta and then enjoy the meat separately. →

You want to have a red wine with nerve here. We suggest Negroamaro from Carvinea.

SECONDI

Make the brasciole: Gently pound the beef using a meat tenderizer to achieve a nice and even thickness.

In a bowl, combine the garlic, parsley, and pecorino. Add a dash of black pepper and thoroughly mix the ingredients. Lay the cutlets flat on a cutting board, placing a slice of lardo on top, followed by 1 tablespoon of the parsley mixture in the centre. Fold the cutlet sides toward the middle lengthwise, then roll from top to bottom. Secure the roll using a toothpick, creating a brasciola or involtino.

To assemble: In a wide and deep pan, warm the olive oil over medium-high heat. Add the brasciole and fry until golden brown all over, 3 to 4 minutes per side. Remove from the pot and set aside.

Reduce the heat under the pan to medium. Add the onion and bay leaves and sauté the onion until soft and starting to take on colour, 5 to 6 minutes. Return the brasciole to the pan and deglaze with the white wine. Add the tomato sauce and gently bring the mixture to a boil. Reduce the heat to a simmer, cover, and cook for 1½ hours. Taste and adjust the seasoning with salt and pepper.

When ready to serve: Bring a generously salted pot of water to a boil. Add the orecchiette and cook for 4 to 6 minutes for fresh pasta (based on its dryness level) or 2 to 3 minutes shy of the package directions if using dried pasta.

Remove the brasciole from the tomato sauce, setting them aside to keep warm. Drain the pasta and add to the sauce, cooking until it reaches the preferred tenderness. For those following tradition, incorporate the ricotta squanta or forte at this stage. Optionally, garnish with grated cacioricotta.

To serve, ladle some pasta into each bowl, then top with 1 or 2 brasciole and serve.

SECONDI

Stinco d'agnello

LAMB SHANKS

SERVES 6

YOU WILL NEED

- Cheesecloth
- Butcher twine
- Large Dutch oven or braising pot
- Food mill or immersion blender

- 2 juniper berries
- 2 bay leaves
- 1 sprig rosemary
- 6 lamb shanks (about 14 ounces/ 400g each)
- Fine sea salt and freshly ground black pepper
- ⅓ cup (80ml) extra-virgin olive oil
- 7 tablespoons (100g) unsalted butter
- 2 garlic cloves, smashed and peeled
- 2 cups (225g) minced onion
- 2 cups (225g) minced celery
- 2 cups (225g) minced carrots
- 2 tablespoons tomato paste
- ⅓ cup (80ml) dry Marsala
- 4 cups (1L) white wine
- 2 cups (500ml) chicken stock or water
- 1 pound 5 ounces (600g) green grapes, halved lengthwise, any seeds removed
- 1 tablespoon pine nuts, toasted

I like a Piedmont red here. Let's drink a delicious Lessona DOC from Colombera & Garella.

Many people are familiar with stinco di vitello, a Friulian dish that's made it to the banquet menu of various Fogolar Furlan clubs (see Note) across the world. We do a lamb shank version at Terroni and it's just what you want on those bitterly cold winter days.

It's one of those dishes that gets an "ooooh" from the crowd when being served in the Terroni dining room; if you're cooking this at home for friends, they are going to be very impressed! Also, it's such a safe recipe, because it basically cannot be overcooked—it's all about the slow braise. The lamb shanks pair wonderfully with mashed potatoes and Braised Greens (page 225).

In a square of cheesecloth, combine the juniper berries, bay leaves, and rosemary and tie it into a sachet with butcher twine.

Rinse the lamb shanks, pat dry, and season them with salt and pepper. In a large Dutch oven or braising pot, heat the olive oil and butter over medium-high heat. Working in batches, sear the lamb shanks, rotating them until a crust forms and they turn a nice golden brown. Once seared, set the lamb shanks aside.

In the same pot, add the garlic, onion, celery, and carrots and cook until they become tender, 5 to 10 minutes.

Add the bouquet garni and tomato paste, stirring everything together. Return the lamb shanks to the pot and deglaze the pan with the Marsala. Add the white wine and enough chicken stock to cover the shanks completely. Bring the mixture to a boil. Reduce to a simmer, cover, and cook until the meat becomes very tender to the touch, about 3 hours.

Carefully remove the lamb shanks and set aside, covered, in a warm spot. (Discard the herb sachet.) Mill the braising liquid through the finest disk of a food mill. (Alternatively, you can use an immersion blender, but a smoother texture is usually achieved with a food mill.)

Return the sauce to the pot and cook over medium heat until reduced by half, about 1 hour (or longer as needed).

Taste the sauce and adjust the seasoning with salt and pepper. Return the lamb shanks to the pot once more and add the halved grapes. Gently bring the mixture to a boil and allow it to simmer until you are ready to serve.

Serve the shanks in their sauce and garnished with the toasted pine nuts.

What Is a Fogolar Furlan Club?

A *fogolar* is a fireplace found in the centre of traditional osterias. It was used for cooking the food and was also, of course, a heat source. The word *furlan* refers to a Friulan, or someone from Friulia. Clubs called Fogolar Furlan were originally set up for immigrants to have a home away from home: a metaphorical fireplace to warm them. In Canada and throughout the world, these clubs have become sort of Italian banquet halls.

SECONDI

Fiorentina stile Terroni

FLORENTINE STEAK, TERRONI-STYLE

SERVES 4 TO 6

YOU WILL NEED

- Cast-iron or other heavy skillet
- Tongs

- 1 (40-ounce/1.2kg) porterhouse or T-bone steak, dry-aged for 8 weeks and cut to about a 3-inch (8cm) thickness
- Fine sea salt and freshly ground black pepper
- Extra-virgin olive oil
- Maldon salt

Terroni has never been a steak joint. On most of our locations' menus you have a choice of a market cut of beef or fish. We keep it simple. Often the option will be rib eye for 1 to 2 people or a nice Fiorentina. And people go nuts over the Fiorentina. A Tuscan speciality from Firenze, it is a thick T-bone steak: on one side is the strip loin, on the other the filet. What makes it "Terroni-style" is that each steak is roughly 1¼ pounds (1kg) and dry-aged for 8 weeks.

Traditionally, and by definition, the meat should be served rare so one can taste the quality of the beef. When we first started serving Fiorentina, we would source it from my good friend Stephen Alexander, whose butcher shop Cumbrae's is a Toronto legend. Dry-aged for 12 weeks, it really elevated our beef offering. Eventually, when Spaccio opened, we created our own butchery and bought directly from Rob Bielak at St. Helen's abattoir. The beef there is from a vertically integrated Ontario supply chain that begins on their family farm in Lucan, Ontario. With a sourcing element of that quality, it makes our job of cooking the meat tremendously easy. Italian technique + Ontario beef is in our opinion the best of both worlds. We cook it for 8 minutes on each side with a similar resting time. Serve with sides such as seasonal grilled vegetables, roast potatoes, a crisp green salad, and grilled mushrooms.

Let the steak sit at room temperature, unwrapped, for at least 1½ hours. Don't touch it.

When ready to cook it, pat the steak dry and season with salt and pepper. Preheat a cast-iron skillet over medium-high heat. Drizzle about 1 tablespoon of olive oil over the steak, and 1 tablespoon in the pan. Place the steak vertically on its bone at the centre of the pan and sear the wide end of the steak for 4 to 5 minutes (you may need to hold it there with tongs). Next, lay the steak flat in the pan and sear it until a dark brown crust starts to form and the steak can be easily flipped, about 8 minutes per side.

Remove the steak from the pan onto a cutting board and again, don't touch it. Let it rest for 5 to 6 minutes. Remove the striploin and filet steak from the bone. Slice each steak against the grain and with the knife at an angle to the cutting board to a thickness of about ¾ inch (2cm). Place the bone at the centre of the serving platter standing up and arrange the sliced meat all around it. Finish with a drizzle of olive oil and Maldon salt.

Since you're already spoiling yourself with the beef, go all the way and drink a Nebbiolo in Barolo form, from Giuseppe Mascarello.

PATATE PEPERONI MELANZANA CIPOLLA OLIO SALE PEPE CICORIA RAPINI BIETOLA CAVOLONERO AGLIO PEPERONCINO RICOTTA BASILICO CICORIA RAPINI CAVOLO NERO POMODORINI

CONTORNI
SIDES

9

CONTORNI

Pipi e patate alla Rita

MAMMA RITA'S POTATOES AND PEPPERS

SERVES 6 TO 10

YOU WILL NEED

- Cast-iron or other heavy skillet about 12 inches (30cm) in diameter
- Spider strainer

- 2 pounds (900g) Yukon Gold potatoes, peeled, halved, and cut into slices 1/4 inch (5mm) thick
- 2 1/2 cups (350ml) extra-virgin olive oil
- 1 pound (450g) orange bell peppers, cut into wedges 1/2 inch (1.3cm) wide
- 1 pound (450g) red bell peppers, cut into wedges 1/2 inch (1.3cm) wide
- 1 pound 10 ounces (730g) eggplant, halved lengthwise and cut crosswise into slices 1/4 inch (5mm) thick
- 6 ounces (175g) thinly sliced yellow onion
- Fine sea salt

This is a staple in any Calabrese household. I grew up with this dish. It was a little like our family's French fries. Growing up in Canada, my friends all got to eat McCain frozen French fries . . . but we *never* had French fries (or ketchup for that matter!) at home. Instead, we had *pipi e patate*: essentially fried potatoes, peppers, and eggplant. It's a great side dish that my mother always makes—and I always ask her to bring over. And Mamma Rita always serves it with bread.

As you slice the potatoes, place them in a bowl of cold water and let sit as you prep the other vegetables.

In a 12-inch (30cm) heavy-bottomed skillet, heat the olive oil over medium-high heat. Drain the potatoes and add them and all the sliced vegetables to the pan. Sauté for a couple of minutes, stirring with a wooden spoon. Reduce the heat to medium and continue cooking, stirring frequently to prevent the vegetables from sticking to the pan, until the potatoes are golden and crispy, about 20 minutes.

Use a spider strainer to carefully lift the fried vegetables from the pan, allowing excess oil to drip off onto a paper towel. Season with salt and serve immediately.

CONTORNI

Verdure saltate in padella

BRAISED GREENS

SERVES 4

- Fine sea salt
- 1 pound (450g) dandelion greens
- 1 pound (450g) rapini
- 1 pound (450g) Swiss chard
- 1 pound (450g) black kale (aka lacinato kale)
- ¼ cup (60ml) + 2 tablespoons extra-virgin olive oil, plus more for drizzling
- 1 garlic clove, smashed and peeled
- 1 small chili pepper
- 1 red onion (12 ounces/350g), cut into slices ¼ inch (5mm) thick (about 1¾ cups)
- Freshly ground black pepper

We have a version of these braised seasonal greens on the menu of all of our restaurants, year-round. It could be chard and dandelion greens, or kale and rapini, or rapini and spinach.

We use the greens on pizza, in panini, in torta salata, or as a side for Florentine Steak, Terroni-Style (page 218) or Mamma Rita's Salted Cod (page 195). We suggest you serve these braised greens with Bread Crisps (page 290).

Bring a large pot of salted water to a boil.

Meanwhile, create a cold-water bath in your clean sink. Immerse all the greens in the bath, allowing them to soak for 5 to 10 minutes, occasionally agitating them in the water. Lift them out of the water and thoroughly rinse under running water for a few minutes. Shake off excess water. Place each bunch on a cutting board, discarding any wilted or discoloured leaves. Trim about 1 inch (2.5cm) from the base of the stems. Chop all the greens into 1-inch (2.5cm) pieces.

Fill a large bowl with ice and water. Once the boiling water is vigorously bubbling, carefully add the greens in thirds. Boil for 3 minutes, then scoop the greens into a colander and submerge them in the ice water to cool. Drain once more, gently squeezing out any excess water. Set aside.

In a sauté pan, heat the olive oil over medium heat. Add the garlic and chili and cook until the garlic turns golden. Add the sliced onion and sauté for 2 to 3 minutes. Reduce the heat to medium-low. Season with salt and pepper, cover, and cook until the onion is translucent, 6 to 8 minutes.

Uncover, increase the heat to medium-high, and add the greens and a generous pinch of salt to the pan, stirring vigorously for 1 minute. Reduce the heat completely, cover, and simmer for 10 minutes.

Uncover, allowing any excess moisture to evaporate, about 2 minutes longer. Drizzle a final touch of olive oil and adjust the seasoning to taste with salt and black pepper.

CONTORNI

Fagiolini alla Elena

ELENA'S GREEN BEANS

SERVES 4 TO 6

- Fine sea salt
- 2 pounds (900g) green beans, trimmed
- ¼ cup (60ml) extra-virgin olive oil
- 2 garlic cloves, smashed and peeled
- 1¾ cups (225g) cherry tomatoes, halved
- Freshly ground black pepper
- ½ cup (60g) finely grated cacioricotta cheese
- 5 or 6 fresh basil leaves

We're gifted with beautiful green beans at the end of summer in Ontario, and this recipe is the perfect excuse to use as much as you can. One of the best bits about this recipe is dipping bread in the residual garlic oil infused with cherry tomatoes and ricotta *(cacioricotta)*. I partly make it just for this! These beans just sing alongside Seafood in Parchment Packets (page 192). In the summer, my wife, Elena, likes to add fresh basil from the garden, freshly torn, into the pan.

Set up a large bowl of ice and water and place near the sink. Bring a medium pot of salted water to a boil.

Add the green beans to the boiling water and cook 5 to 6 minutes. Drain and transfer to the ice bath.

In a 12-inch (30cm) skillet, heat the olive oil and garlic over medium heat and cook until the garlic is golden. Increase the heat to medium-high, add the cherry tomatoes, and cook until they break up and get saucy, 4 to 5 minutes.

Add the green beans and cook them in the tomato sauce 5 to 6 minutes more, mixing well. Season with salt and pepper to taste. Remove from the heat and add the cacioricotta, leaving a couple of tablespoons of it aside for garnish. Toss until the cheese evenly coats the beans, adjusting seasoning as needed.

Transfer to a large platter and finish by garnishing with the reserved cacioricotta and basil leaves.

226

CONTORNI

Cime di rapa saltate in padella

SAUTÉED RAPINI

SERVES 4

- 2 pounds (900g) rapini, ends trimmed by 1 inch (2.5cm)
- ¼ cup (60ml) extra-virgin olive oil, plus more for drizzling
- 1 garlic clove, smashed and peeled
- 1 small chili pepper
- Fine sea salt and freshly ground black pepper

Perhaps my favourite contorno at Terroni. And it's super simple: rapini, garlic, chili pepper, and olive oil. There are two keys to this recipe: The first is to steam the greens in their own liquid for a couple of minutes, just until they are tender but not too soft and still are a bright green colour. You don't want to overcook, or they turn quite bitter. At home we tend to overcook because Elena likes them more bitter; they lose their colour, but they gain so much flavour. The second key point is to make sure when you add the rapini to the pan with the garlic that it is dripping wet. The rapini needs all the moisture. Trim the base first and then wash so it retains water.

In Italy, home cooks tend to use only the tips, but there is a lot of deliciousness in those stems and using them just makes the whole dish moreish.

In a large bowl of ice and water, soak the rapini for 5 to 10 minutes, gently shaking the greens in the water periodically. Drain and rinse thoroughly under running water for a couple of minutes. They should be dripping wet when you add them to the pan.

In a sauté pan, warm the olive oil over medium heat. Add the garlic and chili pepper and cook until the garlic begins to take on some colour. Add the rapini, season with salt and black pepper, cover, and cook the rapini for 2 to 3 minutes, occasionally stirring.

Uncover and let any remaining water evaporate. Finish by adding a generous final drizzle of olive oil. Taste for seasoning, adjusting with salt if needed.

CONTORNI

Peperonata alla Piera

PIERA'S STEWED PEPPERS

SERVES 6

YOU WILL NEED

- Large Dutch oven or sauté pan

- 8 red and yellow bell peppers, a mix (about 2 pounds 10 ounces/1.2kg total)
- ¼ cup (60ml) extra-virgin olive oil
- 2 garlic cloves, smashed and peeled
- Roughly 2 cups (300g) sliced yellow onions, cut ¼ inch (5mm) thick
- 1½ cups (200g) cherry tomatoes, halved
- ¼ cup (60g) Leccino olives or similar
- 1 tablespoon capers
- Fine sea salt and freshly ground black pepper
- 1 tablespoon minced fresh Italian parsley

This is Elena's cousin Piera's recipe. We love Piera and we love this recipe! There are many different types of peperonata, but the recipe here is the most versatile. We use red and yellow peppers (never green ones for this!) and add some capers and olives for the saltiness. The parsley at the end brightens the whole thing up. I leave it in the refrigerator and eat it the next day in a panino, such as the Sea Bass and Red Pepper Sandwiches (page 90); it's also great as a side dish for really any pasta, or as a topping on pizza.

Cut the bell peppers lengthwise into wedges ¾ inch (2cm) wide.

In a large Dutch oven or sauté pan, warm the olive oil over medium heat. Add the garlic and cook until it turns golden. Add the onions and 3 to 4 tablespoons water and sauté for 2 to 3 minutes. Stir in the cherry tomatoes. Reduce the heat and cook until the onions and tomatoes have softened, about 10 minutes.

Increase the heat to medium, stir in the sliced peppers, and sauté for 2 to 3 minutes. Reduce the heat, cover, and let the peperonata cook an additional 10 minutes, allowing the flavours to meld together.

Uncover and stir in the olives and capers. Increase the heat until everything is bubbling nicely, then reduce the heat and simmer for 5 minutes. Taste and season with salt and black pepper as desired. Finally, remove the pot or pan from the heat and stir in the parsley.

Eat it straightaway or store it in an airtight container for up to 3 days in the refrigerator.

CONTORNI

Pasticcio di zucchine con le uova

ZUCCHINI AND EGG HASH

SERVES 4

- 3 tablespoons extra-virgin olive oil
- 2 garlic cloves, smashed and peeled
- 4 medium zucchini (about 10 ounces/ 300g each), cut into rounds $1/16$ to $1/8$ inch (2 to 3mm) thick
- Fine sea salt and freshly ground black pepper
- 2 eggs
- 1 tablespoon grated Pecorino Romano cheese
- 5 fresh mint leaves, roughly chopped, plus a few whole leaves for garnish

This dish is not on the Terroni menu. It's one I make at home with my family and wanted to share. It's a great quick and nourishing dish that I make as one of my numerous sides at the dinner table. I regularly make a version without the egg (see Nota Bene), but I'll add the egg if I'm having it as a meal for brunch; it's very comforting.

In a medium skillet, heat the olive oil over medium heat. Add the garlic and sauté until golden brown. Add the zucchini and cook, stirring every now and then, until golden and soft, 8 to 10 minutes. Season with salt and pepper.

Meanwhile, in a medium bowl, mix the eggs together with the Romano.

Immediately after turning off the heat under the pan, add the eggs to the zucchini mixture and use a wooden spoon to mix quickly. Cover and set aside for 3 to 5 minutes. Add the chopped mint before serving.

NOTA BENE Use less salt here than you normally would to season zucchini. The Romano will give you almost all the salty umami you need.

This dish can be made lighter by omitting the cheese and egg: Follow the recipe as written, cooking the zucchini for 10 to 12 minutes, season with salt and pepper, and stir in the chopped mint. Garnish with whole mint leaves and serve.

CONTORNI

Scarola alla Titina

TITINA'S ENDIVE WITH OLIVES, PINE NUTS, AND RAISINS

SERVES 4 TO 6

- ⅓ cup (30g) raisins
- 2 heads escarole (about 1 pound 10 ounces/750g total)
- Fine sea salt
- 2 tablespoons extra-virgin olive oil
- 1 garlic clove, smashed and peeled
- 2 tablespoons (30g) Leccino olives
- 2 tablespoons (20g) pine nuts
- Freshly ground black pepper

My Neapolitan mother-in-law, Titina, cooked this dish for me and we put it on the Terroni menu whenever we can get our hands on escarole. There are two types of escarole, one that looks a bit frizzy (known as curly endive) and one that looks more like romaine lettuce. The second type is the kind of escarole you want for this recipe. After the initial challenge of finding the right escarole is met, this is a very simple (and delicious) dish.

Soak the raisins in a bowl with some warm water to cover for 10 minutes, then drain.

Prepare an ice bath in your sink and soak the escarole for 5 to 10 minutes, shaking it in the water periodically. Remove the escarole from the water bath and rinse it under running water for a couple of minutes.

In a large pot, bring 6 quarts (6L) salted water to a boil. Blanch the escarole for 1 minute. Drain and rinse in very cold water. Roughly chop the escarole into pieces about 1 inch (2.5cm) thick and set aside.

In a large skillet, warm the olive oil and garlic over medium heat. Sauté until the garlic becomes golden. Increase the heat to medium-high, add the escarole, cover, and steam for 2 to 3 minutes.

Uncover, add the olives, drained raisins, pine nuts, a pinch of salt, and pepper and cook over medium-low heat for 8 to 10 minutes. Discard the garlic. Taste to adjust seasoning and serve immediately.

CONTORNI

Sformato di Fontina

FONTINA CHEESE SOUFFLÉ

SERVES 6 TO 8

YOU WILL NEED

- 9-inch (23cm) casserole dish
- Electric mixer
- A roasting pan large enough to fit the casserole for a bain-marie

- 1 tablespoon (15g) unsalted butter
- ¼ cup (30g) fine dried bread crumbs
- 2½ cups (600ml) Béchamel Sauce (page 294; see Nota Bene)
- 20 slices (7 ounces/200g) Fontina DOP, or a similar cow's milk cheese that melts well
- ½ cup (120ml) whole milk
- Fine sea salt
- 4 eggs, separated

NOTA BENE You will be making the whole recipe for béchamel, which means you will have some left over. This is your chance to try something new, like the Fennel Gratin (page 238).

If you happen to have a convection oven, make sure you do not use it. You need static heat here; a fan blowing would deflate the sformato!

This hasn't ever appeared on any of the Terroni menus, because it's in Elena's home repertoire, but it is so good we just had to include it in the book. It's a luscious Fontina soufflé. (Fontina is a cheese from Val d'Aosta in the northwest of Italy.) And we love having this at home as a side dish. It's great for a larger crowd. But, it's a soufflé, so, yes, a little more technique is required—so make sure you follow the recipe and the timing.

We recommend serving a little square as a side to a big main like the Florentine Steak, Terroni-Style (page 218) or the Braised Beef Roulade (page 211). Another option is to make the soufflé the main attraction and add some sausages or a salad as a side.

Preheat the oven (see Nota Bene) to 350°F (180°C). Grease a 9-inch (23cm) casserole dish with the butter and evenly dust it with the bread crumbs.

Make the béchamel sauce as directed and measure out what you don't need for this recipe and save it for another use (see Nota Bene). Reduce the heat under the remaining sauce and gradually add the Fontina while stirring continuously with a wooden spoon. Once all the cheese is incorporated, adjust the thickness of the sauce by adding just enough milk to make it slightly thicker than the traditional béchamel; check seasoning and add salt to taste if needed. Transfer the sauce to a large bowl to cool.

Whisk the egg yolks into the cooled sauce, mixing thoroughly.

In a separate bowl, with an electric mixer, whisk the egg whites until they reach a slightly stiff consistency.

Gently fold the egg whites into the cooled cheese sauce. Pour this cheesy mixture into the prepared casserole dish. Place the casserole dish into the roasting pan and add enough hot water to reach about halfway up the sides of the baking dish.

Carefully place in the oven and bake until puffy and a delicate golden brown crust starts to form, about 30 minutes.

Turn off the oven and allow the soufflé to rest for 2 minutes before carefully removing it from the oven. The consistency should be custard-like. Serve immediately.

237

CONTORNI

Finocchio gratinato

FENNEL GRATIN

SERVES 4 TO 6

YOU WILL NEED

- 10-inch (25cm) baking pan

- 2¼ pounds (1kg) fennel
- Fine sea salt
- 1 tablespoon (15g)
  softened butter, plus
  2 tablespoons cold butter,
  cut into small cubes
- 2 cups (500ml) Béchamel
  Sauce (page 294)
- ½ cup (50g) finely
  grated Parmigiano-
  Reggiano cheese
- 3 tablespoons fine
  dried bread crumbs

NOTA BENE Freeze the fennel stalk trimmings and fronds and tough outer layer for future use in soups like minestrone or vegetable stock.

A great way to convince your children to eat more fennel! This side dish is a perfect complement to the Lamb Shanks (page 217) or the rib eye steak (see Florentine Steak, Terroni-Style, page 218).

Preheat the oven to 400°F (200°C).

Trim the stalks and fronds off the fennel (see Nota Bene) and quarter the bulbs through the core. Cut the fennel quarters into smaller wedges, each about ¾ to 1¼ inches (2 to 3cm) thick.

Set up a bowl of ice and water and place near the stove. Bring a large pot of salted water to a boil. Add the fennel wedges and boil them until soft, 4 to 5 minutes. Drain the fennel and plunge into the ice water bath.

Grease a 10-inch (25cm) baking pan with the softened butter. Arrange the fennel in a layer covering the pan bottom. Pour the béchamel sauce evenly over the fennel, followed by an even sprinkling of Parmigiano. Finally, add the bread crumbs and cubes of cold butter.

Bake until the fennel wedges achieve a crisp texture, 18 to 20 minutes. Serve immediately.

GLI AVANZI
LEFTOVERS

10

GLI AVANZI

Insalata di pollo

CHICKEN SALAD

SERVES 4

- 7 tablespoons extra-virgin olive oil, plus more for drizzling
- 15 slices guanciale or pancetta (5 ounces/150g), cut into $\frac{1}{4}$ × $\frac{1}{2}$-inch (5mm × 1.5cm) strips
- 3 tablespoons balsamic vinegar
- 5 tablespoons red wine vinegar
- $\frac{1}{4}$ teaspoon granulated sugar
- Fine sea salt
- 2 tablespoons very thinly julienned shallots
- 1$\frac{1}{4}$ pounds (570g) poached chicken (leftover from Chicken Broth, page 295)
- $\frac{3}{4}$ cup (90g) thinly sliced carrots ($\frac{1}{16}$ inch/2mm)
- $\frac{1}{4}$ cup (90g) sliced celery ($\frac{1}{8}$ inch/3mm)
- $\frac{1}{3}$ cup (75g) mayonnaise
- Freshly ground black pepper
- 1 small Belgian endive (75g), washed and torn into 2-inch (5cm) pieces
- 1 small head radicchio (75g), washed and torn into 2-inch (5cm) pieces
- 16 leaves romaine lettuce, washed and torn into 2-inch (5cm) pieces
- Maldon salt
- $\frac{1}{4}$ cup (45g) Parmigiano-Reggiano cheese shavings
- 4 eggs, soft-boiled, peeled, and quartered

This is a recipe for the chicken left over from the making of Chicken Broth (page 295), where a whole chicken is simmered for 4 hours. One could say, we've made this a North American dish with an Italian twist, adding a bit of guanciale or pancetta, making it even more luscious with some crispy bits and pieces. It works great as a packed lunch as well.

Line a plate with paper towels and place near the stove. Heat a cast-iron skillet over medium heat for 3 to 4 minutes. Add 1 tablespoon of olive oil, followed by the guanciale. Fry them until they turn crispy and golden brown, 4 to 5 minutes. Deglaze the pan with the balsamic vinegar and continue to cook for an additional minute. Using a large spoon or spatula, carefully remove the crispy strips from the pan and place them on the paper towels to drain.

In a small bowl, whisk together the remaining 6 tablespoons of olive oil, the red wine vinegar, sugar, and a generous pinch of salt. Whisk together, then add the julienned shallots. Set this vinaigrette aside for at least 15 minutes to allow the flavours to meld.

Meanwhile, place the chicken meat in a large bowl. Add the carrots, celery, half of the shallot vinaigrette, the mayonnaise, a pinch of salt, and black pepper to taste to the chicken, mixing until everything is well combined.

In another bowl, toss together the endive, radicchio, and romaine with the remaining shallot vinaigrette and a pinch of Maldon salt.

Arrange these mixed lettuces on a serving platter and place the chicken salad on top. Sprinkle the Parmigiano-Reggiano shavings over the salad and add the crispy guanciale on top. Finally, add the eggs and season them with a pinch of salt and pepper. Finish with a final drizzle of olive oil and serve.

GLI AVANZI

Verdure come le faceva Terri

TERRI'S SWISS CHARD, MEAT, AND CHEESE CASSEROLE

SERVES 6 TO 8

YOU WILL NEED

- 10 × 13-inch (25 × 33cm) casserole dish at least 3 inches (7.5cm) deep

- ½ recipe Braised Greens (page 225) or 1¾ pounds (800g) any leftover braised greens
- 5 ounces (150g) prosciutto cotto, cut into ⅜-inch (1cm) cubes
- 4 ounces (100g) cubed salame, any Italian type (or use hot soppressata to give your verdure some heat), cut into ⅜-inch (1cm) cubes
- 7 ounces (200g) smoked scamorza (or any cheese like Fontina, provolone, or similar), cut into ⅜-inch (1cm) cubes
- 8 eggs
- ½ cup (120ml) whole milk
- ½ cup (50g) finely grated Parmigiano-Reggiano cheese
- ¼ cup (25g) finely grated Pecorino Romano cheese
- Fine sea salt and freshly ground black pepper
- 1 tablespoon (15g) unsalted butter, for the casserole dish
- 3 tablespoons fine dried bread crumbs

Terri was my mother-in-law's best friend and she was always at the family house. This recipe of hers can't be found on the menu at Terroni, but it's so good I wanted to share. This is also a great way to use up the diced cured meats and cheese that we use in our Neapolitan Potato Cake (page 246). It's perfect for when I have leftover braised greens, otherwise I simply boil some Swiss chard and use that as my vegetable base. Baked with some eggs and Parmigiano-Reggiano, it serves as a great side dish and can even be made a day in advance and just reheated.

For this recipe feel free to use any leftover cured meats or cheese you have in your fridge.

Preheat the oven to 400°F (200°C).

Cut the greens into pieces no larger than 1 inch (2.5cm) and place them in a large bowl. Add all the cubed cured meats and scamorza to the bowl.

In a separate bowl, whisk together the eggs, milk, Parmigiano, and Romano. Season with ½ teaspoon salt and black pepper.

Grease a 10 × 13-inch (25 × 33cm) casserole dish at least 3 inches (7.5cm) deep with the butter and evenly coat it with bread crumbs, shaking off any excess.

Arrange the greens, meats, and cheese mixture evenly in the prepared pan. Pour the egg and cheese mixture over the top, ensuring an even distribution.

Bake until the top becomes golden brown and slightly firm to the touch, 30 to 35 minutes. Serve immediately while still warm.

GLI AVANZI

Gattò di patate

NEAPOLITAN POTATO CAKE

SERVES 6 TO 9

YOU WILL NEED

- 10 × 14-inch (25 × 36cm) casserole dish at least 3 inches (7.5cm) deep
- Potato ricer

- 2 tablespoons (30g) unsalted butter, plus more for greasing the casserole dish
- ½ cup (55g) fine dried bread crumbs
- 3 pounds 5 ounces (1.5kg) Yukon Gold potatoes
- 3½ ounces (100g) prosciutto crudo, cut into ⅜-inch (1cm) cubes
- 5 ounces (150g) prosciutto cotto, cut into ⅜-inch (1cm) cubes
- 3½ ounces (100g) salame, any Italian type (or use hot soppressata to give your gattò some heat), cut into ⅜-inch (1cm) cubes
- 4 ounces (200g) smoked scamorza (or any cheese like Fontina, provolone, or similar), cut into ⅜-inch (1cm) cubes
- 3½ ounces (100g) fior di latte, cut into ⅜-inch (1cm) cubes
- ½ cup (50g) finely grated Parmigiano-Reggiano cheese
- ¼ cup (25g) finely grated Pecorino Romano cheese
- 3 eggs, lightly whisked
- ½ cup (120ml) milk, heavy cream, or Béchamel Sauce (page 294)
- Fine sea salt and freshly ground black pepper

We've been making this since the very beginning. When we first opened in 1992, we were a type of salumeria (i.e., a deli) with four stools and a small counter and we sold all types of Italian cold cuts and cheeses. And because we had a lot of leftovers and end pieces, Elena suggested we use them in a gattò di patate. Quite simply: You gather up all your leftover cold cuts and cheeses, cut them up into little cubes, and mix them with mashed potatoes, eggs, milk or cream, and put it all into a casserole dish. Top it with bread crumbs and some pieces of butter. Super simple, super satisfying, especially when the melted cheese oozes out.

Preheat the oven to 375°F (190°C). Lightly grease a 10 × 14-inch (25 × 36cm) casserole dish at least 3 inches (7.5cm) deep with butter and sprinkle one-third of the bread crumbs evenly across its surface.

In a large pot, combine the potatoes with cold water to cover, bring to a boil, and cook until a fork can easily pierce them without resistance, 30 to 40 minutes. Drain the potatoes and peel them while they are still warm. Use a potato ricer to push the potatoes through into a large bowl.

To the mashed potatoes, add all the cubed meats, all the cheese, the eggs, and milk and season with salt and pepper. Thoroughly mix everything together.

Press the potato filling firmly into the casserole dish and sprinkle the remaining bread crumbs over the top to create an even coating. Dot the surface with dollops of the butter.

Bake until the potato cake is crispy and golden brown, 25 to 30 minutes. If it isn't browned enough at this point, switch on the broiler for a couple more minutes to achieve the desired look and texture. Serve while still warm.

GLI AVANZI

Frittata di spaghetti

SPAGHETTI FRITTATA

SERVES 4 TO 6

- 2 tablespoons extra-virgin olive oil
- 1 tablespoon (15g) unsalted butter
- About 7 ounces (200g) leftover cooked and lightly sauced spaghetti (see Nota Bene)
- 2 ounces (60g) julienned prosciutto or guanciale (optional), fried until crispy
- 2 ounces (60g) Fontina or similar cheese (optional), cut into $3/8$-inch (1cm) cubes
- 5 eggs
- $1/4$ cup (25g) finely grated pecorino cheese
- 2 tablespoons finely grated Parmigiano-Reggiano cheese
- Fine sea salt and freshly ground black pepper

NOTA BENE Best are lightly sauced spaghetti dishes, like butter and Parmigiano, light tomato sauce, or carbonara.

The problem with this leftover spaghetti dish is there is almost never any leftover spaghetti.

But this is worth it! You could probably do it with any kind of pasta, but with spaghetti you get this cool look of a bird's nest. When frying in a generous amount of olive oil, it is essential not to keep interfering. Just let it cook and crisp up. Add some eggs, cold cuts, and cheese, or whatever leftovers you have.

In a medium skillet, gently heat the olive oil and butter over medium heat. Add the spaghetti, distributing it evenly across the pan. If desired, add the crispy prosciutto and cubed cheese.

In a bowl, whisk together the eggs, pecorino, and Parmigiano. Season with salt and pepper. Pour this egg mixture evenly over the spaghetti in the pan, then reduce the heat to medium-low, cover, and cook for 8 to 10 minutes. To ensure that the sides of the frittata are detached from the pan and a crust has formed underneath, gently run a silicone spatula around the edges. If needed, continue cooking for an additional 3 to 4 minutes until the frittata is fully set.

Carefully flip the frittata onto a plate. While the frittata can be enjoyed hot, it is often served as a picnic item and is equally delicious cold.

DOLCI
SWEETS

11

DOLCI

Panettone classico

TERRONI'S PANETTONE

**MAKES 2 PANETTONI,
EACH 8 INCHES (20CM)
IN DIAMETER**

YOU WILL NEED

- Digital scale
- Stand mixer fitted with the
  dough hook and paddle
- Plastic bowl scraper
- Digital thermometer
- Clear storage container
  with capacity of
  3 quarts (3L)
- Two paper panettone
  molds, 8 inches (20cm)
  in diameter and 3 inches
  (7.5cm) in height
- Small bowl, 5 inches
  (12cm) in diameter
- 4 wooden or steel
  skewers at least
  12 inches (30cm) long
- Baking sheet
- Sharp scoring blade
  (if making panettone
  con mortadella)
- Sealable plastic bag
  for final storage
- Offset spatula

Panettone is a legendary egg-yellow cake, studded with raisins and candied fruit, and intended only for the Christmas season. Hailing from the Lombardian capital of Milano, it is delicious, iconic, and extremely labour-intensive: The naturally leavened dough calls for long proofing times, and once the panettone is baked, it needs to be hung upside down while it cools to retain its shape.

Like any Italian bakery, our panettone season really begins in August. Or for some of us, it begins in January, two weeks after the previous season ends. This is when questions like these start coming up: Where are we buying this year's boxes? Where will we source our candied orange from? Which chocolate are we going to use?

We have been making panettone for over a decade and *yet* each year the process is a little like the Abbott and Costello "Who's on first?" skit. We're always trying to improve on the previous year. Depending on the year, we can make up to five thousand panettone per season, all of which are produced between November and the end of December. We even have a special weapon, Luca Rotatori, a dedicated panettone maker who uses Spaccio as his very own panettone headquarters. There was a time when Luca would start his panettone day at midnight, but now, he starts a bit later in the morning, thanks to a camera we've pointed at each of the proofing cabinets and at the hanging site, allowing him relative freedom during this delicate time. Sound obsessive? It is. Panettone is a science, an art, *and* a state of mind.

As any smaller bakery will tell you, panettone, from a business perspective, is a losing game. And tends to take over everything in its path. But it's inherent to the Italian tradition of Christmas, and now the tradition of Terroni, and it is, as a result, most definitely our favourite time of year.

We have a few panettone variations. The recipe here is our traditional version with candied orange and raisins. You can also opt-in for chocolate. In addition, we have included savoury panettone (a version with mortadella that is really out of this world).

This recipe comes together over the course of two entire days (plus several days of feeding up the sourdough starter). We've provided time indicators, but feel free to work around your schedule. There are some recipes in this book where exact measuring is not a necessity. *This is not one of those recipes!* Weighing everything and following the metric system are important if you want to obtain the desired result.

We thought the easiest way to follow this recipe is to have ingredients listed for each step in the process. If you're going to attempt this panettone, please read through the entire recipe first, to understand the journey ahead and the ingredients you will need to have on hand. →

252

DOLCI

NOTA BENE We use the Omega flour from Molino Paolo Mariani. This is a high-gluten strong flour. You can also use Manitoba.

For proofing: Your oven with the light on and a bowl of warm water is a great spot for this step, but the temperature must be monitored. If it gets too hot you can turn the light off.

FOUR DAYS PRIOR

Feed the starter for at least 4 days prior to starting the panettone recipe. (See Day 7 of Sourdough Starter, page 288.) This is to ensure that the starter shows good fermentation activity (bubbles, growth) prior to commencing the recipe.

DAY 1: 7 A.M.

Pull the Sourdough Starter (page 287) from the refrigerator.

DAY 1: 9 A.M. / FIRST FEED

- 100g sourdough starter
- 65g panettone flour (see Nota Bene, above)

Ensure that all your ingredients are at room temperature (70°F/21°C). In a stand mixer fitted with the paddle, combine the starter and flour and mix on medium-low speed until it is smooth and elastic, 6 to 8 minutes. Transfer the dough to a lightly floured work surface and cover with a clean kitchen towel. Let the dough rest for 20 to 30 minutes.

Shape the dough into a tight round ball. Score a cross on top of the dough, wrap it inside a piece of plastic wrap, and place it in the bowl to rest at a temperature of 82°F (28°C) (see Nota Bene, above). The goal is to have a starter that is strong enough to triple in size within 3½ to 4 hours.

DAY 1: 1 TO 1:30 P.M. / SECOND FEED

- 100g sourdough starter (from the first feed)
- 100g panettone flour
- 50g water, at room temperature

In a stand mixer fitted with the paddle, combine the starter, flour, and water and beat at medium-low speed until it is smooth and elastic, 10 to 15 minutes. Transfer the dough to a work surface and cover with a clean kitchen towel. Let the dough rest for 20 to 30 minutes.

Shape the dough into a tight round ball. Score a cross on top of the dough, wrap it inside a piece of plastic wrap, and place it in the bowl. Rest at a temperature of 82°F (28°C).

DAY 1: 5:30 TO 6 P.M. / EVENING RISE (LIEVITO SERALE)

- 75g sourdough starter (from the second feed)
- 135g water, at room temperature
- 1g malt flour (optional; see Pro Tip)
- 95g granulated sugar
- 300g panettone flour
- 90g egg yolks, refrigerated
- 140g unsalted butter, at room temperature

PRO TIP If you can source malt flour, adding a small amount to the water in this mix and into the flour in the second mix will help the fermentation process of your panettone, resulting in better final colouring.

Use a knife to remove the dry skin from around the starter. In a stand mixer fitted with the paddle, combine the starter, water, malt flour (if using), and a pinch of the sugar. Mix on low to medium speed for 30 seconds. Add the flour and 60g of egg yolks from

the fridge and mix on low to medium speed until everything is well combined and smooth.

Change to the dough hook and increase to medium speed. Divide the butter and remaining sugar into three equal parts. Add them to the mix in three stages, increasing the speed to ensure the dough is well mixed at each step. Slowly add the rest of the egg yolks and beat on medium speed until combined. At the end of the mix use a thermometer to check the temperature (see Nota Bene, below). The dough should finish between 75° and 79°F (24° and 26°C) and should look smooth and feel elastic. Transfer the dough into a clear, lightly greased 3 quart (3L) container. Mark the outside of the container with a line or sticky tape matching the dough level. This will enable you to see when the dough has eventually tripled in size. Let it rest for 30 minutes.

Transfer the dough to the counter. Using the plastic bowl scraper gently tighten the dough into a taller mound, pushing it upward by sliding the scraper swiftly beneath the dough. Try to execute this movement as swiftly as possible, using only a couple of moves. It should look shiny and not ripped.

Return the dough to the container, without flipping it, with the seal at the bottom. Allow to rise at a temperature of 73° to 77°F (23° to 25°C) until tripled, about 12 hours.

NOTA BENE When checking dough temperature, ensure your thermometer is calibrated and insert the tip of the thermometer at least 1 inch (2.5cm) into the dough.

→

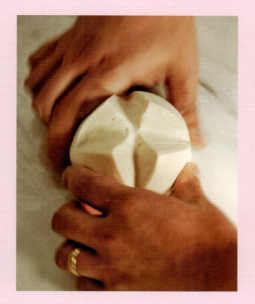

DOLCI

DAY 1: 7 P.M. / MIX-IN PREP

BUTTERCREAM

- 130g unsalted butter, at room temperature
- 75g granulated sugar
- Seeds of 1 vanilla bean
- 20g honey
- 5g fine sea salt

PANETTONE CLASSICO

- 165g high-quality candied orange
- 165g raisins

Make the buttercream: In a stand mixer fitted with the paddle, beat together the butter, sugar, vanilla seeds, honey, and salt. Mix until everything is combined. Store in a container and refrigerate overnight.

If making a panettone classico: Drain the candied orange from any syrup. Carefully wash all the raisins and dry on a baking sheet at 200°F (100°C) for 15 minutes or until almost completely dry.

DAY 2: 6 A.M. / SECOND MIX (SECONDO IMPASTO)

Do not begin the second mix until the dough has tripled in volume. The tripling factor is imperative at this stage.

SECONDO IMPASTO

- Evening rise dough
- 100g panettone flour
- 1g malt flour (optional; see Pro Tip, page 254)
- Buttercream (from Day 1 / Mix-in Prep)
- 110g egg yolks, refrigerated

PANETTONE CLASSICO

- 165g high-quality candied orange (prepped earlier)
- 165g raisins (prepped earlier)

PANETTONE AL CIOCCOLATO

- 335g chocolate callets or feves (see Nota Bene, page 257)

PANETTONE CON MORTADELLA

- 165g Mortadella DOP, cut into 1/3-inch (8mm) cubes
- 165g smoked scamorza (or a good provolone, Fontina, or Emmental), cut into 1/3-inch (8mm) cubes
- 1/2 teaspoon freshly ground black pepper

Place the dough from the previous night, the panettone flour, and malt flour (if using) in a stand mixer fitted with the dough hook. Mix on low-medium speed until well combined, smooth, and elastic, 15 to 20 minutes.

Add half of the buttercream from the previous night and mix it into the dough until it has been completely absorbed. Add one-third of the yolks and keep mixing until absorbed. Add the remaining buttercream, increasing the mixing speed to medium-high to help the dough come together quickly. Slowly add one-third more of the yolks, keeping the speed constant. Once absorbed slowly add the remaining yolks,

DOLCI

slowing down the speed of the mixer to medium. This should take about 20 minutes.

Once all the egg yolk has been incorporated, proceed by adding the flavouring for your chosen type of panettone at low speed. Mix until all the ingredients are well combined with the dough, 3 to 5 minutes.

This process should take you about 1 hour. At this point the dough should look smooth and feel elastic and its temperature should be between 77° and 80°F (25° and 27°C). Transfer the panettone dough back into the lightly greased container for 1½ hours.

If your dough is below 75°F (24°C), place in a warmer place and extend the bulk fermentation, which refers to the phase between the mixing period and the dividing and shaping period. During this time the dough rests and gains strength; this helps the panettone rise in the baking phase.

If your dough is above 82°F (28°C), place in a cooler place and shorten the bulk fermentation.

NOTA BENE We use Domori Morogoro drops, which have a 56% cacao content. We recommend using your favourite high-quality chocolate.

DAY 2: 8:30 A.M. / PRESHAPE (PREFORMA)

Divide the dough into two equal parts, around 1¾ pounds (800g) each. Using the plastic bowl scraper gently tighten the dough into taller mounds, pushing it upward by sliding the scraper swiftly beneath the dough. Try to execute this movement as swiftly as possible, using only a couple of moves. It should look shiny and not ripped. Allow the two doughs to rest on the table in the open air. →

DOLCI

**DAY 2: 9 A.M. /
FINAL SHAPING AND
PROOFING (PIRLATURA
E LIEVITAZIONE FINALE)**

Using the plastic bowl scraper, tighten both doughs into taller, firmer mounds pushing them upward by sliding the scraper swiftly beneath the doughs. Transfer each dough to a panettone mold. Cover with a plastic wrap allowing room for vertical growth and place in a warm spot at about 79° to 82°F (26° to 28°C) for 5 to 6 hours. Take careful note of the temperature as this directly affects the rising time.

DAY 2: 2 P.M. / OVEN PREHEAT

If you are proofing the panettoni in the oven, remove now! Preheat the oven to 350°F (180°C).

**DAY 2: 3 P.M. / GLAZES,
GARNISHES, AND BAKING**

**GLAZE (FOR CLASSICO
AND CHOCOLATE VERSIONS)**

MAKES 2 PANETTONI

- 15g egg whites
- 5g canola oil
- 10g granulated sugar
- 10g icing sugar
- 10g hazelnut flour
- 10g almond flour

**GARNISH (FOR CLASSICO
AND CHOCOLATE VERSIONS)**

MAKES 2 PANETTONI

- ¼ cup (20g) whole hazelnuts or whole almonds
- 3 tablespoons (20g) pearl sugar

**GARNISH (FOR MORTADELLA
VERSION)**

- 1 tablespoon butter

Make the glaze: In a small bowl, mix all ingredients for the glaze together until well combined.

For the mortadella panettone: Simply score a cross with a very sharp blade, being careful to score only the skin without going deeply into the dough. Place the butter at the heart of the cross.

For the classico or chocolate panettone: Uncover the panettone and spread half the amount of the glaze onto each panettone, using your offset spatula. Sprinkle half the nuts and then half the pearl sugar on each loaf.

Place the panettone on a baking sheet and bake for 40 minutes. The panettone is ready when its core temperature reaches 198°F (92°C).

DAY 2: 3:20 P.M. / COOLING

While the panettone is baking, create a structure to allow them to be hung upside down to cool off.

Options for hanging panettone include hanging them between the spreaders of a ladder or two piles of books or between the backs of two chairs.

Once the panettone has reached the core temperature, remove from the oven and quickly insert 2 skewers at the base of each panettone mold—parallel to the base and at each extremity of the mold. Hang the panettone upside down using the ends of the skewers as support for 5 hours as the panettone cool.

DAY 2: 9 P.M.

Flip the panettone and enjoy! If not consuming right away, store in an airtight container or plastic sealable bag.

This will keep for up to 3 weeks, as long as it's wrapped tightly.

DOLCI

Torta di ricotta

RICOTTA CHEESECAKE

MAKES ONE 9-INCH (23CM) TART; SERVES 6 TO 8

YOU WILL NEED

- Stand mixer fitted with the paddle
- Rubber spatula
- Rolling pin
- Parchment paper
- 9-inch (23cm) springform pan
- Baking beans or pie weights

- 1 disk Almond Shortcrust dough (recipe follows)
- Softened butter, for the pan
- 2 cups (455g) sheep's milk ricotta cheese
- 1 cup (200g) granulated sugar
- 3 eggs, separated
- Grated zest of 1 lemon
- ¼ cup (60g) blanched sliced almonds
- 2 tablespoons pine nuts

ALMOND SHORTCRUST DOUGH

MAKES ENOUGH FOR TWO 9-INCH (23CM) CRUSTS

- 3 cups + ⅓ cup (360g) pastry flour
- Scant cup (120g) finely ground toasted almonds
- 2 sticks (8 ounces/225g) unsalted butter, at room temperature
- 1 cup + 1 tablespoon (115g) granulated sugar
- Pinch of fine sea salt
- 2 egg yolks
- Grated zest of 1 lemon

At some point I realized that beautiful, individually portioned desserts were the way to go at the restaurants—quite a departure from the cake slices we served early on. They were delicious, don't get me wrong, but this tart upped our game. We did this first at Osteria Ciceri e Tria and we baked each tart to order. It was a simple dessert, but the crust was nutty and crispy and the ricotta, light, fluffy, and delicately citrusy.

In a bowl, combine the flour and ground almonds.

In a stand mixer fitted with the paddle, beat the butter, sugar, and salt on medium speed until light and fluffy, 5 to 6 minutes. Beat in the egg yolks one at a time, then add the lemon zest. Reduce the speed to medium-low and add the flour/almond mixture gradually. Mix until it forms a well-combined dough.

Place the dough on a lightly floured surface and divide it into 2 equal portions, shaping each into a rough disk. Wrap each disk in plastic wrap and refrigerate for at least 30 minutes (or up to 36 hours) before using. (Or freeze for later use.)

TORTA DI RICOTTA

Make the shortcrust dough and refrigerate as directed.

Grease a 9-inch (23cm) springform pan with butter and line it with a round of parchment paper.

Roll the dough to a thickness of ¼ inch (5mm). Carefully transfer to the springform pan, pressing it along the sides to create a crust that extends about 1¼ inches (3cm) up the sides of the pan.

Line the tart shell with a sheet of parchment paper and fill it with baking beans or pie weights. Refrigerate for 30 minutes.

Meanwhile, preheat the oven to 350°F (180°C).

Bake the tart shell with the baking beans for 10 minutes. Carefully lift out the parchment and baking beans and continue baking until the crust achieves a lovely golden colour, an additional 5 minutes. Remove from the oven, but leave the oven on.

In a stand mixer fitted with the paddle, combine the ricotta, half of the sugar, the egg yolks, and lemon zest and beat on medium speed for 1 to 2 minutes. In a separate bowl, whisk the egg whites with the remaining sugar by hand until fluffy and glossy. Gently fold the beaten whites into the ricotta mixture using a spatula.

Pour this ricotta mixture into the prebaked tart shell, evenly sprinkle almond slices on top, and add the pine nuts. Bake until the ricotta is set, about 30 minutes. Note that there will be a bit of a wobble, and cracks will appear.

Enjoy the tart either warm or chilled, depending on your preference.

DOLCI

Cannoli

TRADITIONAL SICILIAN CANNOLI

MAKES 15 TO 20 CANNOLI

YOU WILL NEED

- Stand mixer fitted with the paddle
- Cannoli tubes (easily sourced online)
- Rolling pin
- Deep heavy-bottomed pot, for deep-frying
- Deep-fry thermometer
- 3¼-inch (8cm) round pastry cutter
- Spider strainer
- Tongs
- 1 piping bag

CANNOLI DOUGH

- 2½ cups (300g) all-purpose flour, plus more for dusting
- 1 tablespoon + 1 teaspoon granulated sugar
- 1 tablespoon cocoa
- ½ teaspoon fine sea salt
- ¼ cup (60ml) white wine vinegar
- 3 tablespoons (45g) unsalted butter, melted
- 2 tablespoons Marsala
- 1 egg white
- Cooking spray or butter, for greasing the tubes
- Sunflower oil (about 4 quarts/4L), for deep-frying
- Egg wash: 1 egg lightly beaten

Every time I walk into Sud Forno and I see the cannoli, I am so proud, as these beauties are the cannoli of my dreams. Simultaneously, they are the cannoli of our accountant Kari's nightmares: The ingredients are cost-prohibitive, and they are labour-intensive to make. You need to make the dough, let it rest, roll the dough out, cut rounds out of it, wrap each round around a steel tube, deep-fry each cannoli shell, pull the cannoli shell off the steel tube while searing hot, and let these cannoli shells rest, making sure they don't break in the process! All this to say, we sell them at Sud Forno despite Kari's misgivings, stuffed the traditional way with sweetened ricotta and topped with the finest pistachios and candied orange bits. For a home cook, it's a fun project to do as a family—just don't let the kids near the deep-frying station. →

FILLING

- 2 cups (450g) sheep's milk ricotta or high-quality cow's milk ricotta, pressed to reduce moisture (see Nota Bene)
- ¾ cup (150g) granulated sugar
- ¾ cup (90g) pistachios, toasted and coarsely crushed
- 4 tablespoons (60g) candied orange strips
- Icing sugar

NOTA BENE The moisture in ricotta can be reduced by wrapping it in cheesecloth and squeezing out excess liquid.

DOLCI

Make the cannoli dough: In a stand mixer fitted with the paddle, combine the flour, sugar, cocoa, salt, ¼ cup (60ml) water, the vinegar, melted butter, Marsala, and egg white and mix on medium speed until well combined, 8 to 10 minutes. Turn the mixture onto a lightly floured surface and knead until a smooth dough is formed. Wrap in plastic wrap and store in the refrigerator for at least 1 hour and up to 36 hours.

When ready to fry: Spray the cannoli tubes with cooking spray or grease each one with butter.

Line a tray with paper towels and place near the stove. Pour 4 inches (10cm) sunflower oil into a deep heavy-bottomed pot and heat over medium heat to 320°F (160°C).

Roll the chilled dough out using a rolling pin to a thickness of $\frac{1}{16}$ inch (2mm). Use a 3¼-inch (8cm) round pastry cutter to cut out rounds. Keep them covered with plastic wrap to ensure they don't dry out. Take each round and tightly wrap it round a cannoli tube, sealing it with the egg wash where the seams come together.

Working in batches of 3 or 4, add the tubes to the hot oil and fry until they rise to the top and become bubbly and crispy, 1 to 2 minutes. Using a spider, remove from the oil, being sure to drain off excess hot oil into the pot. Place the tubes on the paper towel. Use tongs and some of the paper towels to avoid touching the shells and the tubes with your hands and quickly but carefully detach the cannolo shell from the steel tubes while still hot.

Repeat the wrapping and frying process until all the dough rounds have been fried and turned into shells. Allow them to cool completely.

Make the filling: In a medium bowl, combine the ricotta and sugar and mix with a wooden spoon until well combined. Place the filling in a piping bag and cut a hole about a ½ inch (1.5cm) wide. Fill each cannolo shell by piping the ricotta filling through both sides, then dab one end in the crushed pistachios and place a piece of candied orange on the other end. Generously dust with the icing sugar and serve. It is best to fill the cannoli right before serving to ensure the shell stays crisp.

Always enjoy a cannolo immediately, they do not store well.

DOLCI

Crostata di Nutella e crema

NUTELLA AND CUSTARD TART

MAKES ONE 9-INCH (23CM) TART

YOU WILL NEED

- Stand mixer fitted with the paddle
- Digital scale
- Small rubber bowl scraper or spatula
- Rolling pin
- 9-inch (23cm) round tart pan

- 3 cups + 3 tablespoons (340g) pastry flour, plus more for dusting
- 1¼ cups (110g) cocoa powder
- 1 teaspoon fine sea salt
- 1 teaspoon baking powder
- 2 sticks (8 ounces/225g) unsalted butter, at room temperature, plus more for the tart pan
- 1½ cups (300g) granulated sugar
- 3 eggs
- ¾ to 1 cup (250g) Nutella
- 2 cups (650g) Pastry Cream (page 301)

Nutella—the Italian hazelnut and chocolate confection—can be a polarizing commodity . . . but not at Terroni! We all love it. This is Giovanna's baby, a tart she first introduced at Sud Forno. She usually makes a long, rectangular crostata, but this also works well in a round tart form. She came up with the idea when she was very pregnant, and had just moved to Sud Forno Queen because we didn't have a pastry chef. We all love the versatility of this tart . . . it can be dressed up as a special dinner party dessert or kept rustic for a Sunday lunch. Warning: Children love this tart!

Preheat the oven to 350°F (180°C).

In a bowl, combine the flour, cocoa, salt, and baking powder.

In a stand mixer fitted with the paddle, cream the butter and sugar together until light and fluffy, 4 to 5 minutes. Gradually add the eggs, one at a time, mixing at medium speed. Reduce the mixer speed to low and slowly incorporate the flour mixture.

Using a bowl scraper or spatula, transfer the dough from the mixer bowl, wrap it in plastic wrap, and let it rest in the refrigerator for about 30 minutes. (You can keep the dough in the refrigerator for up to 2 days but remember to bring it back to room temperature before using it. It's also possible to freeze the dough for up to 4 months.)

Once the dough is back at room temperature, divide it into 2 portions, one about 60 percent of the total (675g)

and one 40 percent (450g). Lightly flour a work surface and roll out the larger piece of dough with a rolling pin to a 10-inch (25cm) round ¼ to ⅜ inch (6 to 8mm) thick. Grease a 9-inch (23cm) tart pan with butter. Press the round of dough into the tart pan. Using a fork, gently poke some holes across the bottom of the tart. Spread the Nutella over the bottom of the tart shell and then top it with the pastry cream. Roll the remaining dough out to a round ¼ to ⅜ inch (6 to 8mm) thick and cut strips about ⅜ inch (1cm) wide. Arrange these strips across the top of the crostata, spacing them about 1¼ inches (3cm) apart. Create a second layer of strips by placing them perpendicular to the first set, creating a grid pattern. Finally, use some of the strips to create a border around the circumference of the crostata.

Bake the crostata until it is cooked through and has a golden-brown colour, 45 to 50 minutes. Allow it to cool completely before serving.

DOLCI

Sporcamuss

PASTRY CREAM PUFFS

SERVES 8 TO 10

YOU WILL NEED

- Baking sheet
- Parchment paper
- Piping bag
- Plain piping tip (opening diameter 1cm)

- 1 pound (450g) Puff Pastry (page 298)
- 2 egg yolks
- 4 cups (1.25kg) Pastry Cream (page 301)
- ½ cup (60g) icing sugar
- Optional: Nutella, about 1 teaspoon per puff (see Nota Bene)

NOTA BENE Fill each sporcamuss with a little less pastry cream, then dollop a teaspoon of Nutella before closing the sporcamuss.

Sporcamuss is Barese dialect for . . . "dirty your mouth."

The first time I had this dessert, it was over thirty-two years ago at Al Sorso Preferito, a restaurant in Bari. The place blew me away because of the Barese-style appetizers that flooded our table right when we sat down. As our meal progressed toward dessert, everyone started talking about sporcamuss. The treats came to the table and nobody, of course, thought to warn me. I picked it up, not knowing it was filled with lots of delicious cream inside a delicate pastry, and it just exploded all over my hands and face as I bit into it: *Sporcamuss!*

Preheat the oven to 375°F (190°C). Line the baking sheet with parchment paper.

Lightly flour a work surface and roll the puff pastry to a thickness of ½ inch (1.5cm). Cut the pastry dough into 2-inch (5cm) squares. Gingerly transfer the puff pastry squares to the lined baking sheet, leaving at least 1 inch (2.5cm) of space between them. (At this stage, you can freeze the pastry squares until ready to use, then thaw them in the fridge before baking.)

In a small bowl, lightly whisk the egg yolks. Brush the top of each square with the egg. Bake until puffed and golden, 12 to 14 minutes.

Place the pastry cream in a piping bag fitted with a ⅜-inch (1cm) plain tip. Once the puff pastry squares have cooled, cut each in half horizontally (to make 2 squares: a base and its corresponding top). Top each pastry base with pastry cream (about 2 tablespoons) and then cover the cream with the corresponding top. Slightly reheat each filled puff pastry square for 3 to 4 minutes in the oven, dust with icing sugar, and serve while still warm.

DOLCI

Pasticciotti leccesi

FLAVOURED CUSTARD TARTS

MAKES 24 TARTS IN 3 FLAVOURS: PASTRY CREAM, NUTELLA, AND APPLE COMPOTE

YOU WILL NEED

- Food processor or high-powered blender
- 24 tart shells about 2½ inches (7cm) in diameter
- Rolling pin
- Parchment paper
- 3½-inch (8cm) round pastry cutter
- Baking sheet
- 2¾-inch (7cm) round pastry cutter
- Pastry brush

DOUGH

- 2 cups (215g) pastry flour
- 2 cups (240g) all-purpose flour, plus more for dusting
- 2 sticks + 2 tablespoons (9 ounces/250g) unsalted butter, cold
- 4 egg yolks
- 1¾ cups (200g) icing sugar
- Grated zest of 1 lemon
- 1 vanilla bean, split lengthwise

PASTRY CREAM

- 2 cups (500ml) whole milk
- 6 egg yolks
- ¾ cup (150g) granulated sugar
- ⅓ cup + 1 tablespoon (50g) all-purpose flour

This recipe hails from Lecce in Puglia, and although it's an Italian classic, it's a polarizing little tart. Perhaps because it's moreish, in that there is *a lot* of crust and cream, but each bite is balanced. It was my wife, Elena's, suggestion to put it on the menu at Osteria Ciceri e Tria back in 2007, and she and Giovanna worked through different recipes to find the best expression of what you would find at a little *forno* while walking the shaded streets of Lecce. It works for dessert, sure, but I see it as the perfect *merenda* for that 3 p.m. espresso. →

APPLE COMPOTE

- 2 Honeycrisp apples, peeled and cut into ⅜-inch (1cm) cubes
- 2 tablespoons brown sugar
- 2 tablespoons fresh lemon juice

ASSEMBLY

- 1 tablespoon softened butter, for the tart shells
- ¾ cup (170g) pastry cream
- 16 Amarena cherries
- Scant ½ cup (120g) Nutella
- Egg wash: 1 egg beaten with 1 tablespoon whole milk
- 2 tablespoons granulated sugar

DOLCI

Make the dough: In a food processor, combine both flours and the butter and blitz until the mixture becomes crumbly. Add the egg yolks, icing sugar, and lemon zest. Scrape in the vanilla seeds (and reserve the vanilla pod) and pulse 3 to 5 times. Pour the mixture onto a lightly floured work surface. Quickly knead the dough together until it becomes smooth. Wrap the dough in plastic wrap or place inside an airtight container and allow to rest for 30 minutes.

Make the pastry cream: Prepare a large bowl of ice and water. In a medium saucepan, slowly bring the milk and the reserved vanilla pod to a boil over medium heat.

Meanwhile, in a bowl, whisk the egg yolks with the sugar and flour. This mixture will be hard to mix, just do the best you can to combine the ingredients. Slowly pour the hot milk mixture into the egg mixture, whisking vigorously to avoid scrambling the eggs. Pour the mixture back into the saucepan and slowly increase the heat, whisking constantly. As soon as the cream thickens, whisk for another couple of seconds and remove from the heat. Place the saucepan into the bowl with ice to cool off quickly. Discard the vanilla pod. Cover the surface with plastic wrap to avoid a skin forming and place in the refrigerator.

Make the apple compote: In a small pot, combine the apples, brown sugar, ¼ cup (60ml) water, and the lemon juice. Cook over medium heat, stirring, until the apples are soft and all liquids have evaporated, about 5 minutes. Remove from heat and set aside to cool.

To assemble: Preheat the oven to 350°F (180°C). Lightly grease twenty-four 2½-inch (7cm) tart shells with the softened butter.

Using a rolling pin, roll out the dough on a lightly floured surface until it is about ¼ inch (5mm) thick. (Alternatively, you can do this between two sheets of parchment paper or between plastic wrap.) With a 3½-inch (8cm) round cutter, cut out 24 rounds of dough. Gather the scraps and reroll to get all the rounds (but save the scraps for the top crusts). Press the dough into the tart shells. Arrange the tart shells on a sheet pan.

For the classic pastry cream version, fill each of 8 tart shells with 3 table-spoons pastry cream and 2 Amarena cherries per tart. For the Nutella version, fill each of 8 tart shells with 2 tablespoons pastry cream and 1 tablespoon Nutella. For the apple version, fill each of 8 tart shells with 1½ tablespoons apple compote and 1½ tablespoons pastry cream.

Roll the leftover dough to a ⅛-inch (3mm) thickness. With a 2¾-inch (7cm) round cutter cut out 24 rounds and cover the tarts. Brush the top of the tarts with the egg wash and dust with the granulated sugar.

Bake until golden brown, 30 to 35 minutes.

Cool before removing from the tins. These tarts will keep for 3 to 4 days once baked and can be frozen raw or after being baked. They should be consumed within 2 weeks.

CONVERSATION

COLLO QUIO ✕
CONVERSATION

Ralph Giannone

Giannone Petricone Associates Inc. Architects (GPA) is a Toronto-based design firm comprising over forty architects, led by principals Ralph Giannone and Pina Petricone.

Where are you based?

Toronto

What's your relationship to Terroni?

Architect and interior designer for Terroni. Relationship has spanned over twenty-five years. Also, good friend of Cosimo's and member of the brotherhood.

Favourite Terroni dish (including all restaurants, Spaccio, etc.)?

Depends. When I'm being good, the Funghi Assoluti and Carpaccio di Manzo. Favourite pasta is the Arcobaleno. Favourite pizza is the Smendozzata.

Favourite Terroni memory?

My most personal and professional memory: Cosimo and his family had come out of a crushing year, and we sat down to talk about life and work. Given his experience, I assumed that he was going to call it quits, move his family to Italy, and enjoy a quiet life . . . instead, like the force of nature that he is, he looked right at me and said, "I'm here and we are going for it, hold on for the ride," and "Are you ready?!" This caught me completely by surprise . . . I grabbed on to his coattails and have held on tight ever since!

Other memory: Another wonderful memory was the most enjoyable party Pina and I attended. It was on the heels of the opening of Terroni Centrale. Cosimo and Elena decided to celebrate New Year's with a party at Centrale, inviting close friends, family, and collaborators. It was such a great night, full of food, drink, and authentic hospitality. It was a night that made us feel and profoundly understand the ether of Terroni and how special the Terroni community was to us personally and professionally.

Favourite Terroni location?

I would like to say Terroni Price Street, since it is closest to my home and therefore our go-to location for my family, but my favourite is Bettola di Terroni. It is for me, the epitome of what the physical manifestation of Terroni is . . . full of subtle contrasts and touchstone manipulations. It embodies the hyphenated *sprezzatura* that only Terroni can create.

Do you like it sweet or savoury?

Yes and yes.

DOLCI

Biscotti di Mamma Rita

MAMMA RITA'S COOKIES

MAKES ABOUT 65 COOKIES

YOU WILL NEED

- Stand mixer fitted with the paddle
- Bench scraper
- 2 baking sheets
- Parchment paper

- 6 eggs
- 1 cup + 1 tablespoon (210g) granulated sugar
- $^3/_4$ cup (180ml) sunflower oil
- $1^1/_4$ cups (300ml) orange juice
- $1^1/_4$ cups (170g) ground toasted almonds
- 1 cup (170g) dark chocolate chips
- $6^2/_3$ cups (800g) all-purpose flour, plus more for dusting
- 5 teaspoons baking powder

I'll confess that as a child I preferred Oreos and chocolate chip cookies to these shortcrust biscuits. But store-bought cookies were not to be found anywhere inside our house, so, this is what we had, *basta*!

We would have them for breakfast with our milk or caffè latte. My father would dip them in wine at the end of dinner. When we first opened Terroni, my mom baked them for customers. To this day, they are our most popular cookie. When most non-Italians think of biscotti, they picture cantucci biscotti. These have the same shape, but typical cantucci are harder and denser. Our biscotti are lighter . . . and better.

Preheat the oven to 350°F (180°C). Line two baking sheets with parchment paper. (If your baking sheets won't fit side by side, position oven racks in the upper and lower thirds of the oven.)

In a stand mixer fitted with the paddle, beat the eggs and sugar on medium speed for 3 minutes. Decrease the speed, add the sunflower oil and orange juice, and beat for 3 more minutes.

Add the almonds and chocolate chips and mix until combined. Add the flour incrementally and finally the baking powder. Turn the dough onto a lightly floured surface and knead for a couple minutes until smooth. Cut the dough into 6 equal portions and roll each portion into a 15-inch (38cm) log about 1 inch (2.5cm) thick. Place the logs on the lined baking sheets. Using your hand, flatten them to a ½-inch (1.5cm) height.

Bake for 20 minutes (switching racks halfway through if using two racks). Remove from the oven but leave the oven on and reduce the oven temperature to 200°F (90°C).

Place the logs on a cutting board and cut them on a diagonal using a serrated knife to slices ½ inch (1. 5cm) thick. Return them to the baking sheets.

Bake until very crisp, 2 to 2½ hours.

Store in an airtight container. These cookies will keep up to 1 month.

DOLCI

I ricciarelli di Sud Forno

CHEWY ALMOND COOKIES

MAKES ABOUT 22 COOKIES

YOU WILL NEED

- Stand mixer fitted with the paddle
- Sifter or small sieve
- Bench scraper
- Digital scale
- Baking sheet
- Parchment paper

- 8½ ounces (240g) best-quality unsweetened marzipan
- 1 cup (120g) icing sugar, plus more for dusting
- 2 teaspoons baking powder
- Grated zest of 2 unwaxed organic lemons
- 5 egg whites
- 2⅓ cups (200g) blanched sliced almonds

These cookies are so soft, rich, and gentle and another creation from Giovanna. We make them at the bakeries, and they are on the menu year-round. They also work as a great gift for Christmas and are the perfect cookie for that much needed afternoon espresso break.

For almond lovers, these cookies are gluten-free (they're flourless).

Preheat the oven to 300°F (150°C). Line a baking sheet with parchment paper.

In a stand mixer fitted with the paddle, combine the marzipan, icing sugar, baking powder, lemon zest, and egg whites and mix them until they are thoroughly combined.

Dust a work surface with icing sugar by using a sieve and sifting it to completely cover the surface. Place the sliced almonds in a shallow bowl. Turn the marzipan out onto the sugared work surface and roll it into a log about 4 inches (10cm) thick. Using a bench scraper, cut disks that weigh between 20 and 25g.

Roll the disks in the almonds to coat all sides, and then, on the sugared work surface, shape them into parallelograms. Arrange the shaped treats on the lined baking sheet.

Bake for 10 minutes.

Cookies can be stored in an airtight container for 1 week.

DOLCI

Zeppole di San Giuseppe

FRIED CHOUX

MAKES ABOUT 24 FRITTERS

YOU WILL NEED

- Stand mixer fitted
  with the paddle
- 2 piping bags
- 3/8-inch (1cm) star tip
- Deep heavy-bottomed
  pot for deep-frying
- Deep-fry thermometer
- Baking sheet
- Parchment paper
- Spider strainer
- Tongs

CHOUX PASTRY

- 2 cups + 1 tablespoon
  (500ml) water
- 3 sticks + 3 tablespoons
  (13 1/2 ounces/380g)
  unsalted butter
- 4 1/3 cups (600g) pastry flour
- 15 eggs
- 1 tablespoon fine sea salt
- Sunflower oil (about
  3 quarts/3L), for deep-frying

FILLING

- 1 1/2 recipes Pastry
  Cream (page 301)
- 1 1/2 cups (300g) drained
  Amarena cherries
- Icing sugar, for dusting

Zeppole di San Giuseppe are delicious and decadent fried sweet fritters topped with gorgeous Amarena cherries. These pastries mark the feast day for San Giuseppe, Father's Day, which is always March 19 in Italy, and other very special times of the year for us.

These require a bit of time and focus, but are such a special tradition to undertake. They are something that all the Italian bakeries make, so even if this recipe is too heavy of a commitment, make sure to mark your calendars in March to sample the best of what's on Italian offer. Amarena (cherries preserved in sweet syrup) are a speciality item in Canada (and even in Italy) and they are absolutely worth the splurge. Do not even for one moment consider substituting maraschino cherries. Our favourite two brands are Fabbri and Toschi. →

DOLCI

Make the choux pastry: In a large heavy-bottomed pot, combine the water and butter. Bring to a boil over medium heat. Add the flour all at once and stir constantly with a wooden spoon until the flour is fully incorporated and the dough comes together in the pot. Remove it from the heat and transfer the dough to a stand mixer fitted with the paddle and mix until the dough cools down, about 10 minutes.

Crack the eggs into a bowl, and gradually add them to the dough along with the salt. Continue mixing until you achieve a smooth and creamy consistency. Fit a piping bag with a ⅜-inch (1cm) star tip and transfer the dough into it.

Line a tray with paper towels and place near the stove. Pour 3 inches (7.5cm) sunflower oil into a large heavy-bottomed pot or Dutch oven and heat to 330°F (165°C).

Meanwhile line a baking sheet with parchment paper. Pipe out dough circles, each about 4¾ inches (12cm) in diameter. Pipe a second circle of dough on top of the first circle. Cut the parchment paper into squares around each zeppola to make it easier to drop them into the hot oil.

Working in batches of 2 or 3 (this will depend on the size of your pot), carefully lower them into the hot oil with the parchment paper side up. You can help yourself by placing the parchment square on a spider and lowering it into the oil.

Fry the zeppole until they turn a lovely golden brown and become crisp on both sides, 4 to 5 minutes per side. Don't forget to flip them. Use tongs to remove the parchment after flipping. Use a spider strainer to remove the zeppole from the fryer and place them on the paper towels to drain.

Fill the zeppole: Fill a piping bag fitted with the star tip with the pastry cream. The traditional way to finish the zeppole is to simply top them with the pastry cream and Amarena cherries. But, for the Sud Forno zeppole, cut each zeppola in half horizontally and pipe the pastry cream around the inner circle of the zeppola. Cut 2 or 3 Amarena cherries in half and distribute them on top of the pastry cream. Close the zeppola back up and add a tablespoon-size dollop of pastry cream on top. Adorn each zeppola with an Amarena cherry. Finish off with a dusting of icing sugar and savour the delightful flavours.

DOLCI

Torta della Nonna Lucia

NONNA LUCIA'S CAKE

MAKES ONE 9-INCH (23CM) CAKE

YOU WILL NEED

- 9-inch (23cm) springform pan
- Parchment paper
- Sifter or sieve
- Electric mixer or whisk

- 7 ounces (200g) dark chocolate (70% cacao), roughly chopped
- 11 tablespoons (5½ ounces/ 150g) unsalted butter
- ¾ cup (150g) granulated sugar
- 2 tablespoons all-purpose flour (or 1 tablespoon cornstarch for gluten-free)
- 4 eggs, separated
- Icing sugar, for dusting

Nonna Lucia was Elena's grandmother and she made this very simple and delicious chocolate cake, which Elena now makes for the family. And—if you're lucky—you can occasionally spot it on the Sud Forno menu. It's a great last-minute dessert that pleases everyone always. It is very easy to execute, but the baking timing is key. The cake has just five ingredients, so each one really counts. Use the best-quality chocolate you can find because it will make all the difference.

Please note we've added a gluten-free option, swapping out the small amount of flour for cornstarch.

Preheat the oven to 350°F (180°C). Line a 9-inch (23cm) springform pan with a round of parchment paper. You can do this by wetting the inside of the pan and then sticking the parchment paper to it. It may not adhere perfectly, but that's part of the cake's charm.

In a small heavy-bottomed pan, combine the chocolate and 2 tablespoons water. Melt the chocolate over low heat, then add the butter and allow it to melt into the chocolate slowly. Stir in the sugar with a wooden spoon until the mixture is well combined. Remove the pan from the heat, sift in the flour, and stir. Set this mixture aside for about 10 minutes to cool.

Add the egg yolks to the cooled chocolate mixture. In a separate bowl, with an electric mixer or whisk, whip the egg whites until they form soft peaks. Gently fold the whites into the chocolate mixture. Scrape the batter into the springform.

Bake until a skewer into the centre comes out moist but not wet, 25 to 30 minutes.

Let the cake cool in the pan for about 10 minutes. Loosen the sides of the pan and carefully flip the cake onto a serving plate. Dust generously with icing sugar.

DOLCI

Il tiramisù di Terroni

TERRONI'S TIRAMISÙ

SERVES 4

YOU WILL NEED

- Stand mixer fitted with the whisk
- Ceramic baking dish about 10 × 14 inches (25 × 36cm) or similar

- 1²/₃ cups (400ml) espresso (made with a stovetop espresso maker), sweetened to taste
- 4 egg yolks
- ½ cup + 2 tablespoons (120g) granulated sugar
- 2¼ cups (500g) mascarpone cheese
- 1 cup (250ml) heavy cream
- 14 ounces (300g) ladyfingers
- ½ cup (90g) roughly chopped dark chocolate
- ¼ cup (20g) cocoa powder, for dusting

A classic tiramisù is simple: eggs, mascarpone, sugar, and cocoa. I however, like to add a little whipped cream to make it "fluffier," a definite nod to my North American upbringing. But Italy being Italy, everyone is judged on their take on this classic. I think a tiramisù is something very personal and you can make your own adjustments, even when it comes to dipping the ladyfingers in coffee (double dip, dip both sides, etc.). Also, feel free to add some booze to your coffee, or decaf coffee, whatever you prefer!

One thing that is non-negotiable: always use the freshest and best ingredients and Italian mascarpone. We started making this at Terroni Queen Street and as we opened new locations, each specific chef in charge would make their own version. You would think everyone would just follow our main set recipe, but it became a serious competition between locations. Some had a heavier hand, some put more mascarpone, some added more chocolate. At the beginning we made it in banana split boats! Today we make all of our tiramisù at Spaccio so everyone serves it just the way I like it. When Sud Forno opened is when we invented our tiramisù *al volo* ("to go") so you could have tiramisù at any point of the day.

Pour the espresso into a shallow bowl (and let cool if it is freshly made).

In a stand mixer fitted with the whisk, combine the egg yolks, sugar, and mascarpone and beat on medium speed for about 1 minute. Increase the speed to medium-high and whip until the mixture becomes light and fluffy, 3 to 4 minutes. Add the heavy cream and whip everything together for 5 minutes.

Spread a ¾-inch (2cm) layer of the mascarpone mixture into a 10 × 14-inch (25 × 36cm) ceramic baking dish. Dip the ladyfingers into

the espresso for 5 to 6 seconds each, adjusting the time based on your preference. Arrange these espresso-dipped ladyfingers over the mascarpone cream, covering completely. Spread a second ¾-inch (2cm) layer of the mascarpone cream on top. Repeat the process of dipping the ladyfingers in espresso to create a second layer. Finish by covering it with the remaining mascarpone cream and sprinkling it with dark chocolate. Immediately move to the refrigerator and chill for at least 3 hours, or preferably overnight.

Dust with the cocoa before serving.

12

LA DISPENSA

TERRONI

PANTRY

LA DISPENSA

These are the workhorse recipes and components that pop up throughout the book (and in each of our locations) again and again.

NOTA BENE We recommend following metric measurements in all pastry and bakery recipes.

Lievito madre
SOURDOUGH STARTER

This is our baby. Our mother yeast. It's vital for making our natural leavened bread and we care for it very much. Giuliano Pediconi, who is our master baker and has forty years of service under his belt, brought his lievito madre from Italy to us. And so we take very good care of it.

It must be fed every day, and if you don't take proper care of it, it will die, and you must start over from scratch, which takes up to seven days. When all is going well, it just becomes better and stronger with time. It's part of the whole breadmaking experience where you need to touch, smell, and look for signs that something might be off. Breadmaking can become very scientific, so you also have to gain some hands-on experience. This is something we cannot teach you, but we can provide you with some guidelines for making sourdough, and with some great recipes, some practice, and time you'll get the hang of it.

During panettone season, which is the most stressful period for our bakers, the lievito madre plays a key role, and our head baker Luca Rotatori used to come in at 3 a.m. *just to check on it.* Recently, he installed a kitchen camera that allows him to check in and see how much the sourdough has risen without getting out of bed. It's all about getting those extra twenty minutes of sleep!

Normally, we keep the lievito madre in a fermentation tank that keeps it alive and even allows us to go on vacation occasionally.

This is a one-week process, not active time, of course, but from start to finish. And so, for the method, we've provided instructions per day.

YOU WILL NEED

- Food processor or immersion blender
- Two to three glass jars with a lid, each with a capacity of 2 cups (500ml)
- Rubber spatula
- Cheesecloth
- One rubber band

DAY 1: MORNING

- 3½ tablespoons (25g) peeled and diced apple
- 1 tablespoon + 2 teaspoons (25ml) sparkling mineral water
- 3 tablespoons (25g) bread flour or tipo "00" flour

In a small food processor or with an immersion blender, purée the apple together with the sparkling water. Pour the mixture in a clean and dry (this is very important) 2-cup (500ml) glass jar and add the bread flour. Mix well until combined and scrape down the sides using a rubber spatula. Cover with a clean cloth and set aside for 24 hours in a very warm spot in your home, between 82° and 95°F (28° and 35°C).

DAY 2: MORNING

- 3 tablespoons (50g) starter from the day before
- ⅓ cup (50g) bread flour or tipo "00" flour
- ¼ cup (60ml) still mineral water

The starter should smell slightly lactic and acidic and should have some bubbles and be showing signs of evolution. Remove 3 tablespoons (50g) of starter into a new, clean jar. Add the bread flour and water and mix well until combined, scraping down the sides using a rubber spatula. Cover with a lid (don't twist it shut, just simply place it on), add the rubber band to mark the level of the starter, and store in a warm place out of direct sunlight. Discard the rest of the starter from Day 1. →

LA DISPENSA

DAYS 3 THROUGH 6: MORNINGS

- 3 tablespoons (50g) starter from the day before
- $^3/_4$ cup (100g) bread flour or tipo "00" flour
- 7 tablespoons (100ml) still mineral water

The starter might show a few bubbles on the surface. This is a good sign. It means there is some activity happening and the yeast is starting to multiply. Remove 3 tablespoons (50g) of starter into a new jar. Add the bread flour and water and mix well until combined, scraping down the sides using a rubber spatula. Cover with a lid, add the rubber band to mark the stop of the starter, and store in a warm place out of direct sunlight. Repeat this process for the next three days, discarding the starter from the day before.

DAY 7: REGULAR FEEDING

- 3 tablespoons (50g) starter from the day before
- 1 cup (125g) bread flour or tipo "00" flour
- $^1/_2$ cup (120ml) still mineral water

By now the starter should have become predictable in its rising and falling. Remove again 3 tablespoons (50g) of starter into a new, clean jar. Add the bread flour and water and mix well until combined, scraping down the sides using a rubber spatula. From this point on, the sourdough starter can be fed according to the ingredients laid out on Day 7. Follow the feeding routine for at least 2 or more weeks to make the starter stronger and more resilient. After this point, the starter can be kept in the fridge for 6 consecutive days without any feeding. Remember to note the date of the last feed on a sticker on the jar.

Impasto per pizza di Terroni
TERRONI PIZZA DOUGH

MAKES ENOUGH FOR 4 INDIVIDUAL PIZZAS

In 1993, we began making pizza dough from scratch, using a plastic container and no mixer.

We experimented with different doughs after buying our first secondhand (maybe thirdhand) pizza oven at Terroni (there were definitely better ovens out there, but this one was called "Bari," so it was love at first sight). Initially we mixed everything by hand with fresh yeast. Thankfully, we later acquired a proper mixer. It was always a challenge: Either Paolo or I would make the dough in the morning and then switch, and one of us would make a second batch in the evening. Sometimes, if the dough didn't rise properly, we had to start over. Initially, we made around forty to one hundred pizzas per day, but over the years, that number increased . . . exponentially.

In those early days, we relied on instinct rather than written recipes, which led to occasional disappointments due to variable humidity or a weaker yeast strand.

What sets our pizza apart is our *materia prima*, flour from the Marche region grown and milled exclusively for us. We also use the finest olive oil from Puglia, never compromising on quality.

Our dough undergoes a lengthy resting period. Previously, we would make it in the morning to use it at night, but now we follow a three-day fermentation process. Love is also an essential ingredient.

When our bakeries opened, we further improved our recipes, using sourdough and gentler mixers that don't heat up the dough as they work it. This meticulous control ensures that the dough rarely fails to rise or encounters any issues.

I recall the first time we hired a skilled pizzaiolo: His name is Renato Cesar Nicotera and he worked at lightning speed, stretching multiple pizzas, topping them right on the counter, and then scooping them up with his own aluminum pizza paddle to toss them in the oven. I marvelled at how long it took me to make three pizzas compared to him.

From the very start, we used plates from Grottaglie, Puglia, renowned for its ceramics. They are the perfect size for our pizzas and pizza-size plates were scarce in North America—at least when we started.

This is a two-day process, so for the method, we've provided instructions per day.

YOU WILL NEED

- Digital thermometer
- Digital scale
- Proofing bowl
- Plastic bowl scraper
- Bench scraper

POOLISH

- $^1/_2$ cup (120ml) water, at room temperature (70° to 73°F/21° to 23°C)
- 1 teaspoon (3g) instant yeast
- 1 cup (120g) pizza flour tipo "00"

PIZZA DOUGH

- 1 cup (250ml) water at 50° to 60°F (10°C to 15°C)
- 3 tablespoons + 2 teaspoons (45g) sourdough starter (optional; see Nota Bene, page 289), at room temperature
- 1 tablespoon (15g) extra-virgin olive oil
- $^3/_4$ teaspoon (10g) honey

- 4 cups (475g) pizza flour tipo "00"
- 2 teaspoons (10g) fine sea salt
- Semola rimacinata (works best) or all-purpose flour, for dusting

NOTA BENE This recipe calls for a poolish, which is a type of "pre-ferment"—a small amount of dough (made from flour, commercial yeast, and water) that has fermented for 2 to 24 hours. The poolish is added to the main dough of leavened recipes to improve final volume, flavour, and softness of the baked dough.

Sourdough starter is not essential here, because the recipe calls for yeast. However, the use of sourdough is always preferred because it increases any dough's flavour profile. Simply omit it from this recipe if you don't have it handy. You can use your starter directly from the fridge if it has been fed regularly (see Day 7 of Sourdough Starter, page 288). Allow the starter to sit at room temperature for a couple of hours before mixing.

DAY 1: 5 P.M.

Make the poolish: Pour the water into a bowl or container that can accommodate the increased volume of the dough, which can expand up to three times its original size. Add the yeast and stir the mixture with a spatula until the yeast is completely dissolved. Add all the flour and continue mixing until the flour is fully absorbed, which should take about 3 minutes. The ideal temperature for the dough is 70° to 73°F (21° to 23°C). Cover the bowl with plastic wrap. Allow the poolish to rest at room temperature for 1 hour, then transfer to the refrigerator for 18 to 24 hours.

DAY 2: AROUND 3 P.M.

Make the pizza dough: In a bowl, combine the water, sourdough (if using), olive oil, and honey. (If you're not using the starter, add 1 additional tablespoon water to the dough.) Add the poolish and mix everything together using a spatula until the poolish is fully dissolved in the water. Add half of the flour and continue mixing with the spatula for 2 to 3 minutes until all the flour is incorporated. Add the salt and mix for an additional 2 minutes. Add the remaining flour and continue mixing for another 2 to 3 minutes with the spatula. Transfer the dough onto a clean work surface and knead it by hand for 2 minutes.

Cover the dough with either a bowl or a damp cloth and let it rest for 30 minutes.

Use a plastic bowl scraper to work the dough into a ball shape. While working the dough, make sure to keep the top part always facing upward to maintain a smooth surface, moving the dough away from the surface as you work it. Be careful not to overwork the dough, as you want to keep it smooth and free from tears. Place the dough (without turning it) into a greased bowl or food storage container and allow it to rest for an additional 30 minutes covered.

Gently remove the pizza dough from the container and place it onto a clean surface. Using a bench scraper, divide the dough into 4 equal portions of about 220g each. Take each portion and shape it into a ball using your hands, ensuring each ball is taut and smooth. Arrange the pizza dough balls on a tray dusted with flour and cover them lightly with plastic wrap. Allow the dough balls to proof for 2 to 3 hours, adjusting the time based on the room temperature.

DAY 2: AROUND 6 P.M.

Once the dough balls have proofed, they are now ready to be shaped into delicious pizzas. See Shaping a Pizza Round for how to stretch the dough. And for various topping ideas, see Pizza Bufalina (page 65), Pizza Santo Spirito (page 66), or Pizza San Giorgio (page 62).

LA DISPENSA

Shaping a Pizza Round

To stretch a ball of dough into a 10- to 12-inch (25 to 30cm) pizza round, dust some semola rimacinata on your hands and on a work surface. Place the proofed pizza ball on the floured surface. Start by pressing the dough ball down with the tips of your fingers to flatten it into a round. Press around the rim of the dough, leaving about ½ inch (1.5cm) from the edges, and create a valley between the centre and the edges. Using the outer part of your palm (from your little finger to the bottom of your wrist), stretch the dough from the centre outward to the edges while turning the round. Be careful not to thin out the middle too much. Continue this stretching process until the desired diameter is reached.

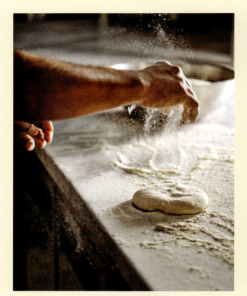

Bruschetta all'olio

BREAD CRISPS

MAKES 6 TO 8 SLICES

Sometimes simple things are overlooked. The first time I had bruschetta all'olio made properly with the right amount of olive oil and salt, I was like "Why have I never had it before?" You have to drench it with EVOO and a "scandalous" amount of Maldon.

- ½ loaf Pane Pugliese (page 80)
- 4 to 6 tablespoons extra-virgin olive oil
- 1 garlic clove, peeled but whole
- Maldon salt

Preheat the oven to 400°F (200°C).

Cut the bread into slices ⅜ to ½ inch (1 to 1.5cm) thick. Place them flat on a baking sheet and drizzle generously with olive oil.

Bake until dark golden, 6 to 8 minutes.

Once out of the oven, rub the whole garlic clove back and forth along each bread slice. Sprinkle well with salt.

LA DISPENSA

Base Brioche

**MAKES 2¼ POUNDS (1KG)
BRIOCHE DOUGH**

This recipe is a staple of the Terroni kitchen. We use it for Stuffed Savoury Brioche (page 115), Bomboloni (page 36), Maritozzi (page 32) . . . It's versatile and a great thing for the home cook to have, even if just making a simple loaf (see Pan Brioche, this page).

This recipe hails from Giuliano Pediconi, our master baker. It has been tweaked through the years by our cooks to be adapted to different preparations and especially to be adapted to Canadian ingredients. All the dough is mixed and transformed into different applications at Spaccio East by our pastry team.

YOU WILL NEED

- Stand mixer fitted with the dough hook
- Baking sheet
- Digital scale or measuring cups
- Plastic bowl scraper

- 1 cup (125g) all-purpose flour
- 3 cups (375g) Manitoba flour (see Nota Bene)
- 1½ teaspoons (10g) instant yeast
- 5 eggs (250g total), fridge temperature
- 2 tablespoons (30g) heavy cream, fridge temperature
- ¼ cup (60g) sourdough starter (optional; see Nota Bene)
- 1½ teaspoons (8g) fine sea salt
- ½ cup (100g) granulated sugar
- 7 tablespoons (100g) unsalted butter, fridge temperature
- Seeds from 1 vanilla bean

In a stand mixer fitted with the dough hook, combine both flours and the yeast. Add the eggs, cream,

and starter (if not using starter, add 4 extra teaspoons of cream). Mix on low speed until everything is combined, 6 to 8 minutes. Stop the mixer and allow the dough to rest in the bowl for 10 minutes. Restart the mixer on low speed for 2 minutes. Combine the salt and the sugar and add them to the mixture one-third at a time, alternating with one-third of the butter and the vanilla seeds. Before you add more sugar or butter, make sure previously added ingredients are completely absorbed. If the sugar sticks to the side of the bowl, pause the mixer, scrape down the sides of the bowl, and continue. Once all ingredients are well combined, remove the dough from the mixer bowl, dust a clean surface with some flour, and knead the dough another 2 to 3 minutes with your hands until smooth. Place in an airtight container that is twice as large as the dough and rest for 20 to 30 minutes. If the dough is too sticky, let it rest uncovered for the last 10 minutes.

This dough is now ready to be used in a recipe. Or it can be frozen for future use (see Nota Bene). Brioche dough can be frozen for up to 1 month since it is naturally leavened, but the yeast will start to die after that.

NOTA BENE Use a strong flour or a bread flour: one that has a protein value of at least 13.5. You can get bread flour at any grocery store, though we use an imported Italian flour called Manitaly flour, which is made with Italian grain.

Sourdough starter is not essential here because the recipe also calls for instant yeast. However, the use of sourdough is always preferred; it really elevates the flavour and texture. Simply omit it from this recipe if you don't have it on hand and add 4 teaspoons of heavy cream. You can use your sourdough directly from the fridge if it has been fed in the past 2 days (see Day 7 of Sourdough Starter, page 288).

If using the brioche to make small shapes, such as Bombolone (page

36), Maritozzi (page 32), or Cornetti (page 40), the best results are obtained if you freeze the unbaked dough in the form (shape) it will be used so that you can thaw and then proof it directly. For example, for bombolone, shape it into bombolone and then freeze it. Then when you're ready to make bombolone, pull the shaped dough from the freezer and then follow the proofing instructions according to the original recipe. However, you need to consider additional time for thawing (typically 3 to 4 hours).

Pan Brioche

YOU WILL NEED

- Bowl scraper
- Plastic wrap
- 2 loaf pans, 9 × 5 × 3 inches (23 × 13 × 7.5cm)
- Pastry brush

Prepare the dough as directed. Transfer to a work surface and divide it into 2 equal portions. Using the plastic bowl scraper, gently tighten each portion of dough into a taller mound, pushing it upward by sliding the scraper swiftly beneath the dough. Try to do this movement as quickly as possible, using only a couple of moves. It should look shiny and not ripped. Cover with plastic wrap and rest for 30 minutes more.

Meanwhile, grease two 9 × 5 × 3-inch (23 × 13 × 7.5cm) loaf pans and line with parchment paper.

Repeat the shaping (see page 82). Place the dough loaves into the loaf pans, cover with plastic wrap, and place in the oven with the light on (but the oven off) and let rise until doubled in size, 2 to 3 hours.

Remove from the oven and preheat the oven to 325°F (160°C).

Glaze the loaves with an egg wash (1 egg yolk beaten with 1 teaspoon water). Bake until a core temperature of 208°F (98°C) is reached, about 50 minutes. Cool in the pan.

291

LA DISPENSA

Pasta all'uovo
FRESH EGG PASTA

MAKES 1 POUND (450G); SERVES 3 TO 4

The ratio is very easy to remember: we use one whole egg for each 100g (¾ cup + 2 tablespoons) flour. We import our flour from the Marche region, but just make sure you source a good tipo "00" flour. The quality of the flour in this recipe is very important. The eggs are also very important. When we started making our pasta, we knew we had the best flour, but we were just not happy with the finished product: The pasta was a good texture, but it looked so very pale. So, we turned our attention to the eggs. We found a farmer in Manitoba who naturally raised chickens and provided us with stunning, rich, orange-yolked eggs (we have since found a local farmer, which is better because it's a smaller carbon footprint). So, if you can't find the greatest flour, try to find the greatest eggs. We use the egg pasta for most of our long pastas such as pappardelle, tagliatelle, or lasagne sheets, or for stuffed pasta like the Ravioli di Zio Paperone (page 168).

YOU WILL NEED

- Large wooden surface, such as a cutting board
- Large resealable plastic bag to store dough and keep it moist
- Bench scraper
- Pasta rolling pin, pasta machine, or stand mixer with a pasta attachment

- 2½ cups (300g) tipo "00" flour
- 3 eggs, very fresh, at room temperature

Spoon the flour onto a clean wooden surface or into a large shallow bowl and make a wide well in the centre. Crack the eggs into the well and, using a fork, swirl the eggs slowly, incorporating the flour into the centre of the well. When the flour is completely incorporated, gather and knead the mixture together to form one large ball. Knead the dough for at least 10 minutes on the counter. Place the dough into a resealable plastic bag and let rest for 30 minutes or up to 24 hours in the refrigerator.

Bring the dough to room temperature before using it. Begin rolling it out with your rolling pin or pasta machine until the desired thickness is reached.

FOR TAGLIOLINI, TAGLIATELLE, AND PAPPARDELLE

Roll the dough out until it has a thickness of about 1/16 inch (2mm). Allow the strips of rolled-out dough to dry a little before cutting them, 10 to 15 minutes. Lightly dust one strip of dough with flour and roll it onto itself from the top, halfway to the middle of the sheeted dough in a roll about 4 inches (10cm) wide. Repeat this from the bottom up as well. When the two rolls meet in the middle, allow them to overlap.

For tagliolini: Use a large chef's knife to cut the dough into strips ⅛ inch (3mm) wide.

For tagliatelle: Cut the dough into strips ¼ inch (7mm) wide.

For pappardelle: Cut the dough into strips ½ inch (1.5cm) wide.

This pasta can be frozen and stored in an airtight container in the freezer for up to 2 months.

NOTA BENE When making all these pasta shapes there will be some extra trimmings that are too short or small to serve. Save and freeze these, they're fantastic in soups.

Pasta agli spinaci
SPINACH PASTA

SERVES 4

For Ravioli di Zio Paperone (page 168), we opted to use this spinach pasta. It makes the ravioli really stand out on the plate but also adds a note of nuttiness that rounds the whole dish off.

YOU WILL NEED

- Food processor or immersion blender
- Pasta rolling pin, pasta machine, or stand mixer with a pasta attachment
- Large wooden surface, such as a cutting board

- 1 tablespoon fine sea salt
- 2¼ ounces (60g) spinach leaves
- 12 ice cubes
- 2 cups and 1 tablespoon (300g) tipo "00" flour
- 3 eggs

Bring a large pot of water to a boil. Add salt.

In a medium bowl, prepare a water and ice bath. Boil the spinach for 2 minutes, strain and transfer directly into the ice bath. Once cooled completely, drain, and squeeze excess water out of the spinach. Using a food processor or immersion blender, puree the spinach until smooth.

On a large, clean wooden surface make a mound with the flour and create a well in the middle. In a small bowl, whisk the eggs together with the spinach puree. Place the spinach/egg mixture in the middle of the well and begin mixing with a fork, adding flour from the mound to the eggs a bit at a time until all the flour is incorporated. Knead the dough, working vigorously with the palm

LA DISPENSA

and fingers of your hands, for 10 to 15 minutes until the dough is smooth and uniform. Place the dough inside an airtight container and let rest for at least 20 minutes up to 1 day in the refrigerator (leave the dough at room temperature for 1 hour before using). Roll the dough out using a rolling pin or pasta machine into the desired format, see Pasta Sfoglia (page 298).

Pasta di semola
FRESH SEMOLA RIMACINATA PASTA

MAKES 1 POUND (450G); SERVES 4

For this recipe, we use semola from Altamura in Puglia and water. That's it. It works because the semola has a very high protein content and does not need the eggs to help support the gluten structure. This is the dough we use to make orecchiette, cavatelli, or capunti.

YOU WILL NEED

- Large wooden surface
- Large resealable plastic bag to store dough and keep it moist
- Bench scraper
- Digital scale
- Table knife or gnocchi board

- 2½ cups (400g) semola flour (see Nota Bene)
- ¾ cup + 1½ tablespoons (200ml) water

NOTA BENE Both semola and semolina flour are made from durum wheat, which is a type of high-protein wheat. Semolina is somewhat coarse, similar to cornmeal, whereas semola rimacinata is much finer, because it's milled twice (which is what *rimacinata* means).

On a clean wooden surface, make a mound with the semola flour and create a wide well in the middle. Add the water to the well and mix it with a fork, working around the circumference of the well and incorporating all the flour into the water. Using the palms of your hands and your fingers, knead the dough until smooth, 10 to 15 minutes. As you knead the dough you will feel it tense up in your hands and become more difficult to mold as the gluten builds through your kneading. Rest the dough in a lightly floured resealable plastic bag for at least 30 minutes or for as long as 24 hours in the refrigerator.

CAVATELLI

Cut the dough into 30g pieces and roll each piece into ropes about ⅜ inch (1cm) thick. Cut the ropes into ⅜-inch (1cm) cubes. Use a table knife and press over each little cube—flattening it, dragging it, and causing it to roll onto itself, making a cavatello.

ORECCHIETTE

Roll, cut, and shape the dough as above. Stick your thumb under a cavatello and flip the pasta in the opposite way from the way it was rolled, almost making a cap over the tip of your thumb. Flick off the tip of your thumb and discover an *orecchietta* or a "little ear."

CAPUNTI

Cut the dough into 30g pieces and roll them into ropes about ⅜ inch (1cm) thick. Cut the rope into 1¼-inch (3cm) rods. Dig the tips of three of your fingers into each rod and flick the dough off your fingers by pressing it off onto the table, creating a pea pod shape known as capunti.

This pasta can be frozen flat on a baking sheet, then once frozen, transferred to an airtight container, and kept frozen for up to 2 months.

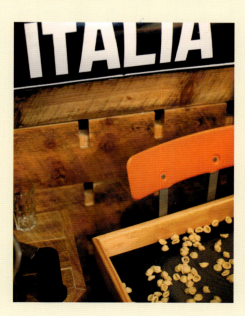

LA DISPENSA

Base di pomodoro
TERRONI TOMATO BASE

MAKES 1L SAUCE

This base is the workhorse for two major recipes in this book: the Classic Tomato Sauce (this page) and our pizza sauce (see pages 62 to 66). If you're one of those home cooks who is all about mise en place, well this recipe is always in the Terroni mise en place. *Always.*

We use San Marzano tomatoes from the Campania region for our tomato sauce and that's really the most important thing in the recipe. Unlike a lot of bigger operations, we do not put the tomatoes through a high-powered blender; we do it all using a hand-cranked food mill. If you don't have a food mill at home, it's possible to roll up your sleeves and press and squish the tomatoes with your hands. We use chopped fresh basil, salt, and olive oil. And that's it.

Please, please, we beg you, do not add dried oregano to your pizza sauce.

YOU WILL NEED

- Food mill with a fine disk

- 2 pounds 2½ ounces (960g) canned Italian San Marzano tomatoes (see Nota Bene)
- 1 teaspoon (5g) fine sea salt
- 2 tablespoons extra-virgin olive oil
- 20 to 25 fresh basil leaves

NOTA BENE We sell our own brand of San Marzanos online and in our shops. We ship across Canada (see Terroni Specialty Products, page 302). But we like Bianco brand, too.

Place a food mill over a bowl or pot. Gradually ladle the canned tomatoes into the food mill while turning the handle to process them. Continue this process until all the tomatoes have been milled. Once the tomatoes are milled, season the sauce with the salt and drizzle in the olive oil to enhance the flavour. Roughly chop the basil leaves and add them to the sauce. Give everything a good stir to incorporate the ingredients.

Store the sauce in the refrigerator up to 3 days, until you're ready to use it in other recipes.

Salsa di pomodoro
CLASSIC TOMATO SAUCE

SERVES 4

This recipe is all about keeping it simple. Whole crushed garlic cloves in olive oil. Once the whole house smells like fragrant garlic, add the tomatoes. You can either take the garlic cloves out or leave it in as a little surprise for someone. Let it simmer, with the lid half on. At the very end, add your fresh basil and . . . *buonanotte*!

Serve it with some delicious spaghetti or homemade Fresh Semola Rimacinata Pasta (page 293) or Fresh Egg Pasta (page 292). This is also one of those rare cases where you should not add Parmigiano-Reggiano at the end.

- ¼ cup + 2 tablespoons (90ml) extra-virgin olive oil
- 2 garlic cloves, smashed and peeled
- 4 cups (1L) Terroni Tomato Base (this page) or canned peeled San Marzano tomatoes milled through a food mill or crushed with your hands
- Fine sea salt and freshly ground black pepper
- 3 to 4 fresh basil leaves

In a large saucepan or Dutch oven, heat the olive oil and garlic cloves over medium heat and cook until the garlic becomes golden. Increase the heat to high, add the tomato base or the crushed tomatoes, and bring to a boil. Reduce the heat to medium-low, partially cover, and cook until the sauce starts to reduce and thicken, 20 to 30 minutes.

Season with salt to taste, keeping in mind that the Terroni tomato base already contains salt, and a pinch of freshly ground pepper. At the very end, add 3 to 4 basil leaves.

Stored in a sealed container, this sauce will keep in the freezer up to 30 days.

Besciamella
BÉCHAMEL SAUCE

MAKES 5 CUPS (1.2L)

This is something I would never have had as a child growing up, seeing as we were from the south of Italy. We did not use béchamel *in any recipes*. I remember finding it very strange the first time I saw it—combine flour and butter, add milk and heat, and . . . this creamy sauce happens. We were always more of a tomato sauce kind of family.

I was introduced to béchamel when my wife, Elena, first made a *pasta al forno* (pasta bake) using béchamel, ham, and Parmigiano-Reggiano. At home, the Mammoliti lasagna was not the traditional kind: We sometimes put meatballs in it, mozzarella, eggs, etc., which is more typical for a southern Italian lasagna. Nowadays, I prefer and love the traditional lasagne Bolognese made with béchamel. This sauce is also delicious in the Fennel Gratin (page 238).

- 1 quart (1L) whole milk
- 6 tablespoons (3 ounces/80g) unsalted butter
- ¾ cup (80g) tipo "00" flour
- 1 teaspoon fine sea salt
- Freshly grated nutmeg

In a medium saucepan, heat the milk over medium heat to just below boiling point, about 197°F (92°C) and set aside.

In a separate medium saucepan, melt the butter over medium heat until it starts to bubble, 2 to 3 minutes. Turn the heat off, add the flour, and mix with a wooden spoon until it looks like a paste. Return to medium heat. Slowly add the warm milk a little at a time, stirring constantly with a whisk until the sauce thickens and begins to bubble, 4 to 5 minutes.

Remove from the heat and season with the salt and some nutmeg. Cover the surface of the béchamel with some plastic wrap to prevent it from forming a skin. Allow hot air to escape through the sides or by puncturing holes in the wrap with a sharp pointy knife. Béchamel can be stored in the refrigerator for up to 2 days.

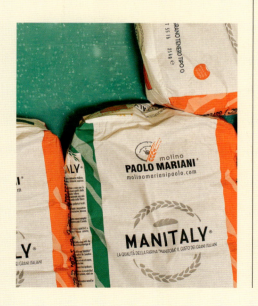

Brodo di pollo
CHICKEN BROTH

MAKES ABOUT 4 QUARTS (4L)

I love making brodo! And I can't emphasize enough how simple or rewarding it is.

My mother would usually make brodo with the chicken bones. So, when I started making brodo myself, I would get this beautiful, whole organic chicken, put the whole thing in the pot, let it simmer for hours, and then either make risotto the next day or freeze the broth in ice cube trays and add them to sauces.

Bring it to a strong boil in the beginning and skim off the foam with a large spoon. We usually use older chickens that are great for stock since they have more flavour. The meat extracted from the broth can be used in the Chicken Salad (page 242).

I was so proud of my brodo that when my meat supplier Rob Bielak brought his eighty-year-old mom to meet me, I shared with her how I make my brodo and I confessed to her that I use a whole chicken, and she just looked straight at me and said: "I use 2 chickens!"

YOU WILL NEED

- 1 large stockpot
- Digital scale
- Fine sieve
- Cheesecloth

- 1 whole chicken/hen, or 2½ pounds (1.2kg) chicken parts
- 3 celery stalks (250g), cut into roughly 2- to 3-inch (5 to 7.5cm) pieces
- 3 small carrots (250g), cut into roughly 2- to 3-inch (5 to 7.5cm) pieces
- 1 or 2 leftover Parmigiano-Reggiano rinds
- 1 large white onion, peeled and halved
- 1 teaspoon black peppercorns
- Kosher salt

In a large stockpot, combine the chicken, celery, carrots, cheese rinds, onion, and peppercorns. Add cold water to cover, at least 5 quarts (5L). Gently bring to a boil over medium heat, skimming off any foam from the top. Reduce the heat to low, partially cover (put a wooden spoon under one side of the lid to prop it open), and simmer very gently for 4 hours.

After the stock has reduced a little and the flavours have developed, taste and season with salt. Achieving the right salt level is the most important part in a successful broth. Extract the meat and vegetables and set aside. Let the broth cool completely. Pour the liquid through a sieve covered with cheesecloth to clarify.

The broth can be stored in the refrigerator for 3 to 4 days or frozen for up to 1 month. You can also pour the broth into ice trays, freeze, and store in the freezer to be used for additional flavour injections in soups, broths, or stews. The chicken meat can be picked from the bones and used in recipes.

LA DISPENSA

Salsiccia di Vincenzo
TERRONI SAUSAGE

MAKES ABOUT 5½ POUNDS (2.5KG)

This is something that my parents used to make in the basement when we were growing up. We always had fresh sausage at home, but they would also hang sausage in the cantina (our cold room), which would dry out and eventually turn into cured sausage. When we opened the restaurant, it was kind of natural that I asked my dad, Vincenzo, if he could start producing sausage for Terroni. In the early days, he was making it at home, but then we moved his operation to the restaurant. My father always said, "Pork is the only meat where the price never changed since I immigrated here in the fifties!" Back when we began, we were making about 100 pounds (49kg) a week; today we make about *ten times* that! At the restaurants you can find this sausage in our Panini con Salsiccia e Cime di Rapa (page 89); Garganelli Geppetto (page 183); Pappardelle alla Iosa (page 163); Salsiccia e Patate (page 202); and Semicalda di Terroni (page 205).

A note on *tastasal* ("to test the salt"): To determine the level of salt in a homemade sausage mixture, it is customary to fry a small patty of the sausage meat, place it in some bread, and eat it as a sandwich. Some areas of northern Italy check the salt by making something called *riso tastasal*, which is risotto made with fresh sausage.

YOU WILL NEED
- Meat grinder
- Sharp boning knife
- Sausage stuffer (optional)
- Digital scale (optional)

- 5½ pounds (2.5kg) boneless pork shoulder
- 3 tablespoons white wine
- ⅓ cup + 1 tablespoon (40g) Spanish sweet paprika
- 1½ teaspoons (3g) crushed dried Calabrian red chili
- 2 tablespoons + 1 teaspoon (40g) fine sea salt
- 2½ teaspoons (5g) freshly ground black pepper
- 8 feet (2.5m) hog casings (optional), 1¼ to 1⅜ inches (3 to 3.5cm) in diameter
- Lemon juice (optional)

Clean the pork shoulder, removing any cartilage. Cut it into 2- to 2½-inch (5 to 6.5cm) cubes. Using the coarsest plate (⅜-inch/10mm) minimum of a meat grinder, grind the pork meat onto a large board or into a large bowl. If you want to achieve a more "artisanal" product, you can cut 20 percent of your meat by hand into ¼- to ⅜-inch (5mm to 1cm) cubes and mix in with the rest.

Add the wine, paprika, Calabrian chili, salt, and pepper to the ground meat and mix well using your hands. If using the sausage meat loose, pack it in small bags and vacuum-seal if possible. The sausage can be kept in the fridge for 2 to 3 days maximum and in the freezer for up to 3 months.

If you plan to case the sausage into links, soak the casings in water and some lemon juice, then wash by running water through the tubes and squeezing out excess water. Twist one end of the casing into a knot to keep the meat in. If you have a sausage attachment for your stand mixer, use that. Otherwise you will need some sort of manual sausage stuffing kit. Pull the casing all the way up on the sausage funnel and push the sausage meat in. Use butcher twine to tie off in links weighing between 90g and 100g. Lightly pierce the links with a needle to release any air. Store as one long rope, with the links just separated by the butcher twine ties.

Pasta sfoglia
PUFF PASTRY

MAKES ABOUT 2 POUNDS (1KG)

As people know, puff pastry can be intimidating, which is why most people buy prepared puff pastry. But the commercial offering is rarely as good as it needs to be. Back when we were a small restaurant and we wanted to try out some dishes with puff pastry, we were really intimidated and thought that it was too much work and would take too much time.

Giovanna took on the challenge and made this puff pastry so delicious that we knew it was worth the effort. But I'm not going to lie, the moment we bought a dough sheeter in 2013, I made the sign of the cross on my forehead because the time you save with the machine vs. doing it by hand is *significant*. The machine allowed us to make much larger quantities. But obviously, you don't have a sheeter at home!

The recipe here is very straightforward and foolproof and we highly recommend you make the full amount, package what you don't need, and freeze so that you always have fresh puff pastry at hand.

This puff pastry recipe is used for Escarole Tarts with Poached Eggs (page 51) and the Savoury Puff Pastry Snacks (page 111), and Pastry Cream Puffs (page 269).

YOU WILL NEED

- Food processor
- Stand mixer fitted with the paddle
- Baking sheet
- Large plastic bag
- Parchment paper
- Rolling pin

BASE DOUGH

- 4 ¾ cups (575g) bread flour, plus more for dusting
- 4 tablespoons (2 ounces/60g) unsalted butter, cold and cut into ⅜-inch (1cm) cubes
- 2 teaspoons (10g) fine sea salt
- 1 cup + 2 tablespoons (270g) cold water
- 2 teaspoons fresh lemon juice

BUTTER SQUARE

- 1 pound (455g) unsalted butter, chilled but pliable, cut into ⅜-inch (1cm) cubes

DAY 1: 6 P.M.

Make the base dough: In a food processor, mix the flour, butter, and salt. Blitz until coarse crumbs form. Add the cold water and lemon juice and pulse 4 to 5 times just until it comes together. Turn the dough (also known as the détrempe) onto a lightly floured work surface and knead it just until it comes together. Press it to form a 3-inch (8cm) square about ⅜ inch (1cm) thick. Tightly wrap the dough in plastic wrap and refrigerate overnight or until chilled, at least 2 hours.

Make the butter square: In a stand mixer fitted with the paddle, cream the butter for 2 to 3 minutes. Remove the butter from the mixer and place on parchment paper. Shape the butter into a 5-inch (12cm) square about ¼ inch (5mm) thick. Wrap in the parchment and refrigerate until the next day.

DAY 2: 8 A.M.

Remove the butter square from the refrigerator and keep at room temperature to soften slightly.

DAY 2: 9 A.M.

Remove the base dough from the refrigerator and from its plastic →

wrap, placing it directly on a lightly floured work surface. Using the rolling pin, roll the dough into a 7-inch (18cm) square. When rolling, move the rolling pin from edge to edge, making sure you have just enough flour underneath, so it never sticks to the surface. Place the dough so that one of the corners is pointing at you. Remove the butter from the parchment and place it at the centre of the square with its base facing toward you. Now fold the corners of the dough over the butter square to cover it. You may need to stretch and pull the dough slightly to cover the butter square completely. Dust with more flour and use your rolling pin to elongate the square to form a rectangle directly in front of you until it reaches a ⅜-inch (1cm) thickness. With a short side facing you, fold one end of the rectangle one-quarter of the way toward the middle and bring the other end up to meet it. Fold the dough in half by flipping the bottom fold over the top fold (like closing a book). You should now have 4 layers of dough, also known as a bookfold or fourfold. Wrap this with plastic wrap and refrigerate for 2 hours.

DAY 2: 11 A.M.

Remove the dough from the refrigerator and from its plastic wrap. Place it directly on the lightly floured surface with a short side facing you. Very lightly dust the dough with flour and use your rolling pin to flatten the rectangle to a ⅜-inch (1cm) thickness. When rolling, be firm and strong, applying even pressure from the bottom to the top of the rectangle. Fold one end of the dough a quarter into the rectangle toward the middle and then bring in the other end of the rectangle to meet it. Make another bookfold. You should now have 4 layers of dough. Wrap it in plastic wrap and refrigerate for 2 more hours.

DAY 2: 1 P.M.

Remove the dough from the fridge and from its plastic wrap. Place it directly on the lightly floured surface with a short side facing you. Very lightly dust the dough with flour and use your rolling pin to flatten the rectangle to a ⅜-inch (1cm) thickness. When rolling, be firm and strong, applying even pressure from the bottom to the top of the rectangle. Fold one end of the dough a quarter into the rectangle toward the middle and then bring in the other end of the rectangle to meet it. Make another bookfold. You should now have 4 layers of dough. Wrap it in plastic wrap and refrigerate for 2 more hours.

DAY 2: 3 P.M.

The dough is now ready to be used and can be divided into the amount you need. If you wish, you can also portion it and freeze it, tightly wrapped, for up to 2 months. Thaw in the fridge overnight before using.

Crema pasticcera

PASTRY CREAM

MAKES ABOUT 5½ CUPS (1.5KG)

This is our workhorse pastry cream that we use for fruit tarts, Maritozzi (page 32), and Zeppole di San Giuseppe (page 278), too. Our current version of pastry cream is inspired from renowned pastry chef Debora Vena. She was with us for the summer of 2023 and shared the recipe from her family's patisserie in Verona. It is simple and tastes deliciously genuine.

- 2 tablespoons + 1 teaspoon (20g) cornstarch
- 2 tablespoons + 1 teaspoon (20g) rice starch (see Nota Bene)
- 10 tablespoons (125g) granulated sugar
- 4 egg yolks (80g total)
- Seeds of ½ vanilla bean
- 1 quart + 3 tablespoons (1L) whole milk
- 3 tablespoons + 1 teaspoon (50ml) heavy cream
- 2 tablespoons (25g) unsalted butter, cut into cubes

NOTA BENE We use rice starch for this recipe and it's ideal, but it is difficult to find. You may substitute with more cornstarch.

In a small bowl, whisk together the cornstarch, rice starch, 6 tablespoons (75g) sugar, and the egg yolks until combined.

In a saucepan, combine the remaining 4 tablespoons (50g) sugar, the vanilla, milk, and cream and bring to a boil over medium heat. Remove from the heat.

Add the cornstarch/egg yolk mixture to the hot milk mixture, whisking constantly until the mixture is smooth. Return the pan to medium-low heat and continue cooking, stirring constantly with a whisk, until the pastry cream just comes to a boil and thickens. Remove from the heat and whisk in the cubed butter until well combined. Transfer to a bowl and let come to room temperature; place plastic wrap directly on top of cream to prevent a crust forming, and refrigerate until ready to use. This will keep up to 3 days.

TERRONI SPECIALTY PRODUCTS

The below items are all tried and true, tested by the Terroni team over many years.

Most can be found on our website (labottegaditerroni.com), and we ship throughout Canada.

DUE VITTORIE BALSAMIC VINEGAR

We love this on tagliata di manzo or ripe strawberries. It has a beautiful viscosity, a great balsamic vinegar for a great price.

ACQUERELLO CARNAROLI RICE

This Carnaroli rice allows you to make a fantastic risotto every single time. It is aged for one to seven years and has all the benefits of brown rice but in white rice form.

MASSERIA DAUNA WHOLE CANNED TOMATOES

These hand-picked tomatoes are sweet and fragrant and deliver summer in every jar.

TERRONI PEPERONCINI PICCANTI

We have been importing these for years. They are so addictive, we know many fans have them shipped all over the world. They make any dish better!

TERRONI EXTRA-VIRGIN OLIVE OIL

Artisanal, 100% extra-virgin olive oil, made by a friend of ours with the Coratina olive in an organic olive grove just outside Bari. The olives are turned into oil and bottled within hours of being harvested. The taste is spicy and pungent and offers a super low acidity, between 0.24% and 0.27%. We use it in almost everything we do. Quite literally the taste of Terroni.

TERRONI PLUM TOMATOES

We work with 3 to 4 family-run suppliers in Puglia and Campania to select the tomato crop that best suits our recipes and matches the quality we demand. The tomatoes are organically grown under the sun and packed full of flavour. The raw ingredient of every tomato-based sauce (and raw on our pizza).

LA PASTA DI CAMERINO

"The best ingredients, slow and careful processing." Here are some of our favourite shapes:

Spaghettoni

This is one of our favourite shapes because of its bite and texture. Try it simply with aglio e olio or with a pomodoro sauce to maximize flavour.

Rigatoni

A must in our sugo della domenica but delicious in any sauce. A great home substitute for the Terroni homemade rigatoni. Also a star of the Arcobaleno (page 164).

Paccheri

We love these in a fishy sauce—lobster or mussels work amazingly.

Calamarata

Calamarata is a nice substitute for spaghetti if you're looking for a short alternative. The perfect pasta for octopus.

Linguine

Amazing with clams or any fish sauce.

Orecchiette

So good with cime di rapa . . . and lamb ragu or a light tomato sauce with ricotta salata. We love this pasta's chewiness and bite

Penne

These have forever been the kid's pasta on our menus, but the taste of these penne will surprise you and have you making puttanesca in no time.

TERRONI SPECIALTY PRODUCTS

OLIVE TERMITE DI BITETTO

This is a pulpy olive, delicious on its own or fantastic eaten with fish or vegetable dishes.

OLIVE BELLA DI CERIGNOLA

This giant of an olive is hand-picked. It is crunchy and fresh and makes an amazing aperitivo.

CUORI DI CARCIOFI

These artichokes are the last to be harvested and are processed within eight hours of being picked. They are delicious right out of the jar or make a great addition to pizzas, focaccia, or salads.

L'ANTICO GRANAIO TARALLI

We carry a variety, savoury and sweet, of these artisanal taralli. Extremely addictive.

MOLINO MARIANI FARINE

A small mill in the Marche region of Italy that produces the majority of the flours we use. They have fields that are dedicated to growing wheat for Terroni and we are proud to be able to offer the retail version in convenient 1-kilogram (2¼-pound) packs.

MALDON SALT

This is Cosimo's favourite finishing salt. He adds it to pretty much everything.

PENTOLE AGNELLI

We use these pans in our restaurants, and they are fantastic. A rewarding pan to have in your home kitchen. Great for tossing pastas or for small batch sauces.

MATTARELLO DA SFOGLINA

This long (43 to 47 inches/110 to 120cm) pasta-making rolling pin (birch or fir) is handmade by a local artisan. Five stars.

303

ACKNOWLEDGEMENTS

I would like to dedicate this book to my father, Vincenzo, my hero, who taught me to work hard, to be honest, to be respectful, to always look after your family, to be on time, and to say good morning to each person you encounter. He dedicated his life to his family. The man I admire most in life.

I feel really fortunate to be able to create and keep this book for my family in the years to come, and grateful for the key people that were a part of this. Those who are family, those who are extended family, some that I have worked with for fifteen to twenty-plus years, and new friends I have shared this special trip with. I hope that everyone gets how deeply personal this project is for me.

Like the recipes in the book, these are some of my personal ingredients, my materia prima, and some of my personal stories.

To my beautiful Elena, the most important person in my life, you have been with me from the start. You have given me room to grow, grow some more, expand, expand some more, opening after opening, put up with my continued distractions because I'm always thinking of the restaurants. Damn!!! How do you put up with all my shit?

But mostly you gave me the strength when I was sick. *La mia roccia!*

You moved to Canada from Italy to be by my side, for love, and I never forget that.

Amore, grazie, I love you.

To Simona, Sofia, Matteo, and Olivia, you inspire me every day to do better and be better and to continue to be a good example. I am so proud of each and every one of you.

I hope you all find love and happiness. Take risks, challenge yourself, fall, and get up. Don't be afraid of failure. Life is dear, live every day to the fullest.

My mamma, Rita, you taught me to be empathetic, to be nice and kind, and share everything you have. Thank you for showing me your traditions, your stories; they inspired me to do what I do. You have made me who I am today.

Anna, my sister who left the teaching world to enter the crazy restaurant world (sorry about that), and to my brother Vince, who has been with me almost since day one, thank you for thinking things really really really really all the way through.

Couldn't have done it without you two.

I love you and appreciate you both more than you can imagine.

Fernando, my brother, who is not in the business but has always supported us and always has thoughtful suggestions.

Joseph, my oldest brother, never forgotten and always with us.

My second family, Titina, Beppe, Betta, and Costantino, spending every summer together, travelling, eating, drinking, laughing, and spending lots of time together as one big family.

Thank you for your acceptance and love.

For Paolo, my best friend, my partner, you have been with me from the first day and every day since. I miss you dearly.

Shereen, who never wanted to sweep the floors when she worked

at Queen. Today, not only a best friend, a true force, and my partner in Los Angeles.

Giovanna, the messiest cook I know, yet the most reliable, and my creative go-to. You have come a long way. Know that this book would have never gotten done without you, Gio. From the bottom of my heart.

Patti, from the first time you came to me about a book in 2018, and me saying NO (how many times?). You convinced me or just wore me down, or the Peruvian in you knew it was time. I know that you are always looking out for me with your heart or armor. And did I say that you are my most favourite Peruvian in the whole world.

My buddy Dale Heslip, although not initially involved in the book, you were the important missing piece. You just jumped into the deep end, my quarterback, you ran with it and showed us your talents. You brought us together creatively and brought that out in each of us. I now understand everything there is to know about natural light and shadow.

Meredith, I never met someone who, in such a brief period of time (once you took the British out of me), understood who I am, what I am all about, where I come from, and who just "got" the Terroni DNA.

And oh yeah, she did it mainly all online—we only met a few times in person.

You just get it, that is talent.

Small Design, Andrew DiRosa, you are the guy who knows the true Terroni gene in every way, superb design and always bang on; and to Bartosz Gawdzik for all your support.

ACKNOWLEDGEMENTS

Our trusted photographer, Jim Norton, for your keen food eye and history with Terroni. Simon Baker, Jim's right hand and the make-it-happen guy, and Tonya Norton for making the schedules work over and over.

Simon & Schuster, Kevin Hanson: Thank you for your persistence and belief by just giving us everything we wanted. To Kirsten Hanson for moving it all forward and putting up with all of us.

Thank you to my friends and longtime regulars, who entered the doors of 720 Queen West and trusted me and followed us through the birth of every location and continue to support us. You help me get better and I will never stop learning.

To the old-school crew: Kari Watson (you are my right hand), Larry (always there for me), and Stephanie D'Andrea, Vince Saroli, Franco Rovazzi, Linda Maione, Tina Debus, Marco Bruno, Johnson Kathiran, Gong Chen, Selvano (Atta) Thiruchelvam, Kumar Sr. Supiramaniyam, Suthan Suppaiah, Francesco Laudini, Fabio Moro, Audley (the Man) Ennis, Shelly Ann Phillip and Bianca Shtapler, Ravi Arumugam, Sanjeevan Sriganesan, Kumar Jr. Vinasithamby, Remo Tantalo, Christine Peever, Music man DJ Ray Gillespie, Valentina and Walter Hysen, Cosi JR. Pagliacolo (LA), Carlo Rota (stand-in owner when he is at Queen St. and basically the guy who got me into the business), Claudia Iacobazzi, Jessie (Jessica Allen to the TV world), Nic Carlino, Ruth Torres, Albion Macleod, Cousin Nat and Andrea Mammoliti, Ersilia Virtu', David Mattachioni, Flaminia Cardoni, Luca Rotatori, Master Baker Giuliano Pediconi, Daniel Mezzolo, Costantino Guzzo, Ruben Rapetti, Francesco Giorgio, Megan Woodhouse.

Ralph Giannone and Pina Petricone (Giannone Petricone Associates).

Making my dreams come to life since 1992. I asked, and you designed beautiful, special spaces that only get better with time.

Stephen Alexander (my best friend, business partner, co-conspirator, and travel mate), the future still waits for more?

To the nuova squadra Ruben Rapetti, Francesco Giorgio, Megan Woodhouse, Leah Del Vecchio, let's go!!!

To everyone, at every location: Dishwashers, our GMs, AGMs, event coordinators, production people, floor managers, bussers, food runners, hosts, bartenders, supervisors, barbacks, expo, servers, line cooks, pizza makers, bakers, chefs, pasta makers, pastry team, bread makers, prep cooks, butchers, our entire marketing team, HR, packagers, drivers, security, warehouse staff, head office, accounting. You are the backbone of Terroni.

To all the amazing Italian winemakers whom I look forward to seeing every year and our continued relationships.

To my olive oil producer, Paolo Lo Monaco. Almost every dish has your hard work and care for the land in it. The Best Olive Oil Ever.

Thank you to the two teachers at De la Salle who didn't know how to teach outside the box, especially the math and English teacher who called me stupid. Thank you for the inspiration.

My grade school teacher at St. Monica's, Mr. Peter Artkin. This guy was instrumental in showing me the joys of learning, sports, and experiencing life, like summer canoe trips in Algonquin park, portaging, and how to make your own canoe paddle.

Mr. Joe Totino, the only bank manager who ever really helped

me when I started and his son Giancarlo Totino.

Dr. Elisa Venier and Chris Zavarce, two very special friends who helped me medically and spiritually.

Dr. Marcus Burnstein (St. Mikes), Dr. Jolie Ringash (PMH), Dr. Malcolm Moore (PMH), for being experts in your field. Thank you.

The original fam jammers: Heslip family (Lukino and Lilah), Alexander family (Bella), Sorbara-Korngold clan, the Harvey family (the blonde family), the Ross family.

I would like to end where it all began, with all my parents' friends and families that immigrated to Toronto in the late '50s and '60s from San Giorgio Morgeto, Calabria. Most with not a penny in their pockets and very little education. They worked hard, risked their lives to cross the ocean to find a better life in a new country, where they didn't speak the language. They stayed close, they kept their traditions. Our big family gatherings were weekly. It was such a beautiful environment to see how they helped one another in growing their businesses, families, and friendships. They were a true inspiration to every one of us (their kids) and helped us to create a new path molded by their values, traditions, honour, and love for family. My deep respect.

INDEX

Page references in *italics* refer to photos of recipes.

Allen, Jessica, 161
Always on Holiday, 121
antipasti, apristomaco e insalate (starters, openers, and salads), 127–41
aperitivo, 93–116. *See also* beverages
Apricot Jam Tart, *44*, *45–46*, *46*
Apulian Bread, 80–83, *81*, *83*

Baccalà, *194*, 195
Baked Oyster Mushroom Salad, 128, *129*
Bardini, Gianni, 86
Bari-Style Focaccia, 76–79, *77–79*
Base Brioche, 291
Base di Pomodoro, 294
beans, chickpeas, and lentils
    Chickpea Pancake with Beet Salad, 132–34, *133*
    Cosimo's Mom's White Bean and Chard Stew, *150*, 151
    Elena's Green Beans, 226, *227*
    Fava Bean Purée and Dandelion, 140, *141*
    Lentil Soup with 'Nduja, 148, *149*
    Pasta and Beans, *146*, 147
    Sausage, Bean, and Radicchio Stew, *204*, 205
    Tria with Chickpeas, *158*, 159–60
Béchamel Sauce, 294–95
beef and lamb
    Braised Beef Roulade, *210*, 211–12, *212–13*
    Cosimo's Sunday Sauce with Rigatoni, 174–76, *175–77*
    Florentine Steak, Terroni-Style, 218, *219*
    Lamb Shanks, *216*, 217
    Meatballs, 206–8, *207*
    Terri's Swiss Chard, Meat, and Cheese Casserole, *244*, 245
Besciamella, 294–95
beverages
    cocktails, 118–21, *119–21*
    wine, 122–25
Biscotti da Inzuppo, *30*, 31
Biscotti di Mamma Rita, 274, *275*
Bombolini Salati, 108, *109*
Bomboloni, 36–39, *37*, *38*
Braised Beef Roulade, *210*, 211–12, *212–13*

Braised Greens, *224*, 225
Brasciole di Manzo, *210*, 211–12, *212–13*
bread and dough
    Apulian Bread, 80–83, *81*, *83*
    Bari-Style Focaccia, 76–79, *77–79*
    Bread and Anchovies, 104, *105*
    Bread Crisps, 290, *290*
    Ciabatta Buns, *84*, 85
    Fresh Egg Pasta, 292
    Fresh Semola Rimacinata Pasta, 293
    Fried Dough Pockets, *106*, 107
    Long Thin Breadsticks, *94*, 95–97, *96*, *97*
    Round Breadsticks, *98*, 99–100, *100*, *101*
    Sourdough Starter, 287–88
    Terroni Pizza Dough, 288–90, *289*
breakfast, 27–59
Brioche Dough, 291
Brodo di Pollo, 295
Bruschetta all'Olio, 290, *290*
Buon per Te, 121

Calamarata with Octopus Sauce (Calamarata al Sugo di Polpo), *178*, 179
Calamari alla Griglia, *130*, 131
Calita, 120, *120*
Cannoli, Traditional Sicilian, 262–64, *263*, *265*
capunti dough, 293
Carlino, Nicholas "Nicolino," 209
cavatelli dough, 293
Cavinona Wine Agency, 18, 122–25
cheese
    Fennel Gratin, 238, *239*
    Fontina Cheese Soufflé, *236*, 237
    Fried Mozzarella Sandwiches, *138*, 139
    Frittata with 'Nduja, Onion, and Fontina, *58*, 59
    Gnocchi with Tomato Sauce and Fresh Ricotta, 184, *185*
    Pizza with Anchovies, Capers, and Fior di Latte, 66, *68–69*
    Pizza with Mozzarella di Bufala, *64*, 65
    "Rainbow Rigatoni," Buffalo Mozzarella in, 164, *165*
    Ricotta Cheesecake, *260*, 261
    Terri's Swiss Chard, Meat, and Cheese Casserole, *244*, 245

Titina's Eggplant Parmigiana, 196, *197*
    in Traditional Sicilian Cannoli, 262–64, *263*, *265*
    See also pizza
Chestnut Soup, 152, *153*
Chewy Almond Cookies, *276*, 277
Chicken Broth, 295
Chicken Salad, 242, *243*
Chickpea Pancake with Beet Salad, 132–34, *133*
Choux, Fried, 278–80, *279–81*
Ciabatta di Terroni, *84*, 85
Ciccio Farcito con Verdure, *70*, 71
Ciceri e Tria, *158*, 159–60
Cime di Rapa Saltate in Padella, *228*, 229
Classic Tomato Sauce, 294
cocktails, 118–21, *119–21*
colazione (breakfast), 27–59
contorni (sides), 221–39
Cookies, Chewy Almond, *276*, 277
Cookies, Dunking, *30*, 31
Cookies, Mamma Rita's, 274, *275*
Corn Crisps, Rita's, *102*, 103
Cornetti, 40–43, *41–43*
Cosimo's Mom's White Bean and Chard Stew, *150*, 151
Cosimo's Sunday Sauce with Rigatoni, 174–76, *175–77*
cream and custard
    Flavoured Custard Tarts, 270–72, *271*
    Italian Donuts Filled with Pastry Cream, 36–39, *37*, *38*
    Nutella and Custard Tart, 266, *267*
    Pastry Cream, 301
    Pastry Cream Puffs, *268*, 269
Cream of Fennel Soup, *154*, 155
Crema Pasticcera, 301
Crostata alla Marmellata di Albicocche, *44*, *45–46*, *46*
Crostata di Nutella e Crema, 266, *267*
Crostini di Mais, *102*, 103

Danese Salata, *110*, 112
dolci (sweets), 251–85
Donuts, Italian, Filled with Pastry Cream or Nutella, 36–39, *37*, *38*
Duck Confit Ravioli, 168–70, *169*
Dunking Cookies, *30*, 31

Egg Pasta, Fresh, 292
Eggplant Parmigiana, Titina's, 196, *197*

307

INDEX

eggs
Eggs in Purgatory, 56, *57*
Escarole Tarts with Poached Eggs, *50*, 51–52
Frittata with 'Nduja, Onion, and Fontina, *58*, 59
Scrambled Egg Sandwich, *54*, 55
Spaghetti Frittata, *248*, 249
Whipped Egg with Espresso, 28, *29*
Zucchini and Egg Hash, *232*, 233
Elena's Green Beans, 226, *227*
Escarole Tarts with Poached Eggs, *50*, 51–52

Fagiolini alla Elena, 226, *227*
Farinata con Insalata di Barbabietole, 132–34, *133*
Fava Bean Purée and Dandelion (Fave e Cicoria), 140, *141*
Fennel Gratin, 238, *239*
Fennel Soup, Cream of, *154*, 155
Finocchio Gratinato, 238, *239*
Fiorentina Stile Terroni, 218, *219*
first courses, 157–85
fish and shellfish
Anchovy-Filled Panzerotti, 75
Bread and Anchovies, 104, *105*
Calamarata with Octopus Sauce, *178*, 179
in Fried Mini Panini, 108, *109*
in Fried Pizza Pockets, 75
Fried Seafood, 188, *189*
Grilled Calamari, *130*, 131
Italian Niçoise, 136, *137*
Mamma Rita's Salted Cod, *194*, 195
Pizza with Anchovies, Capers, and Fior di Latte, 66, *68–69*
Seafood in Parchment Packets, 192, *193*
Seared Octopus, *190*, 191
Flavoured Custard Tarts, 270–72, *271*
Florentine Steak, Terroni-Style, 218, *219*
Focaccia Barese, 76–79, *77–79*
Fontina Cheese Soufflé, *236*, 237
Fresh Egg Pasta, 292
Fresh Semola Rimacinata Pasta, 293
Fried Choux, 278–80, *279–81*
Fried Dough Pockets, *106*, 107
Fried Mini Panini, 108, *109*
Fried Mozzarella Sandwiches, *138*, 139
Fried Pizza Pockets, *72–75*, *73–75*
Fried Seafood, 188, *189*
Frittata alla 'Nduja Cipolle e Fontina, *58*, 59
Frittata di Spaghetti, *248*, 249
Frittura di Pesce e Frutti di Mare, 188, *189*
Funghi Assoluti, 128, *129*

Garganelli Geppetto, *182*, 183
Gattò di Patate, 246, *247*
Geppetto's Sausage and Dandelion Garganelli, *182*, 183
Giannone, Ralph, 273
gli avanzi (leftovers), 241–49
Gnocchi with Tomato Sauce and Fresh Ricotta (Gnocchi alla Simi), 184, *185*
Gnocco Fritto, *106*, 107
Good for You, 121
Green Beans, Elena's, 226, *227*
greens
Braised Greens, *224*, 225
Chard Stew, Cosimo's Mom's White Bean and, *150*, 151
Dandelion, Fava Bean Purée and, 140, *141*
Dandelion Garganelli, Geppetto's Sausage and, *182*, 183
Endive with Olives, Pine Nuts, and Raisins, Titina's, 234, *235*
Escarole Tarts with Poached Eggs, *50*, 51–52
Fennel Gratin, 238, *239*
Fennel Soup, Cream of, *154*, 155
Greens, White Pizza with, *70*, 71
Radicchio Stew, Sausage, Bean, and, *204*, 205
Rapini, Sautéed, *228*, 229
Rapini Sandwiches, Sausage and, *88*, 89
Swiss Chard, Meat, and Cheese Casserole, Terri's, *244*, 245
Grilled Calamari, *130*, 131
Grissini, *94*, 95–97, *96*, *97*

Il Tiramisù di Terroni, *284*, 285
Impasto per Pizza di Terroni, 288–90, *289*
Insalata di Pollo, 242, *243*
I Ricciarelli di Sud Forno, *276*, 277
Italian Croissants, 40–43, *41–43*
Italian Donuts Filled with Pastry Cream or Nutella, 36–39, *37*, *38*
Italian Niçoise, 136, *137*

jam and marmalade
Apricot Jam Tart, *44*, 45–46, *46*
Italian Croissants (with marmalade), 43
in Sweet Buns, 32–35, *33*, *34*

La Coccola, 120, *120*
La Dispensa, 286–301
Lamb Shanks, *216*, 217
leftovers, 241–49
Lentil Soup with 'Nduja, 148, *149*

Lievito Madre, 287–88
Long Thin Breadsticks, *94*, 95–97, *96*, *97*

Mamma Rita's Cookies, 274, *275*
Mamma Rita's Potatoes and Peppers, 222, *223*
Mamma Rita's Salted Cod, *194*, 195
Mammoliti, Cosimo, biographical information. *See also* Terroni Group
Maritozzi, 32–35, *33*, *34*
Mau, Bruce, 47
Meatballs, 206–8, *207*
meats. *See* beef and lamb; fish and shellfish; pork and sausage; poultry
Minestrone, 144, *145*
Mozzarella in Carrozza, *138*, 139
mushrooms
Baked Oyster Mushroom Salad, 128, *129*
in "Pasta Mayhem," *162*, 163
Pizza with Button Mushrooms and Soppressata, 62, *63*

Neapolitan Potato Cake, 246, *247*
Nizzarda, 136, *137*
Nonna Lucia's Cake, 282, *283*
Nutella
and Custard Tart, 266, *267*
Italian Croissants with, 43
Italian Donuts Filled with, 36–39, *37*, *38*

Orecchiette con Cime di Rapa, 180, *181*
orecchiette dough, 293
Orecchiette with Rapini, 180, *181*

Pan Brioche, 291
Pane e Acciughe, 104, *105*
Pane Pugliese, 80–83, *81*, *83*
Panettone Classico, 252–58, *253–59*
Panettone French Toast, 48, *49*
Panettone Gastronomico, 115–16
Panini con Branzino e Peperonata, 90, *91*
Panini con Salsiccia e Cime di Rapa, *88*, 89
Panino all'Uovo, *54*, 55
Panzerotti, *72–75*, *73–75*
Pappardelle alla Iosa, *162*, 163
pappardelle dough, 292
Parmigiana di Titina, 196, *197*
pasta
Calamarata with Octopus Sauce, *178*, 179
Egg Pasta, Fresh (Pasta all'Uovo), 292

INDEX

Garganelli, Geppetto's Sausage and Dandelion, *182*, 183

Gnocchi with Tomato Sauce and Fresh Ricotta, 184, *185*

Orecchiette with Rapini, 180, *181*

Pasta and Beans (Pasta e Fagioli), *146*, 147

"Pasta Mayhem": Sausage, Peas, and Mushrooms, *162*, 163

"Rainbow Rigatoni," 164, *165*

Ravioli, Duck Confit, 168–70, *169*

Rigatoni, Cosimo's Sunday Sauce with, 174–76, *175–77*

Semola Rimacinata Pasta, Fresh (Pasta di Semola), 293

Spaghetti Frittata, *248*, 249

Spaghetti with Lemon Sauce, *166*, 167

Spinach Pasta, 292–93

Tria with Chickpeas, *158*, 159–60

Pasta agli Spinaci, 292–93

Pasta Sfoglia, 298–300, *299, 300*

Pasticcio di Zucchine con le Uova, *232*, 233

Pasticciotti Leccesi, 270–72, *271*

Pastry Cream, 301

Pastry Cream Puffs, *268*, 269

Peperonata alla Piera, 230, *231*

peppers

Mamma Rita's Potatoes and Peppers, 222, *223*

Piera's Stewed Peppers, 230, *231*

Sea Bass and Red Pepper Sandwiches, 90, *91*

Pesce al Cartoccio, 192, *193*

Piera's Stewed Peppers, 230, *231*

Pipi e Patate alla Rita, 222, *223*

pizza

Fried Pizza Pockets, *72–75*, 73–75

Pizza with Anchovies, Capers, and Fior di Latte (Pizza Santo Spirito), 66, *68–69*

Pizza with Button Mushrooms and Soppressata (Pizza San Giorgio), 62, *63*

Pizza with Mozzarella di Bufala (Pizza Bufalina), *64*, 65

Terroni Pizza Dough, 288–90, *289*

White Pizza with Greens, *70*, 71

pizza e pane (pizza, focaccia, panini), 61–91. *See also* bread and dough; pizza; sandwiches

Pizzette, *110*, 111

Polpette, 206–8, *207*

Polpo Scottato, *190*, 191

poolish, about, 288

pork and sausage

in Braised Beef Roulade, *210*, 211–12, *212–13*

in Chestnut Soup, 152, *153*

in Chicken Salad, 242, *243*

in Fried Pizza Pockets, 75

Geppetto's Sausage and Dandelion Garganelli, *182*, 183

Lentil Soup with 'Nduja, 148, *149*

in Neapolitan Potato Cake, 246, *247*

in Pasta and Beans, *146*, 147

in "Pasta Mayhem," *162*, 163

Pizza with Button Mushrooms and Soppressata, 62, *63*

Pork Roast (Porchetta di Terroni), *198*, 199–200, *200, 201*

Sausage, Bean, and Radicchio Stew, *204*, 205

Sausage and Rapini Sandwiches, *88*, 89

in Scrambled Egg Sandwich, *54*, 55

in Spaghetti Frittata, *248*, 249

in Stuffed Savoury Brioche, 115–16

tastasal (testing salt) for, 296

in Terri's Swiss Chard, Meat, and Cheese Casserole, *244*, 245

Terroni Sausage, *296*, 296–97, *297*

Terroni Sausage with Potatoes, 202, *203*

potatoes

Mamma Rita's Potatoes and Peppers, 222, *223*

Neapolitan Potato Cake, 246, *247*

Terroni Sausage with Potatoes, 202, *203*

poultry

Chicken Broth, 295

Chicken Salad, 242, *243*

Duck Confit Ravioli, 168–70, *169*

primi (first courses), 157–85

Puff Pastry, 298–300, *299, 300*

Puff Pastry Snacks, Savoury, *110*, 111–12

"Rainbow Rigatoni": Zucchini, Cherry Tomatoes, and Buffalo Mozzarella, 164, *165*

Ravioli di Zio Paperone, 168–70, *169*

Ricotta Cheesecake, *260*, 261

Rigatoni Arcobaleno, 164, *165*

The Right Spritz, 119

Rita's Corn Crisps, *102*, 103

Round Breadsticks, *98*, 99–100, *100, 101*

salads

Baked Oyster Mushroom Salad, 128, *129*

Beet Salad, Chickpea Pancake with, 132–35, *133*

Chicken Salad, 242, *243*

Salatini di Pasta Sfoglia, *110*, 111–12

Salsa di Pomodoro, 294

Salsiccia di Vincenzo, *296*, 296–97, *297*

Salsiccia e Patate, 202, *203*

sandwiches

Fried Mini Panini, 108, *109*

Fried Mozzarella Sandwiches, *138*, 139

Sausage and Rapini Sandwiches, *88*, 89

Scrambled Egg Sandwich, *54*, 55

Sea Bass and Red Pepper Sandwiches, 90, *91*

Stuffed Savoury Brioche, 115–16

See also bread and dough; pizza

sauces

Béchamel Sauce, 294–95

Classic Tomato Sauce, 294

Cosimo's Sunday Sauce with Rigatoni, 174–76, *175–77*

Lemon Sauce, Spaghetti with, *166*, 167

Octopus Sauce, Calamarata with, *178*, 179

Terroni Tomato Base for, 294

Tomato Sauce and Fresh Ricotta, Gnocchi with, 184, *185*

sausage and pork recipes. *See* pork and sausage

Sautéed Rapini, *228*, 229

Savoury Puff Pastry Snacks, *110*, 111–12

Scarola alla Titina, 234, *235*

Scrambled Egg Sandwich, *54*, 55

Sea Bass and Red Pepper Sandwiches, 90, *91*

seafood recipes. *See* fish and shellfish

Seared Octopus, *190*, 191

secondi (second courses), 187–219

Semicalda di Terroni, *204*, 205

Sempre in Vacanza, 121

Sformato di Fontina, *236*, 237

Sfumato, 119, *119*

sides, 221–39

snacks. *See* aperitivo; dolci (sweets)

soups, 143–55

Sourdough Starter, 287–88

Spaghetti al Limone, *166*, 167

Spaghetti Frittata, *248*, 249

Spaghetti with Lemon Sauce, *166*, 167

Spinach Pasta, 292–93

Sporcamuss, *268*, 269

starters, openers, and salads, 127–41

Steak, Florentine, Terroni-Style, 218, *219*

Stinco d'Agnello, *216*, 217

Stuffed Savoury Brioche, 115–16

Sugo della Domenica, 174–76, *175–77*

Sweet Buns, 32–35, *33, 34*

INDEX

sweets, 251–85
tagliatelle dough, 292
tagliolini dough, 292
Taralli, *98*, 99–100, *100*, *101*
tarts
    Apricot Jam Tart, *44*, 45–46, *46*
    Escarole Tarts with Poached Eggs
        (Tartine con Scarola e Uova), *50*,
        51–52
    Flavoured Custard Tarts, 270–72, *271*
    Nutella and Custard Tart, 266, *267*
Taschina, *110*, 111
tastasal, about, 296
Terri's Swiss Chard, Meat, and Cheese
    Casserole, *244*, 245
Terroni Group
    conversations about, 47, 84, 161, 209,
        273
    history and growth of, 3–25
    Los Angeles locations, 18–19
    Spaccio, 20–23
    specialty products, 302–3
    STOCK T.C, 23–24
    Sud Forno, 20
    Terroni name, 2–3
    Terroni Pantry, 286–301
    Toronto locations, 6–9, 11–14, 19–24
Terroni Pizza Dough, 288–90, *289*
Terroni Sausage, *296*, 296–97, *297*
Terroni Sausage with Potatoes, 202,
    203
Terroni Sour, 121, *121*
Terroni's Panettone, 252–58, *253–59*
Terroni Tomato Base, 294

Tiramisù, Terroni's, *284*, 285
Titina's Eggplant Parmigiana, 196, *197*
Titina's Endive with Olives, Pine Nuts,
    and Raisins, 234, *235*
Tomato Sauce, Classic, 294
Torta della Nonna Lucia, 282, *283*
Torta di Ricotta, *260*, 261
Traditional Sicilian Cannoli, 262–64,
    263, *265*
Tria with Chickpeas, *158*, 159–60

Uova al Purgatorio, 56, *57*
Uovo Sbattuto con Caffè, 28, *29*

Vegetable Soup, 144, *145*
Vellutata di Finocchio, *154*, 155
Verdura di Mamma Rita, *150*, 151
Verdure Come le Faceva Terri, *244*, 245
Verdure Saltate in Padella, *224*, 225

Whipped Egg with Espresso, 28, *29*
White Pizza with Greens, *70*, 71
wine, 18, 122–25

Zeppole di San Giuseppe, 278–80,
    279–81
Zucchini, Cherry Tomatoes, and
    Buffalo Mozzarella, "Rainbow
    Rigatoni," 164, *165*
Zucchini and Egg Hash, *232*, 233
Zuppa di Castagne, 152, *153*
Zuppa di Lenticchie e 'Nduja, 148, *149*
zuppe (soups), 143–55

TERRONI
LA BETTOLA
LA BETTOLA
SUD FORNO
SPA
TERRONI
BETTOLA

SUD FORNO

SPA

ONI

LA BETI

CAVINONA

BAR

BAR CENTRALE

CENTRALE

TERRONI

TERRONI

BAITO

TER